THE RAF'S
AIR WAR
IN LIBYA

THE RAF'S
AIR WAR
IN LIBYA

*New Conflicts in the Era
of Austerity*

Dave Sloggett

Pen & Sword
AVIATION

First published in Great Britain in 2012
By Pen and Sword Aviation
an imprint of
Pen and Sword Books Ltd
47 Church Street
Barnsley
South Yorkshire S70 2AS

ISBN 978 1 78159 060 7

Printed and bound in England by
CPI Group (UK) Ltd, Croydon, CR0 4YY

Typeset in Times New Roman by
Chic Media Ltd

Pen & Sword Books Ltd incorporates the imprints of
Pen & Sword Aviation, Pen & Sword Family History, Pen & Sword Maritime,
Pen & Sword Military, Pen & Sword Discovery, Wharncliffe Local History,
Wharncliffe True Crime, Wharncliffe Transport, Pen & Sword Select,
Pen & Sword Military Classics, Leo Cooper, Remember When,
The Praetorian Press, Seaforth Publishing and Frontline Publishing

For a complete list of Pen and Sword titles please contact
Pen and Sword Books Limited
47 Church Street, Barnsley, South Yorkshire, S70 2AS, England
E-mail: enquiries@pen-and-sword.co.uk
Website: www.pen-and-sword.co.uk

Contents

Preface and Acknowledgements

In the immediate aftermath of publishing its much-maligned Strategic Defence and Security Review (SDSR) the United Kingdom's coalition government became embroiled in a military adventure in Libya. Somewhat unexpectedly this would shine an intense spotlight on the outcome of the SDSR. It would also provide an immediate opportunity to conduct a detailed assessment of its impact on the United Kingdom's ability to project military power onto the world stage using the outcome from the campaign to validate the decision-making that took place in the SDSR.

The Prime Minister, David Cameron, perhaps tiring of all the criticism of the SDSR, seemed really keen to prove his doubters wrong. At the time of writing, as aircraft from many of the coalition partners involved in the Libyan campaign return home and the newly-recognised National Transitional Council (NTC) gets down to work to create a new Libya, the final outcome is far from certain.

Gaddafi's death draws part of a line under the mission. The regime has been replaced and plans are already in train in Libya to provide an opportunity for its people to elect their own government. Something they have been unable to do for over forty years. For many Libyans that will be a hugely welcome moment. However, not all the indicators emerging from Libya are positive.

The southern parts of Libya, traditionally loyal to the Gaddafi regime, remain largely unconquered. The border areas, which have the potential to provide a sanctuary to those who wish to seek retribution for the demise of the regime, are inherently difficult to secure; providing the kind of challenge that exists in Afghanistan. The Al Qaeda affiliate in the area, Al Qaeda in the Islamic Maghreb (AQIM), is moving its focus towards the south east of Algeria. They may be intent on exploiting a post-Gaddafi situation in Libya to ferment an insurgency. The possibility for Libya to descend into the kind of chaos witnessed in Iraq in the aftermath of the invasion in 2003 haunts political nightmares.

The intervention in Libya had been seen to be necessary as forces loyal to the regime of Colonel Gaddafi had overcome an initial advance along the coast by rebels seeking to overthrow his regime, forcing them back towards Benghazi. The virus at the heart of the Arab Spring, the clamour for a new form of democracy based on Islamic ideals, had spread from Tunisia to Egypt. Regimes that had previously seemed stable had fallen. All bets, it would appear, were now off. Any of the regimes in the Middle East were now vulnerable.

Against this backdrop, and to the surprise of many including Colonel Gaddafi, the virus spread to Libya. Many Libyans had spontaneously risen up in local towns and communities across the country. An insurrection initially gained a foothold in some areas. But the regime was swift to mobilise its military to try and re-establish control over the rebel areas. The uprising had not been confined to a single geographic area. This complicated the regime's response. It had to adopt a mode of fire-fighting each uprising. The scenes that initially emerged from Misrata were especially disturbing and gave an insight into just how far the regime would go to hold onto power. This was a no-holds-barred approach to suppressing a rebellion.

A swift rebel advance from Benghazi across the desert towards Tripoli, and to provide a link up with other centres of the rebellion, was quickly thrown back. Gaddafi's forces rapidly headed for a showdown with the main centre of the rebellion, Benghazi. The prospect of a massacre loomed large as Gaddafi's rhetoric indicated he was hell-bent on revenge. A political consensus emerged at the United Nations that saw two resolutions adopted. The first creating an initial set of limitations on the freedom of manoeuvre of members of the regime, with specific actions to seize financial assets held overseas, the second authorising the deployment of a limited mission with an aim of enforcing a no-fly zone.

Working under the legal umbrella of two quickly formulated United Nations resolutions, the United Kingdom and French military – working in tandem with a number of coalition partners – launched a series of raids aimed at immediately degrading the Libyan air defence systems. Superiority over the Libyan skies was quickly achieved.

However, the initial objective of the campaign sanctioned by the United Nations, to secure the safety of the citizens of Benghazi, rapidly suffered the kind of mission creep that is often associated with contemporary wars. As the air and naval bombardment moved from suppressing the Gaddafi forces on the outskirts of Benghazi to helping them advance against Tripoli, a number of diplomatic arguments broke out. The mission, it appeared, had morphed. Regime change was now the order of the day.

For some countries, Russia being amongst the most vociferous, this was not what had been intended. Russia, of course, had an economic axe to grind. Its arms industry had a large number of orders that it was working on for the Gaddafi regime. Any attempt to replace him would have seen those orders potentially cancelled. Other countries, however, saw Libya through the blood and treasure invested in Iraq. They wanted nothing to do with what they saw as another potential nightmare, a war without any defined endpoint.

For David Cameron and the French President Nicolas Sarkozy, some tough decisions had to be taken. Could they risk becoming involved in another military quagmire? In both countries the public would not be forgiving if what was sold as a limited military intervention to protect the people of Benghazi suddenly unfolded into a wide ranging attempt at regime change. The initial signs were not good. The imposition of an air exclusion zone swiftly saw NATO aircraft bombing Tripoli. The public and the media were almost duty bound to ask the question. How does bombing Tripoli save people in Benghazi several hundreds of miles away to the east?

As the campaign unfolded Cameron came under a lot of pressure, as critics used the faltering campaign to highlight inconsistencies in the SDSR process; which many claimed had been rushed. The early retirement of the Harrier Force and HMS *Ark Royal* were foremost amongst the concerns of the critics. They consistently used these two decisions to suggest that the government had emphasised cost-cutting over the need to undertake a carefully considered, and long overdue, strategic assessment of where the United Kingdom may need to exert military power in the future.

The cancellation and rapid scrapping of the Nimrod MRA4 maritime surveillance aircraft upgrade was also amongst the most contentious outcomes of the SDSR. Given the United Kingdom's dependence upon trade routes and the enduring threat in the Indian Ocean and Gulf of Aden from piracy, this specific decision seemed to beggar belief – underlining a viewpoint of an intellectual vacuum at the heart of political understanding of the maritime domain and its importance. With one element of the Libyan campaign being to enforce a trade embargo on Libya, which relied heavily on its daily output of crude oil, the removal of the Nimrod MRA4 force seemed specifically short-sighted.

The situation was also not helped as the Prime Minister was also arguing strongly for a shift in the balance of expenditure apparently away from the military towards interventions designed to prevent war. This was a clear strategic shift from the use of what is often called hard power to soft power; using money to invest in nation states in ways that avoided these countries becoming failed states which might then require some form of military intervention. The much heralded ring-fencing of the Overseas Development Aid budget being a vital part of the coalition government's approach to foreign policy.

That its outcome will be seen as a success is not in doubt. David Cameron will want to have his moment in the limelight over Libya. But, below the surface, complex issues exist that need to be discussed before too many dramatic conclusions are drawn over the Libyan campaign. Any detailed reflection raises a great many questions. Some commentators have even ventured to suggest that David Cameron and Nickolas Sarkozy were lucky to have achieved the removal of the regime – implying that circumstances favoured them that might not apply in a different context. For that read Syria or Yemen.

The Libya campaign therefore presents an ideal opportunity to place the magnifying glass over the outcome of the SDSR and to look at how Cameron's philosophy for conducting future military campaigns emerges. Set in the context of the campaigns in Iraq and the likely outcome in Afghanistan, this book will analyse the emergent Cameron Doctrine for military interventions, asking the question is this a blueprint for future wars?

In this book we place the SDSR under the microscope of a specific campaign and its utility against a range of wider potential limited interventions, taking Syria and Yemen as potential case studies. This book specifically avoids any mention of the elephants that were in the room during the SDSR process, but which were specifically ignored; Iran and China. Any consideration of the likely use of military power in conflicts involving either of these two states would have sharply biased the SDSR process. To have made the SDSR contingent upon future United Kingdom military operations in Iran or against China was simply not feasible. That analysis, and its implications, is subject to an on-going debate that will shape the way the next SDSR develops.

In the meantime this book looks at the ways the United Kingdom military forces conducted their operations in Libya alongside their coalition partners. It concludes that whilst the outcome shows the SDSR in a favourable light the Prime Minister would be wise not to suggest that it alone provides a practical validation of the SDSR. The situation that prevailed in Libya suited the emphasis on air power and the secondary role of the Royal Navy in enforcing an embargo and providing a platform for attacks on the coastal areas when the need arose. The inherent agility of the Royal Air Force and the Royal Navy to deliver combat power into this situation cannot be underestimated. Libya was a good place to test out the aftermath of the SDSR.

These circumstances allowed the Prime Minister to embark upon the campaign in Libya whilst not removing any focus from the on-going operations in Afghanistan – retaining the United Kingdom's centre of gravity militarily. Aside from the very public rebuke given by the Prime Minister to the First Sea Lord, when he went public on his concerns at the implications for the Royal Navy of trying to juggle its assets, the media have not provided any great commentary on the operational stretch these two campaigns have placed upon the United Kingdom's military forces. That the Royal Air Force had to juggle its already overextended transport force cannot be in doubt. For them the adage that it was a close-run thing applies.

By analysing the Libyan campaign in detail the SDSR will be tested. Coming as it does as the process for looking in depth at capabilities ahead of the next SDSR gets underway, this analysis is hopefully timely. It also provides some insights into the way the Prime Minister is thinking about the way military power needs to be projected in the future.

PREFACE AND ACKNOWLEDGEMENTS

As the Libyan campaign draws to a close and the head of the TNC has taken up residence in Tripoli it is hard not to wonder what the future holds for Libya. It is to be hoped that a descent into chaos and an Iraq-style insurgency can be avoided. If that is the future, many of those that forecast an uncertain and bloody future will be proved to have been wrong. For some it will provide the basis around which future military doctrine concerning short-term interventions will be written. They need to take care to avoid the classic problem of preparing our military forces to fight the last war. For others it will provide a moment of reflection. What can we learn from Libya that is more widely applicable?

The book develops some insights into the Prime Minister's formula for future warfare that emerges from the SDSR process and its first validation in the Libyan campaign. By providing a forensic examination of the circumstances surrounding the campaign it aims to contribute to the emerging debate about the impact of the SDSR and how that will shape future military interventions.

Before anyone jumps to wide-ranging conclusions about the outcome in Libya, a moment to pause, reflect and probe the actual events in the campaign is valuable. The Libyan campaign provides a perfect opportunity for mature reflection and debate ahead of the next SDSR slated for 2015. It is a window that should be seized with both hands by military and political leaders. The outcome of any future military engagement will depend upon it.

*   *   *

I am honoured in the course of my work to spend time visiting our armed forces as they work overseas in what are often dangerous and arduous conditions. I never fail to be amazed by their fortitude and professionalism. These men and women really do exemplify an approach to problem solving that is so very different. It is always a pleasure to do anything I can to assist them in their aims. Their intellectual challenge and curiosity is always a stimulation to develop greater insights in the pursuit of how to help them do even better at the projection of military power, both in its hard and soft forms.

I am also very fortunate to be involved in the United Kingdom in work alongside the emergency services community. My lectures on the threat from international terrorism bring me into contact with another superb group of people whose desire to do good things is truly inspiring. Their voracious appetite for knowledge and insight is the highlight of many training sessions that I conduct all over the country. I rarely emerge from any of these sessions without being surprised by the detailed nature of the questions I am asked. As a citizen of the United Kingdom it is very reassuring that such people exist.

This book is dedicated to all of those, wherever they may work, with whom I have the pleasure to work on a day-to-day basis. I am so very lucky to be able to get up each day and look forward to another stimulating day looking at the possibilities of developing new ways of applying military power. There is never a sense of Groundhog Day, for that I am intensely grateful to all of those who dedicate such time and effort to protecting the United Kingdom.

I sincerely hope that those who read this book find within its covers some thoughts and ideas that are valuable. It has been a real pleasure to write it and I thank John Grehan for his initial suggestion that I take the project on. His help in getting the project approved and his advice in helping develop a real focus for the book are seriously appreciated.

I also want to thank my friend James Green and his colleagues at IHS Janes. They always provide me with opportunities to write ideas and make contributions to the kind of open-source analysis and publishing at which they excel. The Editor of *Warships International Fleet Review*, Iain Ballantyne, has also been a huge influence on me over the past five years, allowing me to express my ideas and thoughts in his magazine. Sir Jeremy Blackham who brilliantly edits *The Naval Review* has also been a long term source of encouragement for my writing. I also wish to acknowledge the help of many individuals who I cannot name in the United Kingdom armed forces for their insights and assistance in preparing this book.

I am also extremely fortunate to have such an understanding wife who is always able to keep herself busy whilst I am upstairs in my study. Jo is the light in my life that lifts my every waking day. She also has a rare talent, an ability tease out from me what are often confused thoughts in my head into a sense of order and structure. Her contribution to all my efforts is immense and so really important.

Data Analysis Note

The book contains an analysis of the attacks carried out in the campaign. The data used for this analysis was derived from two principle sources. The first of these was the dataset assembled by the *Guardian* newspaper *Datablog*. This data was assembled by the *Guardian* analysts from information published by NATO sources – see www.guardian.co.uk/data.

However, in a complex battlefield environment it is entirely possible that some incorrect definitions of targets occurred and NATO may have not used a standard lexicon for their day-to-day reports – introducing an apparent bias in the data. In particular, I am slightly worried by the low level of Armoured Personnel Carriers that have been reported as being destroyed. Given the large inventory owned by Gaddafi's forces at the outset of the campaign that seems slightly unusual. There are several plausible explanations. Many may have been destroyed in garrison or holding areas and not defined as individual targets.

I mention this to council anyone using the data as a definitive source of reporting. It provides excellent indications of the way the campaign unfolded, but only a detailed breakdown of the actual data stored by NATO on the war could ever produce a final comprehensive analysis.

The second source was reports published by the United Kingdom Ministry of Defence on the activities of the Royal Air Force, the Royal Navy and the Army Air Corps Apache aircraft on missions they had completed. Neither of the datasets that I have used should be regarded as complete or absolute. They are a sample of the full set of data. This is what has been placed in the public domain.

Both of the two data sources used are taken on face value in terms of their veracity and accuracy. The analysis presented in the book should therefore not be regarded as absolute, but indicative of the numbers of sorties undertaken and the patterns of targets attacked. My aim in looking at the data was to see to what extent I could see the shifting priorities of the mission unfolding and to determine if there were subtle shifts in the targeting that was being conducted in the course of the campaign.

It is for the reader to decide if I have used this data and added any value to the understanding of the Libyan campaign. Any errors or mistakes that emerged in the course of the data analysis are my responsibility.

Dr Dave Sloggett
Ryde, Isle of Wight
November 2011

Introduction

This book sets out to provide a detailed chronology of the events that occurred in Libya and to draw out important lessons for the future. It is the first campaign undertaken by NATO where the United States stood back, this campaign was politically and militarily led by the European partners in NATO. As such it provides a benchmark for analysis and debate. The insights that emerge should be the subject of mature reflection and not seen through the distorting lens of the celebrations that were seen in Tripoli when the Gaddafi regime was overthrown.

Some of the lessons that can be learnt are hugely important in areas such as campaign planning and in terms of the current balance of forces that exist in the United Kingdom. If boots on the ground are something to be avoided at all costs where does this take the argument on the future of the British Army?

For the Chief of the Defence Staff (CDS) in the United Kingdom this must be a critical concern. Already some are suggesting that the Army may well be the focus of any future rounds of defence spending as the effort in Afghanistan is scaled back. Some commentators are already re-writing elements of British defence doctrine suggesting that the British Army will do little more than help train countries to develop their own armies in the future.

Supporting security sector reform, something that naturally emerges from the latter work of the British Army in Afghanistan, may well provide a new focus. But that would hardly require a large standing army. The emphasis being placed on reserve forces provides another element of a form of thinking that is not looking to conduct brigade-formation led interventions in the future.

The RAF, above all of the armed forces in the United Kingdom, has the most to draw from the Libyan campaign in terms of lessons learnt. From the point they were 'asked to go and do something' they responded magnificently, despite the lack of forewarning of the mission and the cut backs that had been imposed upon them in the SDSR.

The role played by the Royal Navy, as so often is the case, did not have the same drama as RAF jets hitting targets across Libya on a daily basis. But its mission to work within a multi-national naval coalition to enforce the arms embargo was an important one – adding to the pressure on the Gaddafi regime. In the course of the campaign the RN was to play an additional role, bombarding coastal areas and attacking regime targets to protect Libyan citizens. These shore bombardments were highly reminiscent of the Falklands campaign. Some firing missions were carried out to protect the fleet from action by the pro-Gaddafi forces. On a large number of occasions naval gunnery was also used to place star shells over key areas to help illuminate targets on the ground. It had a marked impact on those trying to conduct clandestine activities in the vicinity of the coastline.

At the outset of the campaign, and in the course of the war, the Royal Navy would also launch a number of Tomahawk cruise missiles from a submarine in the Mediterranean Sea. The targets were hardened command and control facilities being used by the regime to coordinate its forces and vehicle assembly areas. Apache helicopters would also be launched from HMS *Ocean* to attack targets along the coast and, on at least one occasion, deep into Libyan territory to attack targets whilst being protected from above by Typhoon aircraft operating as 'overwatch' on the mission; ready to come to the help of the Apaches if they were suddenly to be placed in danger.

On all of these missions the Intelligence, Surveillance, Target Acquisition and Recognition (ISTAR) assets of the RAF, the RN – through the venerable Fleet Air Arm's Sea King Airborne Surveillance and Control (ASaC) helicopters – and United States aircraft provided the timely intelligence feeds required to conduct a successful campaign against what were often fleeting targets.

Of all the armed services it is the work of the RN that seems so distant from the mind of the politicians. The sea blindness that pervades the United Kingdom government is one that simply has to be addressed. The simple purchase of an aircraft carrier and deploying it at the end of the decade does not in any way enable the United Kingdom to remain a maritime power.

Without their presence alongside other forces in the Mediterranean,

INTRODUCTION

Gaddafi could still have been re-supplied by sea, prolonging the conflict. Fighting wars in the twenty-first century is not all about combat operations. Shaping the campaign battlespace requires a government and its military forces to manoeuvre, using all of the instruments of power, economic, political and military. These are matters that are developed in the book in the context of the Libyan campaign and the lessons that can be drawn to help guide and shape future military spending.

Chapter two provides the context to the outbreak of the protests from a political, economic and military standpoint and asks the question why did NATO feel it had to intervene? Chapter three looks at the transition to conflict, as things in Libya started to get out of control and Gaddafi's initial overtures promising reforms to the rebels in Benghazi were rejected. It describes the political manoeuvres that created a basis for two United Nations Resolutions to be passed providing a legal basis for an intervention by NATO.

Chapter four addresses the initial stages of the campaign with the creation of the no-fly zone and the naval embargo and the mission creep that then started to shape the campaign as regime change became an undeclared and yet understood objective for the military effort. The question of how to pressurise Gaddafi from power without having to commit NATO ground troops into the conflict became a major talking point.

Chapter five deals with the period which seems to occur in all contemporary military campaigns, where military progress appears to stall. The media language turns to describing a stalemate and analysing in detail the burgeoning costs of the campaign. Any initial wave of public support for the campaign starts to evaporate as the aim of protecting citizens whose life is in immediate danger becomes shifting sand, the end-point of which seems uncertain and indeterminate. This chapter details that emerging sense of frustration at the intermittent progress made by the rebels and their set-backs as they tried to quickly cross the desert and attack the Gaddafi strongholds in the west of the country.

With little evident progress, many commentators resorted to drawing comparisons with the fluctuating progress made across the very same tracts of desert by soldiers involved in the Second World War. The length of the logistical supply routes being a challenge for the mechanised forces of the Allies and Axis powers in the 1940s as much as it was for the largely ad-hoc degree of mechanisation achieved by rebel forces.

However, when such forces confronted trained Army units that were loyal to the Gaddafi regime, the initial progress of the rebel fighters stalled. When faced with the kind of firepower available to Gaddafi's troops, the improvised nature of the rebel forces quickly lost the initiative. This would be an issue that would dog the campaign, as pro-Gaddafi forces proved resilient in the face of NATO's firepower. As the battles moved from the rural to the urban environment, the tempo in the campaign would inevitably falter. In towns and cities even the precise application of air power has its limitations if civilian casualties are to be avoided at all costs.

With media expectations set high of an imminent collapse of the forces loyal to the regime, the lack of progress brought fears of a long campaign and the unsettling vision of Iraq and Afghanistan back into the forefront of the media commentators. One important lesson to emerge from this is that as soon as a campaign stalls, which it inevitably will, political leaders need to prepare themselves for the inevitable burst of media speculation and accusations that the military effort is at a stalemate.

In actual fact this was not a time of stalemate at all, it was just that progress was difficult to define as NATO and the rebels started to increase their degree of cooperation, and the activity settled into a phase of attrition where NATO sought to erode the military capacity of the forces loyal to Colonel Gaddafi.

Chapter six considers the sudden change of atmosphere as a tipping point in the campaign was reached. Whilst it is hard to define this point in terms of a specific day or event in the campaign, a detailed analysis of the attacks reported by NATO does provide some clues, with hindsight, as to how the point arose. The pattern of attacks carried out by NATO, in the middle of July, were crucial to shaping the battlespace. It helped create the conditions for Tripoli to fall at the end of August.

This of course arose in part because of the closer cooperation that NATO had taken to establish with the rebels. Special Forces inserted on the ground provided advice and brought a greater sense of cohesion to the activities of the rebel forces. Suddenly they were acting in ways that appeared concerted, with a clear focus on a main effort in contrast to making progress in fits and starts. That a breakthrough would eventually occur was then never in doubt. Surrounded on all sides it was simply a matter of time before Gaddafi would lose control of Tripoli and withdraw to his tribal homeland to make one last, defiant stand.

Chapter seven of the book looks at where Libya goes from here. The unfreezing of assets held in overseas banks provides an important start-point for the Libyan people. The sight of the Royal Air Force flying large amounts of freshly minted currency into Benghazi was not one that had been seen in previous conflicts. The sense that some of the lessons of Iraq had been learnt was clear. Planning for the post conflict stage had rightly started earlier, with maintaining the nascent governance structures that had emerged within the National Transitional Council being a core objective. The chapter looks towards a hopeful future and not one that sees Libya descend into the chaos of Iraq. The early signs are positive.

The book comes to a close with chapter eight. This looks at the lessons to emerge from the campaign for NATO and specifically the United Kingdom. It tries to answer the question of where now for the counter-insurgency (COIN) doctrine of NATO and the United Kingdom? If future interventions were necessary in other parts of Africa would we have to tear up the rule book and start again? Or does the Libyan campaign provide another example of the ways in which the ideas forged in the battles in Iraq can be adapted and changed?

After all, if there are to be watchwords for COIN, they are agile and versatile. These are the words used by the RAF to describe its new military posture. The Libyan campaign was to prove just how versatile the youngest member of the United Kingdom's military forces had become. Kosovo is a distant memory for the air power protagonists. The RAF delivered in Libya, and this book explores how it used the full spectrum of its capabilities to assist the rebels operating on the ground.

The book tries to provide an objective analysis of the outcome of the Libyan campaign. Whilst the mood of celebration in Tripoli that surrounded the overthrow of the Gaddafi regime is understandable it did arise because of a specific set of circumstances that developed. The book is clear in it is conclusion. Libya is no panacea for future conflict. Whilst some generic elements can be drawn from the campaign that will help shape future military interventions, it would be unwise of the government and of NATO to think that they have suddenly found a new formula for regime change. The Libyan military were no match for NATO. It was a one-sided fight. Other adversaries would provide a greater test of the political and military cohesion of the alliance.

CHAPTER 1

Cameron's War

The Celebrations in Tripoli

David Cameron must have been delighted with his visit to Tripoli on 15 September 2011, as the international community was rushing to acknowledge the interim government of Libya as the country's legitimate representatives. The Prime Minister's standing across the world had just taken another crucial step. Cameron was now a war leader, tested in the heat of what was a limited application of military power – but it could all have turned out so very differently.

The younger and relatively inexperienced political leader had applied military force, and replaced a man that had dominated Libyan politics for over forty years. This was quite an achievement. Standing shoulder-to-shoulder with him on that visit to Tripoli was the President of France. This was the man with whom the British Prime Minister had set out to establish a new Franco-British military axis at the start of his premiership in 2010. A year later they were celebrating its first application. Together, in one relatively simple war, they had re-cast the European defence landscape and its relationship with the United States. Or had they?

For David Cameron the shouts of joy and the melee he faced must have been both a slightly worrying moment and yet one that offered so much hope. His language seemed to capture the significance of the occasion. This he stated 'goes beyond Libya'. As if caught up by the atmosphere, he went on to say that, 'this is a moment when the Arab Spring could become an Arab summer and we see democracy advance on other countries too.'

President Sarkozy also hailed the moment saying, 'As I flew over Tripoli today, I thought about the hope that one day young Syrians will be given the opportunity that young Libyans have now been given.'

Adding, 'perhaps the best thing I can do is to dedicate our visit to Tripoli to those who hope that Syria can one day also be a free country.' Was Cameron so buoyed up by the success in Libya that in his wildest dreams he saw a similar application of the kind of clinical military power applied by NATO in a Syrian context?

The rhetoric of the day, it would appear, was simply a rush of blood to the head. Since the end of the campaign in Libya was declared wiser heads, it would seem, have prevailed. For the moment Syria appears to be off the hook despite the carnage that is being metered out to its citizens on a daily basis. Sadly, international politics is rarely a place which makes a great deal of sense to the common man. A NATO-led coalition went to war to protect the people of Benghazi from being slaughtered by a tyrannical dictator hell-bent on revenge. How is that not different from Syria or for that matter Yemen?

David Cameron may well have reflected on the C-17, as it flew back that night to land on the short runway at RAF Northolt, that his gamble in pushing for a United Nations resolution to help the people of Benghazi had been vindicated. He may also have thought that it showed that those who that had lambasted his hastily-undertaken Strategic Defence and Security Review (SDSR) had been wrong to say it was flawed.

But, despite the scenes of undoubted joy in Tripoli, the international community does not seem able to come together to protect other nation states in similar circumstances to those experienced by the Libyan people. States like China, India and Russia have seen how David Cameron and Nickolas Sarkozy were able to manipulate the English language and give themselves sufficient room to manoeuvre that allowed them to start a mission with the aim of defending a city and end it replacing an entire regime. The uprising in Syria is not about to falter any time soon. President Assad has warned off the west. His threat of an 'earthquake' across the fault line that Syria sits on in the Middle East is one that many will take seriously. Until countries like China, India and Russia, all of which have vested interests in Syria, decide to act against the regime in Damascus Assad will survive. He will do so by brutalising his people in the full view of the world's population. The inability for the west to help the Syrian people bring the leaders of such a regime to account will rankle with many leaders. Syria's status as a pariah nation is unlikely to change.

The sense of a job well done by the NATO-led coalition was a satisfying moment ahead of the party conference season. David Cameron knew he would face a restless party at the Conservative conference, with some critics arguing he had sacrificed too many Tory principles in establishing a coalition government. Now, though, the Prime Minister was a man who had led his military into a campaign and he had come out on top. He had, quite literally, defined and applied a new approach to war in a very short period of time, one that was compatible with the need to re-balance the national debt. To his mind perhaps the downfall of Gaddafi had seen the SDSR pass its first test. The situation was not bad, not bad at all.

The cold light of dawn, however, often brings with it a more sober reflection. Each day the Prime Minister receives his daily intelligence briefing. As the war with Libya unfolded it is likely that one feature of that briefing would have been the whereabouts of Colonel Muammar Gaddafi and the members of his immediate family. Whilst they were free and had access to money and weapons, the campaign in Libya could not be declared closed. Whilst Colonel Gaddafi was to die in a confusing and complicated situation a matter of days later, several of his sons remained at large. The lessons from Iraq and Afghanistan are simply too painful to ignore. Whilst former regime leaders are free it is difficult for societies to move on. The headline writers remain poised, pens at the ready, to record how the situation in Libya had descended into chaos in the aftermath of what had been a relatively straightforward application of military power.

Fortunately for David Cameron part of that dilemma was quickly resolved. The headline writers had to start writing the obituary of the Libyan leader, not his re-birth at the head of an insurgency. The death of Colonel Gaddafi came swiftly as the last vestiges of resistance crumbled in Sirte – his birthplace – in October. The initial announcement of his death was uncertain, reflecting the chaotic nature of the situation. Reports and rumours abounded at the time. For several hours Gaddafi's fate was unsure.

Gradually, through the modern-day phenomena of social media, images emerged that captured his final moments. Dragged away from a tunnel in which he had sought refuge, Gaddafi's end seemed so reminiscent of that suffered by Saddham Hussein. His lying in state in a cold box for thousands of Libyan's of all ages to file past and take photographs of his bloodied body seemed to send a message out to other dictators. This is how it ends for those that repress their people. His burial in a remote desert strip in Libya was designed to draw a line under the activities of his regime. The question is, will it?

Emerging from Number 10 Downing Street to announce the death of Gaddafi must have been a satisfying moment for David Cameron. He had taken on his critics and won. The cost had also been relatively low. No British or coalition casualties, a first for any war fought by the United Kingdom's armed forces, and a total reported bill of £300 million. A snip when it came to the vast resources poured into Iraq and Afghanistan.

Another bonus was that the military forces had also largely been able to avoid civilian casualties. Throughout the campaign NATO had worked tirelessly to avoid what in military parlance is known as collateral damage. Its daily public pronouncements laboured the point. They were doing all they could to avoid unnecessary casualties. That effort is borne out in the mission statistics. It was not just a statement for the public. It was part of a mantra that governed how NATO would conduct itself in the campaign. Apart from some regrettable incidences early on, that aim had also been achieved. The Prime Minister had reasons to be cheerful and the mood could have been a celebratory one. That temptation, however, was avoided.

His body language and composure was aimed at sending a different message to the people of the United Kingdom. He resisted the language of triumphalism. The images of President Bush aboard an aircraft carrier declaring mission accomplished ahead of the development of a disastrous insurgency in Iraq were all too raw and vivid. His tone and style of delivery was one that befitted the occasion. Not the rhetoric of rejoice used by Margaret Thatcher but a far more measured language.

He set out to remind the British people of what Gaddafi had done to foster terrorism around the world and its consequences for the people of Scotland at Lockerbie, events in Northern Ireland and the death of Police Constable Yvonne Fletcher in London. Gaddafi was dead and now it was time for the Libyan people to decide how they wanted to develop their future. They had won the right to plan that future. NATO, its ships and warplanes, had provided assistance to the Libyan people. It was their victory and it was now for them to plan their future. The Prime Minister's announcement, for it was not a speech, was short, to the point, and delivered with more than a modicum of humility. The spring in his step however as he retired to Number 10 could not be mistaken.

Coming as it did a few days before the Tunisians turned out en masse to vote in their first ever free elections it was a moment when the Arab Spring really did start to look more like a moment in history rather than a passing fad. In Damascus, Sana'a and in the capital cities of many African countries ruled by despots, nerves must have been frayed. The political fault lines that exist in the world often come to the fore at these times.

The leaders of Zimbabwe, Venezuela, Syria and many other countries whose leaders may have felt threatened by the regime change in Tripoli were swift to condemn the manner of his passing. People power had demonstrated what it could do even when faced by a national army and regime intent on suppression and maintaining the status quo. The chances that the virus of the Arab Spring could yet spread further could not be dismissed. The reverberations from the death of Colonel Gaddafi would echo around the Middle East and Africa for some time to come. There are times when history perceptibly changes. October 2011, and the success of the Libyan rebels in taking control of their country back from a dictator, would swiftly be recognised as one of those events.

Gaddafi's Journey: Oblivion or Insurgency?
The regime of Colonel Muammar Gaddafi had long been portrayed as that of an international pariah state. Whilst not specifically named in the famous 'axis of evil' speech given by President Bush, Libya was known to be a country that was involved in a range of destabilising activities across Northern and Central Africa. In parallel it was also simultaneously developing its own brands of toxic weapons systems and their means of delivery. For many in the right wing of American politics the difference between Lockerbie and the events of 11 September 2001 was a matter of semantic nuance. For them Al Qaeda and Colonel Gaddafi could readily be bracketed together as people that had to be dealt with in some way shape or form.

It was Prime Minister Tony Blair, operating with the help of the United Kingdom Secret Intelligence Service (SIS), which managed to create the conditions in which Gaddafi was brought in from the cold. Hindsight, that well-known nearly perfect form of science, reveals that Gaddafi read the straws in the wind and decided to remove himself from the target list of regimes that an emboldened United States President Bush had clearly placed in his cross-wires. Gaddafi chose to be pragmatic. He offered up the one thing he knew would bring his regime in from the cold, his nuclear weapons program and his long-range ballistic missile program. It was not such a hard decision for Gaddafi. His economy was on its knees anyway, and he needed to move Libya back into the world's economy. The sacrifice of a weapons program that in all honesty was going nowhere fast was not such a big gesture. He really had nothing to lose.

The offer to dismantle his nuclear weapons program was hailed as a huge diplomatic success for the British government. That he also offered to bulldoze 3,300 aerial bombs designed to carry chemical weapons was a measure of his anxiety. For Gaddafi the regime had to endure no matter what the short-term cost. The lessons from Iraq, and the way that Saddam Hussein was deposed, did rather provide a reality check for Gaddafi at the time. Little could he have realised that his own end, when it came, would be so reminiscent of the downfall of the leader of Iraq.

In practise, of course, what Gaddafi said and what he actually did differed. It was the way of things with the regime. Promises made rarely lived up to much in reality. In a cable released in November 2009 by the international organisation called Wikileaks that seeks to bring secure information into the public domain, the concerns of the Americans in Tripoli became very clear. Gaddafi was well known to be a mercurial leader and one prone to outbursts of temper and acts of irrationality. But his reaction, when a Russian aircraft that had been scheduled to depart Tripoli with the remnants of his nuclear stockpile on 25 November 2009, provided an insight to how the political sands had shifted in the six years since his rapprochement with the international community.

In what was reported by the *New York Times* to have been a 'fit of pique', Gaddafi suddenly refused to allow the nuclear material to leave the country. The additional handling this caused could have led to the accidental release of the small quantity of highly enriched uranium that was supposed to have been sent to Russia for safekeeping. Whilst the quantities involved were small it was the principle that mattered. If Gaddafi genuinely wanted to disarm why throw such a temper-tantrum?

Apparently Gaddafi had thought that his magnanimous offer to eviscerate his program to develop weapons of mass destruction had not brought about sufficient return for him and Libya. His delaying tactics, not unlike the kind of tactics used by one of the named members of the 'axis of evil', North Korea, were designed to get people's attention.

As it turns out it was a temporary glitch as far as the nuclear stockpiles were concerned. On 21 December 2009, barely a month later, a Russian transport plane left Tripoli bound for Russia. The last element of Gaddafi's nuclear program had been removed from Libya. With this he lost one element of his negotiating power. To retain some control his next step was to delay the program which would have removed his chemical weapons program.

Gaddafi wanted to slow the rate of reduction of the capability and gain more concessions from the international community. He was clearly playing a long-term game. A matter of twenty-two months later Gaddafi was dead and his regime had been toppled by an ad hoc group of rebels who had come together against the backdrop of the Arab Spring. How times had changed. He had gone from international political hero to zero in a matter of less than two years.

The Conflict between NATO and Gaddafi
The conflict between NATO and the forces of Colonel Gaddafi that lasted from the spring of 2011 into the autumn was a pivotal moment for David Cameron. It took place against the backdrop of the initially chaotic political upheavals in the Middle East that saw the regimes in Tunisia and Egypt toppled. The wave of protests started in Tunisia was really important and has not been understood by the media. It had been a beacon of stability, the subject of a great deal of positive commentary by political leaders in the west. Had the Arab Spring started anywhere else it is highly likely that the overall reaction across the Middle East would have been very different. Many would have been wary to go on the streets to try and eject their government. But the fact that Tunisia of all places was able to achieve a successful transition encouraged many that may have been deterred by previous attempts at change, such as the Green Revolution in

Iran. Memories of the terrible civil war in Algeria would also have haunted some that may have been tempted to take to the streets.

The widespread slaughter that occurred in Algeria, as political change swept that country in 1991, resulted in many thousands of people being killed. The memory of that attempt to introduce political change into the Middle East lives on. The Algerian experience of trying to marry up the competing ideals of democracy and Islamic teachings provides a lesson that those writing the constitution in Tripoli would do well to read.

That Tunisia should have been vulnerable and act as the catalyst for the Arab Spring was really difficult to anticipate. As a failure to read the signs it ranks alongside the end of the Vietnam War and the fall of the Berlin War. Such was the confusion in the immediate outbreak of violence in Tunisia that the French government initially offered to deploy police forces to assist the regime of Zine El Abidine Ben Ali.

For French foreign policy this was to be a disastrous move that would eventually cause the downfall of the then French Foreign Minister Michèle Alliot-Marie. The offer to support the regime in Tunisia as people were dying in the streets, provided ammunition to those critics of President Sarkozy that enabled him to be portrayed as a friend of dictators. The contrast with his pre-election commitment to be a defender of global human rights could not have been any plainer.

Even in this globally-connected world there are still ways in which the political landscape can be shaken. As a tidal wave of protests swept throughout the area, the eastern part of Libya spontaneously rose up against the Gaddafi regime.

The east-west fault line in Libya had been known about for some time. The geography of Libya modulated what was already a clearly defined tribal split between the two regions. Ironically it was the east that generated the wealth through the exploitation of the oil reserves, which was hoarded and spent by the regime in the west. This social juxtaposition left the people in the east feeling disadvantaged and oppressed. Once the fuse had been lit in Tunisia it was not difficult to see that others may wish to follow.

This social juxtaposition is one that is not unique to Libya. Yemen is a country that has a similar fault line, although this is aligned north-to-south. The Sudan, whilst recently divided, has a massive north-south fault line that is defined by tribal allegiances and a wealth of oil in the south that had previously been exploited by Khartoum in the north. In Pakistan the fault line between the wealth generation based on the exploitation of gas in Balochistan in the west and the capital Islamabad in the east is equally divisive. This 'compass point' polarisation of nation states can only lead to further tensions and internal insurrections in time.

Saudi Arabia is another example with the wealth being generated in the east of the country by a marginalised minority that has been promised numerous reforms for it to be spent in the west on major projects and infrastructure. The iniquity of this situation, and its obvious potential long-term implications for stability in the countries involved, is often glossed over and ignored. As the wave spread throughout the Middle East the Saudi response was to promise additional expenditure aimed at those who might feel deprived. Similar efforts to neutralise the impact of the Arab Spring in Libya were attempted too late and came in the wake of many previous promises that had amounted to little actual reform for those most deprived in the east.

The timing of the commitment of United Kingdom military effort into Libya in support of the rebels in Benghazi was extraordinary. It was to provide a stern and immediate test of the so-called 'adaptable posture' that now underpinned the thinking in Whitehall. Coming as it did hard on the heels of the publication of the much vilified SDSR it provided an immediate opportunity for the development of Cameron's new ideas on how and why the United Kingdom would resort to force to achieve a political objective.

It was to provide a calibration that would have provided some satisfaction for the Prime Minister, who was quick to chide those who had tried to seize upon the way the campaign in Libya had been conducted as a litmus test of the effectiveness of the SDSR. Whilst Cameron was able to take away some positive elements of the outcome of the campaign, he would be wrong to think that he has just developed a new form of interventionism. The situation in Libya, as we shall explore, is far from generic. The specific characteristics on the ground suited the kind of air campaign that NATO could muster. Colonel Gaddafi, for all his bluster and rhetoric, proved to be an inept military campaigner. His tactics and use of the arsenal at his disposal could have created many more problems for the international alliance set against him.

Defence Reviews

For the United Kingdom, as indeed for many other western countries, defence reviews have become part of the political landscape. On each occasion so-called strategic decisions are made about the composition of the armed forces whose role it is to protect the interests of the state from a defined threat. In the Cold War the definition of the threat was straightforward. The Warsaw Pact loomed large over Europe.

But that focus on the Warsaw Pact, and its potential to invade Europe on some pretext or other, disguised a deeper and longer-term problem that was developing as a result of the proxy wars that were being fought on the periphery of the international political scene. Numerous places around the world were used as testing grounds for various armaments as the west sparred with the Warsaw Pact. Those wars, such as the support provided by the West to the resistance fighters opposing the Russian occupation of Afghanistan, would in time create the conditions for the chaotic world in which we live today.

Past United Kingdom defence reviews have had a relatively simple equation to consider. If social services required a large amount of government spending then the percentage of the tax revenues allocated to defence was bound to decrease over a period of time. Defence reviews were all about taking decisions that made those cuts palatable to the wider population. Where conventional forces could no longer be afforded a nuclear deterrent would provide the weapon of last resort against a potential aggressor. Where conventional forces would be required Western technological superiority would carry the day.

Gaining more capability from fewer platforms has been a mantra that has been echoed by governments past and present for a long time. The problem is that there are lower limits below which the armed forces simply cannot go in order to maintain the missions designated by the government of the day. Many political leaders, barely versed in the history of defence matters when they take up their roles, struggle to understand this fundamental point.

The other shaping factor that has changed the nature of the defence reviews has been the growing, albeit slowly, integration and mutual dependence that exists in NATO and in other collaborative ventures. In the past, debates have often focused on the degree to which the United

Kingdom has been able to project force on its own. In the defence reviews of 1957 the primary task of Duncan Sandys was to create the conditions for a rationalisation of the United Kingdom aircraft building industry and to take a huge step in reducing the size of the army. Sandys' review was hugely influenced by the developments in technology that were changing the nature of warfare. The Royal Navy was to emerge from that review relatively unscathed.

Nearly ten years later, in the 1966 defence review led by Dennis Healy, the withdrawal from operations east of Suez was the main outcome. On this occasion the Royal Navy was not to get off so lightly. The plans to develop a new aircraft carrier (CVA-01) were abandoned. The squabbles between the RN and the RAF that occurred at the time over the nature of air power, saw the TSR-2 project that was to provide the backbone of the RAF's strike attack aircraft for the future, also cancelled.

The Falklands crisis, coming in the wake of the infamous defence review of 1981 led by Sir John Nott, still causes intense debate in historical circles. Had the measures outlined in the review been implemented the chances of the United Kingdom being able to launch OPERATION CORPORATE to re-take the Falklands would have been seriously affected.

The discussions at the time were wide ranging. Nott appeared to favour placing greater emphasis on a Royal Navy with an increased submarine force. He seemed ready to give up the Royal Marines as an amphibious fighting force. One only has to look at today's world to realise what a catastrophic mistake that would have been had it gone through. The Falklands aside, the ability to project maritime power into the littoral and onto the land from the sea is more relevant today than it possibly ever has been.

The *Options for Change* review in 1990 was conducted against the backdrop of the end of the Cold War and the euphoria concerning the peace dividends. For a brief moment there were many that had forgotten how the proxy wars fought in the Cold War may have a legacy that might still affect the international security landscape. The threat from the Warsaw Pact had gone and the wake up call to the legacy of the Cold War that was to occur on 11 September 2001 was twenty years away. Now was the time to cut defence.

Sadly, of all the defence reviews that have been undertaken since the Second World War, it was this review in 1990 that was to set a course that others have followed. The realignment of the British Army created a fighting force that was no longer going to be able to launch a major operation on its own again. In Iraq in 1991 and elsewhere since, the British Army has fought alongside multi-national coalitions of the willing. Of all the services at the moment it is the British Army that must be the most worried post the withdrawal from Afghanistan in 2014. What its role will be in the future will be the major theme to emerge from the next SDSR in 2015.

There are some other points to consider from *Options for Change*. It first cancelled the Brimstone missile. As we shall see this played a crucial part in Libya and is a fundamental component part of the air power activities over Afghanistan. That the program was re-instated at a later date is a tribute to those who argued for its development. In Libya the missile showed its versatility.

Eight years were to pass before, in the wake of their election victory in 1997, the Labour Government would publish its own Strategic Defence Review (SDR). Today, looking back on its analysis and conclusions, it is hard to fault the thought processes and analysis that went into the review. Given the pragmatic view that needed to be taken of the world at the time – and 11 September was still three years away – it remains a point in recent defence reviews where the outcome was validated and tested in a yet to be understood and uncertain world. The re-structuring that took place as a result of the SDR in 1998 enabled the United Kingdom's armed forces to retain a broad range of capabilities and to project power overseas where British interests were at stake.

The fact that the follow-up review in 2002 ordered by the Prime Minister, Tony Blair, in the wake of the terrorist attacks on 11 September in the United States did so little to change what had been published in 1998, is a tribute to the thoroughness of the analysis that went into its development. The additional resources to emerge from the New Chapter exercise would also lay the ground work for facilities that were to prove themselves in combat in Libya. The investments in intelligence collection, networking facilities, unmanned drones and Special Forces were to pay off in Libya.

It would be twelve years before another review was to occur. In that time the United Kingdom's armed forces would maintain an operational tempo that was extraordinary by any supposed peace-time standards. The 2010 SDSR could have been a point for a mature debate on how to re-shape this pressure, re-defining priorities and setting more modest goals for the range of missions to be performed by the United Kingdom's armed forces. Sadly, due to the pressure to reduce the national debt, the political leaders involved decided to cut a range of capabilities whilst shying away from changing the mission profile.

The United Kingdom armed forces were, yet again, to do more with less. The SDSR in 2010 cut a swath through the capabilities of the United Kingdom's armed forces. The loss of naval capabilities and the cut-backs to the RAF seemed ill-conceived and rash given the lack of compromise on redefining the mission profile.

Within weeks of the ink drying on the SDSR, in an eerie echo of the Nott Review in 1981, the United Kingdom's armed forces would again be at war. The outcome of the SDSR, and all its decisions, were about to be tested for real. How that turned out was going to, in part, define the historical view of the premiership on David Cameron. At the start of the Libyan campaign, that outcome was far from certain.

That the United Kingdom's armed forces would undertake the task in hand quickly and professionally was never in doubt. That they would forge an excellent partnership with their coalition colleagues was also clear. The alignment of French and British interests provided an excellent opportunity to forge a new military alliance – one where Europe would show its capabilities to secure its own back yard.

But their ability to maintain a campaign and secure a positive outcome from it over a period of months was less certain. The main effort in Afghanistan would be maintained. But the operational stretch on the RN and the RAF was to test its people to the limit.

Updating the Entente Cordiale
With the United States turning its primary attentions to its major debtor, China, and to what it regarded as more important issues associated with trading with its partners in the Pacific Rim, David Cameron must have known that when he became Prime Minister he would have to redefine

the 'special relationship'. For too long the United Kingdom had appeared to be joined at the hip with the United States. Tony Blair's willingness to deal with the right wing American President George Bush in the wake of 11 September had surprised many commentators.

The part played by the United Kingdom in helping forge the arguments for war against Iraq and the unreliable sources of intelligence on which that was based, are now a matter of public record. For David Cameron that relationship needed to be redefined. In President Obama he found a willing ally. Whilst the public rhetoric would remain clear, some room for manoeuvre would be created for both parties. Military collaboration and intelligence sharing would remain a priority, but when it came down to specific military interventions one could no longer take the participation of the other for granted. For the United Kingdom this was quite a significant, if not profound, shift in its approach to the international security situation.

The SDSR did, however, mean that David Cameron would have to reach out into Europe for cooperation. That created political differences for him with his party which is naturally Euro-sceptic. To re-define the nature of the military links with European countries would be hard. But it was going to have to occur, and where better to start than France? After all, he might have reasoned, had not the original entente cordiale been signed on the 8 April 1904 to redefine the nature of the relationship with France? It was not such a hard thing to find ways to resurrect it and adapt it to the prevailing situation.

A similar test awaited President Nicolas Sarkozy about how to define France's role on the international stage. His much-vaunted desire to ensure that France would be a global player in support of human rights was also to come under the microscope in the Libyan campaign. His decision in 2009 to re-integrate with the NATO command structure would also be scrutinised. He had staked a great deal of his reputation on the move to reverse the decision taken by President De Gaulle in 1966.

Libya was to be the first Franco-British led war that was placed under the banner of NATO. This was not to be a United States dominated campaign. Europe was to step up to the plate and take responsibility for conflicts in its immediate area that might threaten its own interests. For many Americans of a right-leaning political persuasion, this was music to their ears. At last, it appeared, Europe would shoulder its share of the burden of policing the international security landscape. However, it is axiomatic that appearances can be deceptive. Europe is a very long way from being able to achieve that level of autonomy from the United States.

That the Franco-British alliance achieved some of what it set out to accomplish in Libya cannot be in doubt. But could it be the precursor to other joint Franco-British military efforts that no longer place NATO as the main vehicle through which international coalitions are assembled? The outcome of the conflict, that was to last until the end of October, delivered one hugely important lesson. Europe is not capable of conducting military operations on its own. It still needs the direct involvement of the United States if it is to project military power.

In the existing fiscal climate no country could go it alone, so why not have some arrangements in place that you can use if you feel they are appropriate? For France and the United Kingdom to collaborate against a regime on its southern border that was persecuting its people is clear. If you cannot pass that sort of test what is the purpose of having armed forces anyway?

The centrepiece of the Franco-British agreement was that all of the branches of the armed forces would work together where national interests were at stake. It would certainly play to the kind of agility and flexibility that Cameron had seen at the heart of the SDSR.

In Libya they had the prefect opportunity to see how this doctrine might develop. By avoiding the need to field a major land component, and by focusing on supporting the Libyan rebels from the air, the concept of interoperation, could be tested in a relatively controlled environment where the air domain had primacy and the maritime domain would play a controlled secondary role. As a laboratory test of the outcome of the SDSR it was a good exam question to be set.

In one of the more controversial decisions made by the newly incoming coalition government in the United Kingdom, David Cameron had finally addressed the issue of the degree of cooperation that was now required with France in military affairs. It was an important moment. Until then any ideas of a Franco-British defence pact had largely seemed to be not worth the paper they were written on at the time. The previous Labour administration had signed a number of cooperative defence research efforts but had shied away from developing much closer ties. The 'special relationship' between Britain and America always took centre stage when such discussions were going on. Cameron, however, realised that America was starting to look east towards the Pacific Rim. Europe was yesterday's issue. For the United Kingdom, forging a closer alliance with France made a lot of sense. It was, after all, not the first time it had been done.

The St Malo declaration signed by the then Prime Minister Tony Blair and President Jacques Chirac in 1998 focused on cooperation in a European context. The agreement Cameron and Sarkozy signed in London on 2 November 2010 went further, formalising bilateral cooperation in a number of military matters between France and the United Kingdom. Prior to that, the two countries had started to increase their cooperation in 2008 to reflect, somewhat pragmatically, the increasing fiscal constraints that threatened their ability to manoeuvre militarily on the international stage. By gradually joining forces the two countries might gain additional flexibility where joint deployments were contemplated. The agreement of course was met with howls of derision from its critics who tried to point out how often British and French interests had diverged in the past.

Somewhat contrary to his declared indifference towards the European Union, in a stance taken to placate the hard right in his party, the Prime Minister moved to establish a joint Franco-British Combined Joint Expeditionary Force (CJEF) as one of a number of measures included in the agreement.

For many Euro-sceptics this was the slippery slope towards the final dénouement of NATO and its replacement with a European Union army. It was not a decision that was welcomed widely in his political party. That it sent a clear signal, however, that the United Kingdom was determined to be flexible in its relationships with the United States was clear. In the wake of what was characterised on many occasions by the British media as the United Kingdom being at the beck-and-call of the United States wherever it wanted to go and wage war, it was an important moment.

Whether future military campaigns might then be conducted by the Franco-British Brigade, that had been agreed in November 2010 at a summit meeting between Cameron and Sarkozy, is a matter of debate. But in a twist of fate the first major exercise called FLANDRES 2011 involving the new Brigade structures took place between 22 and 29 of June 2011, in parallel with the period where the campaign in Libya appeared to be grinding to a halt. The aim of the exercise was to test the levels of interoperability between the armies against a backdrop of a variety of different types of missions that spanned offensive and defensive operations; securing operations and reconstruction operations – any one of which might have significant overlap with any land component being deployed into Libya.

Whilst the options of placing troops on the ground in Libya was never high on the agenda of either David Cameron or Nicolas Sarkozy, it is likely that when they conceived the idea of the joint Brigade, should it ever be deployed, one of its missions might have been the kind of quick intervention operation that could have tipped the balance in what had become a stalemate on the ground in June and July 2011. As it was, other factors came into play that prevented the need for placing any significant numbers of troops on the ground.

The Legacy of Iraq and Afghanistan
The application of military force can be likened to a super-tanker ; once set on its course it is very hard to change its direction. The initial military campaigns in Iraq and Afghanistan made a range of mistakes as commanders set about conducting brigade-level sweeps through areas, before retiring into their fortresses. Whilst this had an immediate effect of clearing an area, as soon as the forces withdrew the insurgents simply moved back into an area, coercing the population and creating a sense of fear of reprisals for those seen to have cooperated with coalition military forces. It took the military in Iraq many years to determine that their approach to the conduct of military operations was not bringing any sense of progress.

The publication of Field Manual 3-24 in December 2006 by the Headquarters Department of the Army was a turning point. Its title was simple: *Counterinsurgency.* Its content however was revolutionary. It was to define an entirely new approach to warfare. The manual provided 'A guide for action' and included appendices on linguistic support, legal consideration and the role of air power in an insurgency.

The main body of the document contained a blueprint for future warfare and was immediately put into action as General David Petraeus was appointed to command the United States military forces operating in Iraq. He arrived at a propitious time.

Whilst the initial invasion of Iraq had almost gone like clockwork, with technology providing coalition forces with a battle-winning advantage over the poorly equipped Iraqi forces, the situation in the country rapidly descended into chaos. What appeared to be a limited mission to remove the threat from weapons of mass destruction suddenly became a campaign to remove Saddam Hussein from power.

The psychosis that prevailed with many political leaders at the time over the potential threat of such weapons being deployed by terrorist groups against the West saw a fundamental re-appraisal of previously held political views. After nearly 3,000 people died in America on 11 September 2001 the need to go upstream to prevent future attacks which might be much worse suddenly became a sound idea.

The development of the insurgency in Iraq was unexpected. In part it was fuelled by local issues as war lords and criminal gangs vied for position as normal governance and security structures were removed. The decision to disband the Iraqi Army being specifically fateful as it provided a semblance of control and social identity for men who, in its absence, sought security by being part of new organisations that emerged to fill the power vacuums that existed across Iraq. Fairly quickly the nature of the threat to coalition forces on the streets changed. The insurgency started to take hold.

The events that then took place have been well captured and explained by a wide range of authors. Of all of them however it was perhaps the book *The Utility of Force: The Art of War in the Modern World* by General Sir Rupert Smith that provided the most compelling insight into how current and future military campaigns needed to set out their objectives. It remains a definitive and timeless contribution to the debate on the future of war with its central theme of 'war amongst the people'.

The legacy of the campaign in Iraq and the subsequent lengthy operations in Afghanistan provided a backdrop to the Libya campaign that saw the international community very wary of being drawn into a similar quagmire in the largely unpopulated and tribally divided country that Colonel Gaddafi had forged. The parallels with what happened in Iraq and Afghanistan were all too clear.

Libya: Another Insurgency?

The decision to deploy military forces to protect the population of Benghazi was taken whilst the blood and treasure invested in Iraq and Afghanistan was still quite raw. The ubiquity of the Improvised Explosive Device (IED) and the enduring resilience of terrorist networks meant that victory in any sort of asymmetric warfare was not going to be easy to achieve.

For the people of the United States, tired by the continuous campaigns against Al Qaeda in the wake of the attacks on 11 September, the idea of conducting yet another military campaign in some far-off field had little attraction. Time had deflated the memory and the anger that existed in the immediate aftermath of 11 September. The continuing sacrifices being made by the United States and their coalition colleagues, in the pursuit of what seemed like a hopeless cause to bring democracy to a country that had barely emerged from what many commentators have classified as a medieval past, was harder to justify.

President Obama, in the wake of his losses in the mid-term elections, faced a hostile Congress that was simply unwilling to put up with yet more American-led interventions in the Middle East. The visual images of Somalia, Iraq and Afghanistan were simply unable to be readily forgotten. If Europe wanted to go to war to defend the citizens of Benghazi then it would have to take the lead. America would commit resources in terms of aviation and naval power, but it was not about to place any boots on the ground to help secure the country. There was not going to be another twenty-first century colonial war which could be labelled as an occupation by those enemies of the United States who loved to exploit its military adventurism for their own purposes.

President Obama did not want Libya to provide a distraction to his urgent need to address the level of debt in the United States and one of its main drivers was the costs of keeping troops in Afghanistan. For President Obama upstream activities were now to be conducted by drones and Special Forces, not large concentrations of troops on the ground. There were also those in Washington who chose to take the moment to suggest that the intervention in Libya could have been carried out mainly using America's obvious capability in cyber space. For an administration embarked on withdrawal from Iraq and Afghanistan, getting involved in an uncertain military adventure in Libya was the last thing it needed. The opportunity to use attacks in the cyber domain must have been an attractive one.

It is important to realise that America is not alone in this desire to reduce the tempo of military operations. Other countries in NATO also joined in the campaign in Libya despite reservations by some political commentators at home. Denmark is one country which has been juggling the need to keep its army deployed in Afghanistan, at the same time maintaining its naval presence off the coast of Somalia whilst its air force contributes to the NATO air operations over Libya. Though being a relatively small partner in NATO Denmark regularly contributes to all its missions. It is one of the most dependable partners in NATO. However for a country trying to cut two billion Euros from its current military expenditure this is a difficult juggling act. Denmark will not be alone within NATO in wishing to take time to reflect on the optimum balance of forces that it wishes to have for the future.

The intervention in Libya therefore raises a number of issues that this book will attempt to address. For David Cameron, at the point where Tripoli was released from the iron grip of the tyranny that was Gaddafi's regime, this was a personal success story. Not quite a defining moment for his premiership but pretty close. For President Nickolas Sarkozy the economic imperative was clearly to the fore in his thinking. A new political climate in Libya could have all sorts of potential for French arms dealers. His pleasure at the outcome of the campaign will be measured in terms of French jobs secured as a result of new contracts with the leadership in Tripoli.

The leadership being shown by the Qataris in helping Libya move on in the immediate aftermath of the death of Colonel Gaddafi, helps Nicolas Sarkozy. Qatar is a major client for French arms. So, as Gaddafi's body was moved from its showcase refrigerator in Misurata to be buried at a secret location in the desert, it is possible to see the future for Libya through a pair of rose-tinted glasses. International relations, however, rarely develop along predictable trajectories and traps lie in wait for the unwary. What is required now, and what this book hopes to contribute to, is a measured analysis of the campaign and its outcome. For those tempted to delve a little deeper some important insights emerge.

Does the campaign in Libya suddenly provide the West with a new formula for conducting overseas interventions that avoid placing 'boots on the ground' and becoming labelled as 'occupiers'? Can democracy actually be defined from 25,000 feet? Or is it more complicated than that? What does this mean for NATO? What are the implications for the Arab Spring? Will a similar military operation in Syria be next? Perhaps most importantly for the United Kingdom, what does Libya mean for its armed forces as they start to gear up to defend their corners in the next SDSR at the end of the current Parliament?

CHAPTER 2

The Context of the Libyan Campaign

By many measures, Tunisia should be a close US ally. But it is not. While we share some key values and the country has a strong record on development, Tunisia has big problems. President Ben Ali is aging, his regime is sclerotic and there is no clear successor.

Extract from a United States Embassy Cable dated 17 July 2009
leaked by Wikileaks on 7 December 2010

The Political Landscape

To understand the events that shaped the uprisings in Libya it is important to revisit the tensions and issues that existed prior to the outbreak of the civil unrest. This must be done from a number of viewpoints. These include Libya, its neighbouring countries, and from a political and defence standpoint, those nation states that would commit resources to the military campaign that NATO would mobilise.

This also provided the context against which David Cameron took his decision to get involved militarily. When he took office the Prime Minister could have had little idea or warning about the political upheaval that was about to the sweep the Middle East. As ever, events shaped policy. Cameron may, for a moment, have reflected on MacMillan's answer to the question he was asked about what keeps him awake at night. His answer 'events, dear boy, events' are one that has adorned many a political thesis since his time as Prime Minister.

In part MacMillan may have been thinking about the kind of events that unfolded around the Cuban missile crisis and the potential for global nuclear war when he made his remark. Whilst hardly reaching that level of gravity, the dramatic political changes in the Middle East provided a window to send a message to the people of the countries involved. The gist of that message was, if you seek democracy the West will do its best to help. In time the practical limitations of the extent of that help will become increasingly apparent as far more complex situations in Syria and Yemen are not likely to receive the same degree of military intervention, leading to accusations of inconsistency – the bane of a political leader's life.

For Cameron, however, the situation in Libya was an opportunity he felt he could not miss. Political obituaries have a habit of being written in ways that are unkind to the subject involved. For the British Prime Minister the situation in Libya gave him a hugely important opportunity to at least shape one part of that early in his tenure. The confrontation with Gaddafi had come at a time at which his sincerity with respect to the military was also being called into question.

In a high profile address on board HMS *Ark Royal*, he underlined his commitment to creating a new military covenant. This was one that he said would be 'refreshed'. In a speech that was to be quoted widely a few months later as the implications of the SDSR were to become clear, Cameron also praised the role of the Royal Navy. His comments, praising the rich history and traditions of the Royal Navy, were clearly aimed at his immediate audience. His reference to the need for that to be locked into the curriculum of schools added another dimension to the speech. But his observation that that 'we have a great naval future and well as a great naval past' cannot have failed to chime with the 1,000 people assembled on the deck.

For those listening to his words it would appear the future of the HMS *Ark Royal* was secure. If the 'Ark' was secure it was reasonable for the Royal Navy to also expect the Harriers to be kept in service as well. To have a gap in the capability of the Fleet Air Arm was unthinkable if the new aircraft carriers were to enter service on schedule.

Months later, Cameron had to go public defending the action to retire HMS *Ark Royal* and the associated Harrier force from duty. This decision, above all else, was to come to plague Cameron's subsequent attempts to justify the SDSR and its efficacy. One minute he was praising the role and importance of the RN. The next he was cutting to the heart of its capability. If he could appear to be that fast and loose about the future of the last aircraft carrier in the RN, what trust could people place in his words and determination to reform the military covenant?

Having taken what for many were quite extraordinary decisions to cut back on existing military capability, the timing of an intervention in Libya was to say the very least unfortunate. With HMS *Ark Royal* and its sea-based Harrier jump jets consigned to the scrap heap, alongside the Nimrod MRA4 long range maritime patrol aircraft program, it was really not a good time for military adventurism. There were huge risks involved.

No doubt in his daily briefings by the Secret Intelligence Service (SIS) various scenarios would have been played out. But the fall of the regime in Tunisia was difficult to foresee. That, like the end of the Cold War, was a strategic shock. But political careers can be defined over seizing a passing moment and Cameron quickly set his course.

At the outset Cameron had to define a case for an intervention in Libya. What he could not afford to do was to appear to be launching another full scale military intervention, such as those in Iraq and Afghanistan. His early statement, where he said that 'Britain has no intention to get involved in another war in Libya' was clearly aimed at dispelling the idea that a full-scale invasion was going to happen. Cameron's rhetoric was matched from an unlikely corner. The French President was also on a mission.

Nickolas Sarkozy had been quick to call for the assets of the Gaddafi regime to be frozen and for an imposition of sanctions by the European Union. These measures however are never likely to make a dictator quake in his boots. Whilst many other political leaders started to look down at their feet, avoiding eye contact when the key decision needed to be taken, Sarkozy took a lead.

His call for military action against the Libyan regime was to startle many observers. His statement that, 'the continuing brutal and bloody repression against the Libyan population is revolting', laid out the message in less than diplomatic language. His follow-up observation that, 'the international community cannot remain a spectator to these massive violations of human rights', opened up a whole new ball game. A military intervention was on the table. It would be for the United Nations to decide if it were to be implemented.

At the time the British government's message was more circumspect. British citizens were still in Libya and could be taken as hostages if David Cameron and his Foreign Secretary William Hague's language were to appear too bellicose. Cameron's observation at the time that, 'I do not think we are at that stage yet. We are at the stage of condemning the actions Colonel Gaddafi has taken against his own people', was a holding position. Nothing was ruled in or out, although Cameron and Hague both saw problems at the United Nations in getting a resolution passed to take some sort of military action, such as the imposition of a no-fly zone.

Ironically it was the RN that provided the Prime Minister with some much-needed room for manoeuvre as the situation in Libya descended into chaos. The warship HMS *Cumberland* was in the area returning from protecting the United Kingdom's interests in the Persian Gulf. Its diversion to evacuate 454 people from the anarchy in Libya came at an awkward time.

Officially she was on her way home to be scrapped. In rescuing 129 British Nationals and 325 other 'entitled persons' (the official language for people that were the subject of a United Kingdom evacuation program – made up of European and Commonwealth passport owners) HMS *Cumberland* again demonstrated the underlying versatility of the RN. Within days HMS *York*, diverted en-route to her mission in the South Atlantic, joined the operation helping to evacuate another forty-three people from Benghazi whilst also delivering medical and food supplies into the city.

The evacuation from Libya was very reminiscent of OPERATION HIGHBROW in 2006 when people were lifted out of the conflict in the Lebanon. Yet again the RN had reaffirmed its ability to use the 'commons of the oceans' to mass military capability and undertake an unexpected operation.

The RN also provided the Prime Minister with another piece of flexibility. The first deployment of the Response Force Task Group (RFTG) was underway in the area under the mantle of the Cougar Task Force. This is the United Kingdom's military quick reaction force and is led by Commander United Kingdom Task Group (COMUKTG).

Whilst not officially acknowledged at the time, the presence of the

RFTG gave military planners the option to divert the Royal Marines from their original exercise schedule to conduct a limited humanitarian relief operation in Benghazi. Their capability, based on HMS *Albion* and its associated task force and equipment, would have provided a potent intervention force had it proved necessary to intervene on the ground in Benghazi for humanitarian purposes. It is important to understand that the Cougar Task Force schedule, to conduct exercises in the Mediterranean Sea and then move through the Suez Canal to operate in the Indian Ocean, had been planned for some time, before the Arab Spring had even started. Its presence in the area at the time the Libyan campaign was being developed was one of happy coincidence not design.

If the situation had deteriorated rapidly that option would have had a greater role and Cameron would have had to argue that a limited humanitarian intervention – placing the Royal Marines on the ground in Benghazi – was not going to erupt into a full scale military operation. For the public the sign of Royal Marines landing on amphibious craft on Benghazi beaches is one that would have easily recalled memories of another Tory leader reclaiming the Falklands.

Cameron risked backing himself into a major corner, as military interventions do have a habit of having some unpredictable elements. For political leaders, having military planners with options available, is always useful. In this case, as events unfolded, the need for a ground intervention did not arise.

The Risk Environment
The decision to go to war over Libya was layered with numerous risks and unknowns, one of which was the inevitable mission creep that occurs as military campaigns unfold. Despite the careful attention to the wording of United Nations resolutions, with its obvious emphasis on restricting the kind of military venture that might unfold, Cameron and the French President were able to find enough room to manoeuvre in the original wording to cater for the mission creep as it unfolded.

The potential for unintended outcomes was therefore writ large across the campaign from the outset. For many it was a very brave decision to take, given the immediacy of the images of Iraq and Afghanistan in the British public's mindset.

In Libya one of the key factors that kept Gaddafi in power was his knowledge of, and relationship with, key power brokers in the tribal dynamics that punctuated the country's societal landscape. Key tribal leaders were important to Gaddafi. How they might react to any attempt to remove him from power was important. There were other pressing concerns. Libya had a track record of many of its countrymen going to join the insurgency in Iraq. Reports from a number of sources suggested that Libyan nationals were the second most important source of recruits for Al Qaeda's activities in Iraq. With many of them having returned to Iraq, media reports were quick to highlight the issue that yesterday's foes may have become today's allies.

Behind all of these thoughts the issue of Al Qaeda's franchise operating in the region, Al Qaeda in the Islamic Maghreb (AQIM), cannot have been far from the minds of the various intelligence agencies involved. Could a military intervention in Libya somehow create the conditions in which AQIM could thrive? Given the proximity of Libya to the southern borders of Europe this would have been a factor that would have concerned many of those with knowledge of the security landscape in the region.

The physical landscape and barrier of the Sahara Desert may have prevented some of the Islamist extremists from reaching the coastline and embarking upon journeys to spread terrorism in Western Europe. If that was replaced by a new-found reservoir of enthusiastic people that now desired to use the changing political and security landscape in Libya as a platform on which to build to attack France, Spain, Germany and the United Kingdom, the view of the final outcome of Cameron and Sarkozy's War might be so very different.

Another vexing question would be how might Gaddafi react to an attempt to overthrow his regime? His threat, early on in the campaign, to send suicide bombers onto European streets must have caused the odd flutter in Cameron's and Sarkozy's hearts. A few well-placed bombs, or another Lockerbie, may well have tested European public opinion. After all, Europe's political leadership were hardly putting on a united front over Libya.

The Impact of the Arab Spring
As the Arab Spring spread throughout the Middle East the inherent power

of social networks was unleashed as people used all of the varying forms of social networking to issue a call for arms. This kind of spontaneous uprising had not been seen before across more than one country. In the failed Green Revolution in Iran, in the wake of the suspect elections that saw President Ahmadinejad returned to power, social networking sites did provide a means of mass mobilisation and of reporting the violence metered out by the Iranian security forces.

But those events did not have the same impact as the catalyst that occurred in Tunisia. The initial uprising occurred after the immolation of a twenty-six-year-old Tunisian named Mohamed Bouazizi. He set himself alight after the Tunisian Police allegedly seized his grocery cart. The reaction to his sacrifice, and the fact that he was portrayed as a man struggling to make ends meet, chimed with many in Tunisia who were clearly in equally difficult situations.

A combination of price rises, high levels of unemployment and a ruling class that was seen to be distant from the people, created an atmosphere where people were ready to challenge existing governance structures. When this sense of anger was combined with leaked reporting of confidential United States cables from its Ambassador in Tunis, concerning the stability of the regime, the potential for domestic unrest to be unleashed onto the streets was clear.

The Tunis regime was described as 'sclerotic' – rigid and unresponsive. This is hardly the kind of diplomatic language that normally gets aired in public. The additional observation that the President's wife was intensely disliked, also added colour to what was already a frank cable from the United States Ambassador, Robert Godec.

The sacrifice by Bouazizi, and the power of the words he wrote to his mother before he killed himself, provided the catalyst that drove many of them onto the streets, initially in a local protest in the area where he committed suicide, before spreading quickly across the country. He delivered the narrative and the opportunity for the social movement to gain traction, the mobile phone network created the resources.

The authorities in Tunis were completely overwhelmed by this reaction and within days the regime had fallen. The tinderbox that has long been the area from the west coast of Africa to the heart of the Middle East had been lit. For many in Syria, Bahrain and Yemen there would be no going back. The events sent shock waves throughout the region. Regimes, whose grasp on power depended on similar abuses of power, suddenly saw themselves being challenged by the population at large.

The Initial Uprisings in Libya

In order to gain some understanding of the spark that ignited the revolution in Libya it is important to gain an appreciation of the historical background to the societal landscape of Libya. This modulated the emergence of the social movement that acted as the catalyst for the revolution.

Libya's societal backdrop shares a similar but less complex tribal backdrop to countries such as Iraq and Afghanistan. At most Libya has around 140 tribes. Indeed it is estimated that between 15-20 per cent of Libyans have no tribal affiliations. Despite Libyan society being predominantly Muslim Arabs, the social structure is not homogeneous. There are ethnic differences that are important to understand.

The Berbers in the Nafusa Mountains are part of a very distinct ethnic group that is spread out across the Maghreb, now located in one major area in Algeria and several smaller communities that have dispersed over a period of time. Other ethnic divisions occur between the Tuareg's in the south west of Libya and the Toubou in the Cyrenaican part of the Sahara Desert. Demographically the Arabs form the largest single grouping in Libya, although the underlying heterogeneous nature of Libyan society is clear when the multiplicity of dialogues are considered.

Traditionally the major societal fault line that exists in Libya arises over the natural geographic divide that exists between Tripoli in the west and Benghazi in the east. Historically Libya comprised three independent regions of Tripolitania, Cyrenaica and Fezzan. Occupation of these regions has passed from the Greeks to the Romans and Arabs along with the Ottomans and the Italians and British. They were all colonisers, seeking to exploit the natural resources available in the area. Such is the history between the west and east of Libya that in the time after Libya gained independence it was understood to have two capitals, Tripoli and Benghazi. This ended when Gaddafi gained power in Libya in a coup in 1969.

The coup saw the reign of the only King of Libya (Muhammad Idris bin Muhammad al-Mahdi as-Senussi) brought to a premature end. With

British backing he had proclaimed the independent Emirate of Cyrenaica in 1949. At the time Idris was also invited to become Emir of Tripolitania. The King based himself in Benghazi from where he conducted negotiations with the British and the United Nations over independence.

Having successfully completed those discussions Libya was proclaimed as an independent sovereign state on 24 December 1951. Throughout his reign Idris sought to tread a difficult line between the Arab nations, such as Egypt who wanted to move away from the former colonial powers, and remaining in contact with the United Kingdom and the United States. His failure to produce a male heir created an opportunity for Gaddafi and members of the Libyan army. Idris, recognising his own failing health, signed a proclamation appointing his brother's son as his heir. This was to take effect from 2 September 1969.

In the last hours of his reign his wish to pass the responsibility for Libya onto his designated heir was halted as Gaddafi led an uprising that was to last for nearly forty-two years. The symbolism of the era however was to emerge in the traditional Senussi stronghold of Cyrenaica as the flag of the TNC became the catalyst from which the new revolution in Libya would arise.

After the coup, as if to distance itself from the past, Tripoli became the capital of Libya and Benghazi was relegated into being a secondary city. This loss of status was to create a fault line in Libyan society that would be at the heart of the movement that saw the Gaddafi regime replaced.

Gaddafi sought to establish in Libya his own vision of how a state should be run. The new approach was to be called *Jamahiriya* – a state of the masses. It was a very new idea. His approach to re-designing the state's apparatus for governance gave him a huge advantage. He could shut down and disband all of the potential sources of opposition.

By offering the population a vision of a Libya that distanced itself from the past excesses of being ruled by a small elite, and offering to re-distribute wealth amongst the people, Gaddafi was setting out to create his own unique form of socialist state. This would be one with Arab and Islamic overtones that had parallels with Nasser's Egypt and Assad's Syria.

The Gaddafi political vision and ideology was one that ultimately would fail in its own way. As power became more centralised in Tripoli, and the historical east-west fault line across the centre of Libya deepened, the dye was cast. Libya would eventually implode as the communities in the east felt the injustice of a very different form of wealth distribution emerge. This was one that filled the pension pots of Gaddafi's family and also benefited those people who were close to the regime. The east, as it was rapidly apparent to those that lived there, was out of sight and out of mind of those in the regime.

It was also the cause of the grievances that fuelled the rise of the Libyan Islamic Fighting Group (LIFG) which was founded in 1995 by Libyans returning from Afghanistan. Its initial aims were to establish an Islamic state in Libya and took the view that the Gaddafi regime was oppressive and brutal and anti-Muslim. Rumours associate the LIFG with an attempt on the life of Gaddafi in 1996. In an act of reconciliation over ninety members of the LIFG that had been imprisoned by Gaddafi were released as a result of an initiative of one of his sons, Sayif al-Islam Gaddafi.

LIFG always maintained an ambiguous and distant relationship with Al Qaeda despite several of its leaders having established contacts with senior members of the trans-national terrorist group. Whilst sharing a similar vision of an Islamic Libya, LIFG saw that objective being achieved through local action against Gaddafi and not as part of an international effort directed against the West. It is to be hoped that any of those still associated with the LIFG take a similar view of the need to reject terrorism, as Libya shapes its future as a modern Islamic state.

The rhetoric of the recently-anointed leader of Al Qaeda, Dr Ayman al-Zawahiri, was clearly angling to claim some of the plaudits for the overthrow of some of the regimes in the Middle East. His statement that, 'we see through our very own eyes the fall of godless, sinful and unjust tyrants and the crumbling of their thrones', is one that is clearly designed to chime with those who still retain allegiances to Al Qaeda. His warning that, 'the first thing NATO will demand of you is to relinquish your Islam', is also designed to alarm those who have been calling for the introduction of Sharia Law into Libya.

NATO's governments have been quick to make it clear that it is time for the Libyans to decide what kind of government they want. The idea of parachuting democracy in from 25,000 feet is not on the political agenda. After all it was the Libyans that fought the ground war. They invested the blood in displacing the Gaddafi regime, even if the West paid the treasure. But the point was stressed by the Dutch Foreign Secretary on 10 October 2011, 'that Libya must abide by the Universal Declaration of Human Rights (UDHR)'.

For those whose entire ideology is fashioned around a view of Sharia Law, that is quite contrary to the UDHR principles, these will have provided some comfort. For them this kind of theological debate is good ground on which to create problems in the future. The idea that Al Qaeda would sign up to the UDHR is at best far-fetched. Creating a post-Gaddafi government in Libya that marries up the principles of the UDHR and the complex theological interpretations of the Muslim faith is likely to be a challenge. It is one the West would be wise not to underestimate.

For Zawahiri however, another even more important sharp contradiction exists in his most recent claims. It goes directly against Al Qaeda's previous approach of trying to overthrow regimes in the area by attacking the West. The aim of cutting off the money supplies to despotic regimes in the Middle East by attacking Western targets has clearly failed. If Zawahiri is to be consistent, an unlikely outcome, a new focus on the so-called 'near enemy' should emerge.

What would be of great concern is the emergence of an alignment or split in the LIFG that sees potential in joining ranks with AQIM. This would give the new government in Tripoli a real headache as it would face a two-pronged insurgency from the east and west of the country. Egypt's uncertain future development might also throw up political alignments that might also help shape any nascent insurgency in Libya.

This task falls initially to the National Transitional Council (NTC) in Libya that became the internationally recognised government of Libya.

For the NTC, healing that open sore is going to be one of the important issues it needs to address as it tries to build a united Libya. With many of the members of the NTC coming from the eastern side of the country it is clear that the NTC has to create a wider constituency if it is to gain a mandate to govern. History in Libya, as it is in other parts of the world, is punctuated with examples of where power vacuums have been exploited by those with a very different vision of the future. Any military campaign that was set against this backdrop needed to be carefully navigated. There were lots of traps awaiting the unwary.

Libya: The Expression of a New Military Doctrine?

It is easy to see why the potential for a massacre in Benghazi was simply too awful for David Cameron and Nicolas Sarkozy to contemplate. For Cameron it was a test of his apparent zeal for foreign affairs and an opportunity to re-define liberal interventionism post-Iraq, and as the campaign in Afghanistan was winding down. For Nicolas Sarkozy, languishing in the opinion polls ahead of a presidential election, it was an opportunity to regain the political initiative.

It is possible to suggest that, at the time both men urged countries to support a United Nations resolution, they did not fully understand the underlying social and tribal factors that governed the way Libya works. It was, after all, a conflict that had appeared out of left field. This was not easy to anticipate and therefore the required degree of pre-planning was not possible before the commitment of forces. It was possible for lots of surprises to emerge as the campaign unfolded.

Regardless of those immediate concerns, for Cameron one thing was clear. Here was an opportunity to show what he meant when he had spoken of compassionate conservatism on the international stage. He wanted to create a new vision of the ways in which liberal democracies could argue that it was right to intervene in the affairs of other countries.

Such a line was far too reminiscent of a speech that Prime Minister Blair had given in Chicago on 22 April 1999 in which he laid out his 'Doctrine of the International Community'. Cameron needed to distance himself from the words of Blair and also show that the SDSR had not decimated the United Kingdom's military capacity and ability to intervene. It was going to be a hard argument to develop. For Sarkozy it was the moment to show that he meant it when he said 'no more Rwandas'.

Of all the many reforms to the process of government that have been brought in by the coalition government in the United Kingdom one of them met only limited public disquiet, the SDSR. The arguments over its efficacy have largely been limited to a number of exchanges in the media conducted between Ministers and members of the Treasury and a number of high-profile retired military officers. The public mood was not inclined to support calls for even maintaining defence spending. If cuts had to be made then everyone should chip in.

These were not the days of the Cold War when the Russian bear was seen to be hours away from launching an all-out attack on the West. This was a very different situation. Whilst being supportive of the military forces on deployment in Afghanistan, public opinion was not ready to dispute the outcome of the SDSR. The efforts made by the arm-chair admirals and generals to stir up trouble simply gained no traction with public opinion. Cameron had got off lightly. SDSR had been dramatic, but hardly any opposition to its outcome had been voiced. The Labour Party was still neutered by its earlier handling of the British economy.

The huge black hole that had been left to fester at the heart of the British military equipment program had been trailed many times by coalition leaders as an example of the ineptitude of the previous government. The political landscape was therefore favourable towards a major revision of military spending. The coalition government had got off virtually free of criticism as it made what it had trailed as 'difficult decisions'.

One of the difficulties that the military have is the lack of an immediate threat to the homeland of the United Kingdom. Barring terrorist events, and even they occur mercifully infrequently, the population at large does not really grasp the issues concerning the deployment of military forces overseas. The Labour administration under Gordon Brown failed to articulate why troops had to be maintained in Afghanistan. Vague references to the need to prevent more terrorist training camps being built in Afghanistan did not resonate with the public.

Whilst the sacrifices of the men in uniform were all felt acutely by the population, the case for a continuing presence in Afghanistan was not clearly made. From the outset of the coalition government their desire to see a line drawn under Afghanistan was clear. Cameron wanted out.

Changing the Nature of Warfare
On arrival in government David Cameron knew he had to make some tough decisions. It was a mantra that he had opined upon on a number of occasions whilst avoiding the pitfalls of being too specific. In the run up to the general election in the United Kingdom in May 2010 a small number of departmental budgets were ring-fenced. Two of those were the funding for the Health Service and the Overseas Development Aid

(ODA). These were essentially political moves by Cameron to maintain his drive to detoxify the brand his party had received.

Of the two, the ring-fencing of the ODA budget provides some insights into the mindset of the Prime Minister in the run up to the conflict with the Libyan regime. It is a well known axiom that prevention is better than cure. It is not difficult therefore to suggest that David Cameron's views on military interventions are that they should be used sparingly. Far better to spend money avoiding wars than to get stuck in prolonged campaigns for which it is almost impossible to define an end point. It also provided further support for those who wished to argue that Cameron was trying to detoxify the brand that had become associated with the Conservative Party under Margaret Thatcher.

The decision to protect the ODA budget, whilst taking a hard line over what was then an unfunded black hole in the defence budget, is revealing. It is hardly the act of a hard-line Tory leader. It provides an illustration of the emerging Cameron Doctrine towards using the military instrument of power. This is no longer going to be based solely on the application of force. From now on military power will be used as part of a re-balanced approach to the ways of using the traditional political, economic and military levers of power. Where austerity rules, defence budgets have to follow and each pound of tax payers money that is spent counts.

By ring fencing the ODA budgets the Prime Minister was sending out a signal, that money spend in prevention might be more effective at delivering an outcome than that expended in fighting wars with no discernable end. The problem with that view is that it does break the mould of established thinking in the world of international relations. It tests the widely held view that money invested in failing and failed states rarely gets channelled to those most able to turn around the situation. Corrupt officials and political leaders often choose to take the investments intended for their people and hide it away in overseas bank accounts.

The intention to spend the money, and help countries develop their infrastructure and education systems, is well meaning but achieves little in practise. To base an emerging stabilisation policy on the hope that British taxpayers' money might no longer go missing and not reach the audiences for whom it was intended is, to coin the famous insight of Samuel Johnson, as 'the triumph of hope over experience'.

35

This kind of intervention is now referred to as one element of the application of soft power. A term that has recently entered the military lexicon as the lessons emerging from the military campaigns in Sierra Leone, Iraq and Afghanistan have been compared and contrasted to the military interventions in Malaya, Oman, Kenya and Cyprus in the middle of the twentieth century.

Soft power is supposed to achieve results in military campaigns without having to resort to the application of kinetic force or hard power, where actual weapon systems are deployed. This is about shaping the wider battlefield, leading to the notion of the 'battle for the hearts and minds' of the people as well as activities that manoeuvre equipment and manpower in the physical landscape.

One of the enduring lessons of the campaign in Iraq and Afghanistan is that you cannot kill your way to success in a counter-insurgency campaign. There are simply too many things against you, such as tribal and family loyalties and societal customs and traditions that dictate behaviour. Military commanders have to become adept at the psychological aspects of warfare, to manoeuvre in the cognitive, as well as the physical domains.

Intriguingly, given the time it has taken for British military doctrine to catch up with the lessons identified in the campaigns in Iraq and Afghanistan, the intervention in Libya has actually tended more towards the traditional use of kinetic effects, applying hard power to shape the battlefield. In this regard the Royal Air Force and its counterparts took the lead.

In the course of the campaign there were few opportunities for applying soft power, perhaps as the dust settles and Libya moves on, its time will come. It has to be hoped that this will not occur against a backdrop of the kind of insurgency that the world saw develop in Iraq in the immediate aftermath of the initial military campaign in 2003, or the creeping insurgency that developed over a longer period of time in Afghanistan.

The Cameron Political Philosophy
The NATO mission was sanctioned by a United Nations Resolution that was steered through the Security Council by a Franco-British alliance

based around the personal chemistry and similar political views of President Sarkozy and David Cameron. It was also built upon a new political pragmatism in Downing Street that acknowledged the United States as the United Kingdom's primary partner in defence matters, but sought a bridge into a European dimension that would also take some of the pressure off the Americans.

David Cameron's actions, in working with President Sarkozy and other members of a hastily assembled coalition of the willing, will have won him the gratitude of the occupant of the White House in the short term and whoever occupies it in the future. America had been drained by Iraq and Afghanistan. It simply could not step up to the plate over Libya. As far as the Obama Administration was concerned this was a problem in Europe's back yard, if they wanted to sort it fine, the United States would offer its warships and aeroplanes to help defeat Gaddafi militarily. But they would not contemplate ground forces and any leadership of the campaign.

The initial mission was clear, to save the people of Benghazi from the kind of indiscriminate retribution which had punctuated previous conflicts in Africa. The call, 'let there never be another Rwanda', rang out clearly even in the more left wing elements of the media. This was an opportunity to set down a marker that Sarkozy and Cameron were not prepared to overlook.

When he became Prime Minister on 11 May 2010, his first address to the nation contained no reference whatsoever to defence and security. David Cameron's initial focus was on what he referred to as the 'broken society' and the issues of the social underclass that exists in the United Kingdom. Fifteen months on, this is a subject to which he has had to return in the wake of the riots on the streets of London and other major cities around the United Kingdom.

The absence of any mention of defence and security in his initial address is interesting. It follows a pattern where the Prime Minister can be seen to blow slightly hot and cold over the subject, appearing to swing with the prevailing mood in the country. Having become Prime Minister, Cameron was yet to define his thinking on defence. The Libyan campaign provided him with his own opportunity to do this without having to pick up the entrails on someone else's war. The Libyan campaign gave David Cameron his own war; one which could be fought on his terms.

Before he became Prime Minister his speeches on defence and security appeared to say all the right things that one might expect of a candidate for Britain's top job, but his lack of action in some areas was all too easy to contrast with the rhetoric. From a defence and security viewpoint Cameron appeared to be an enigma.

For those used to Conservative Governments spending more money on defence and security, the omens prior to the election were not good. Whilst making defence specifically, and his commitment to the mission in Afghanistan in particular, the opening theme of his address to the party faithful in Manchester in October 2009, his main themes shifted away from the topic as the date of the election came closer.

For any aspirant Prime Minister the obligatory visits to Afghanistan to look at what was happening on the ground ticked the boxes that showed he cared. The speed at which after his election he created the National Security Council (NSC), a move welcomed across the political divide in the United Kingdom, also appeared to reveal that the subject was high on his list. He chaired the opening meeting of the NSC the day after he became Prime Minister. The discussion at the NSC that day focused upon Afghanistan, Pakistan and the threat of terrorism to the United Kingdom.

In launching the United Kingdom's military into another round of operations in Libya the Prime Minister would have realised that he was asking much of a military force that was already really overstretched. The legacy of the war in Iraq that had spiralled out of control was a deep one, its roots running right into the soul of the United Kingdom's political establishment. The blood and treasure invested in Iraq is a long way from over, as far as the Iraqis are concerned. Theirs is a country that once knew a form of autocratic security, delivered by a man who was unable to encourage or tolerate any debate with his ideas, ruthlessly suppressing anyone who stepped out of line.

The legacy of the operations to change the regime in Baghdad will for some time to come haunt western political leaders. For the Prime Minister, deciding to send the United Kingdom armed forces into an operation that almost inevitably would result in a mission that would change, cannot not have been entered into lightly.

But to a person with the beliefs and values he holds, the idea of standing to one side when the people of Benghazi were threatened by the overwhelming military might of the war machine controlled by Colonel Gaddafi, was simply intolerable. If it meant that to get a United Nations resolution passed, the initial aims and objectives of the mission should be worded in ways to avoid any mention of regime change, then so be it. The imperative of helping the people of Libya rode roughshod over the political niceties of the usual round of complex negotiations at the UN. It was a pragmatic approach, and time was not on his or the President of France's side.

This then, was the background against which Cameron's War was launched. Given the narrow timetable over which the forces had to be assembled, the fact that the campaign got off to such a positive start is remarkable. As ever it is a testament to the attitude and professionalism of the armed forces of the United Kingdom, France, the United States and all of those countries that so quickly became involved in helping to shape the environment. It could have all been so very different. Cameron's decisions on the SDSR were about to be placed into the spotlight of a limited military campaign whose aims had been clearly defined by the United Nations. This was not all-out war.

By any measure of Iraq and Afghanistan this was a limited, small-scale intervention. If the SDSR could not pass this test Cameron would be damaged goods. There is only so far out on a limb that a political leader can go without risking that the branch may break. The outcome would be both politically and militarily crucial for the British government. With the stain of Iraq and Afghanistan still drying on the history of the United Kingdom armed forces it would provide some interesting insights for how future warfare should be conducted. The outcome, as ever in warfare, was to be inconclusive.

CHAPTER 3

Transition to Conflict

The Pressure Builds

Clearly when the uprisings started in Libya the Gaddafi regime was surprised. For them it was a strategic shock. They cannot have imagined how the uprisings from a tentative start could suddenly gain such traction with the wider population. The regimes in Syria and Yemen are going through similar challenges. The people that they thought were under their control have risen up against the leadership. That they have sustained their protests in the face of the full military might of the country being sent against them is remarkable.

In Libya the initial wave of the Arab Spring caught a mood in the eastern part of the country that had long been developing. They were the wealth generators of Libya, but the people in the west of the country were those that benefitted. Too many broken promises littered the highway between Tripoli and Benghazi.

Gaddafi's heir-apparent Saif al-Islam, had made numerous overtures to the authorities in Benghazi promising additional expenditure and greater autonomy in terms of decision making. These were the typical hollow promises that are made by regimes that have a sense of invincibility. They make the promises with simply no intention whatsoever to follow through on them and delver tangible change. After all, who will question them if they do not deliver?

The leaders of such regimes never bother to take any lessons from sociology or basic human behaviour. They ignore the fact that countries like Libya have failed to forge a national sense of identity. Whilst many Libyans do support the idea of a single country the history of the three major regions of Tripolitania in the west, Cyrenaica in the east and Fezzan in the south provides challenges that the mere imposition of a central regime in Tripoli cannot overcome. Whilst Gaddafi was good at manipulating tribal relationships through patronage networks even they have a limited shelf life.

The initial signs as the Arab Spring swept through Tunisia should have provided a warning for a regime whose hold on power was far more tenuous than they appreciated. The simmering cauldron that was Benghazi benefitted from its own social identity and a distance from Tripoli. Some of this attitude had a history that many in the east were not prepared to forget. Tribal rivalries between the Gaddafi's tribe – the Qadhadfa – and the dominant tribes in the east did not help. Many also had not forgotten how Gaddafi had toppled the Libyan's only reigning monarch Idris al-Senussi in 1969. This was one in a number of grievances that the regime did not address through Gaddafi's rule.

What compounded this already volatile situation was that Gaddafi did not use any form of carrot-and-stick approach to try and reconcile those grievances. If anything his approach was based solely on repression. He maintained military units in the east whose orders were to clamp down on any sign of insurrection. Any potential rebellion in the east was also disrupted, as networks of spies and informers ensured that anyone expressing opposition to the regime was quickly imprisoned. The fate of many of these people will probably never be known. Some burial sites are beginning to reveal their secrets, but it is likely that for many people in Libya, whose loved ones were arrested for opposing the regime, the fate of their kinfolk will never be known. Opposition in Libya under the Gaddafi regime was not an exercise without risk.

The second element of Gaddafi's approach was to punish the population in the east by withholding investment from the oil wealth that they generated. Gaddafi kept the east in a permanent state of underdevelopment; a term used by Alison Pargeter in her article in *Janes Intelligence Review* published in April 2011 entitled *Rebels with a cause: Libyan rebels struggle to hold the east.* Gaddafi's actions exacerbated the divisions in the country rather than trying to heal them.

Whilst the regime used its networks of spies and informers to enable it to disrupt and eliminate dissent at source, before it could gain any meaningful following, it failed to aggregate what it was hearing into a wider view of actions it could and should have taken to reconcile those in the east. It allowed the situation to fester. The infection took hold. It was only a matter of time before the contagion would start to spread. All it needed was a catalyst. The upheaval to sweep across Libya had been waiting to happen. Gaddafi, like many dictators before him, simply was unable to read the signs.

For him, in his isolated and privileged position, all Libyans loved him. That was a view that did not reflect the wider population in Libya, many of whom lacked jobs and a decent education. They were envious of those that had manipulated tribal and kinship relationships in Libya to gain positions. Patronage networks have their uses, but they can create the kind of grievances that fuel dissent.

Responding to the initial wave of protests in Tunisia, in January some people in Benghazi mounted their own protests with many Libyans moving to occupy government housing projects across the country. The regime's initial response clearly paid attention to what had happened in Tunisia. The speed with which the regime in Tunis had been replaced was a shock to the international system. Its rather crude attempts to impose what equated to marshal law on the country had singularly failed. Once the protests in Tunisia had started its outcome was inevitable.

The question was would Libya follow a similar route? Some analysts argued that the situation in Libya was very different from that in Tunisia and that Gaddafi always had the money from oil and gas sales to 'smooth things over'. One initiative taken by the regime at that time was to promise students a larger number of generous scholarships abroad. Other hints emerged from the regime of salaries being reviewed and increased.

Gaddafi's classic tactic of trying to bribe people was being used to placate the protestors without getting to specific proposals.

These half-hearted efforts at conciliation were too little and much too late. When they had little impact, Gaddafi was to react in the only way he knew. He decided the rebels would have to be crushed. His intransigence was to lead to his downfall.

The initial wave of protests that were sparked by the Arab Spring did not, however, gain sufficient traction in Libya. The regime had played its first hand well. Gaddafi himself even moving to make statements about how he was on the side of the people, handing out criticism against the very people whose power and authority he alone underpinned.

That situation was not, however, to last. It was always going to be a question of how the transition would be handled. Sensing their own opportunity many Libyans decided it was also time for action. The Gaddafi regime had to go. Others, however, remained staunchly loyal to the regime with people coming out onto the streets of several Libyan cities in support of Gaddafi. The situation in Libya rapidly fragmented into two quite distinct groupings; the ingredients of a civil war were rapidly coming into place.

The Formation of the National Transitional Council

Very quickly out of the turmoil at the heart of the uprisings, a sense of order started to appear. The National Transitional Council (NTC) was one element of this new order. It was formed on 27 February 2011 at the end of several days of meetings that had taken place between former military officers, tribal leaders, academics and businessmen in the city of al-Bayda.

The meetings had been chaired by the former justice minister, Mr Mustafa Abdul Jalil, who had been born in the city in 1952 – the historic seat of the Senussi dynasty and one of the first places to revolt against the Gaddafi regime. This has added significance as it was the last surviving member of the Senussi dynasty that Gaddafi had deposed on 1 September 1969 whilst King Idris was away in Turkey receiving medical treatment.

The location of this meeting was therefore highly symbolic. In the early part of the twentieth century the Senussi movement had fought against French colonialism in the Sahara, and Italian attempts to create an empire in North Africa in 1911. Despite the history associated with the Senussi nearly one third of all Libyans still affiliate themselves with the Senussi movement and its mix of Salafi and Sufi interpretations of Islam.

After graduation Abdul Jalil was to take up an appointment in the public prosecutor's office in al-Bayda. He was appointed to be a judge in 1978 at the age of twenty-six. In 2002 he rose to the appointment of President of the Libyan Court of Appeal. He was to go on to become the Chairman of the NTC.

Jalil had only recently resigned from the regime. On 21 February he had been sent to Benghazi by Gaddafi. Upon witnessing the levels of violence being used by the regime against the protestors he resigned and joined the rebel cause. This was to be the first of several high profile defections that saw the Gaddafi regime weakened as their power base started to erode.

For Abdul Jalil this was not the first time he had disagreed with the Gaddafi regime. He had been appointed to the role of justice minister at a time when Saif Gaddafi was trying to create an image of himself as being in favour of political reform in Libya. He served in that position for four years before defecting from the regime.

The attempts at reconciliation with the eastern part of the country in 2007 were all about positioning Saif Gaddafi as the natural heir-apparent to Gaddafi. If he could pull off a rapprochement between the east and west of Libya it would strengthen his claims to succeed his father. These efforts were not to bear fruit. Indeed as the east became more belligerent in its attitude towards Tripoli so Gaddafi obfuscated on certain reforms. He even refused to release some people held in jails in the east who were accused of political activism when they had been released by the judicial system. This frustrated Jalil. He was often critical of the regime and, at one point in January 2010, openly disagreeing with Gaddafi on television over the issue of releasing political detainees and resigning his post in a very public display of anger. Gaddafi refused to accept his resignation.

It was at this time that Jalil met with the United States Ambassador to Libya, Gene Cretz, on 25 January 2010. A copy of the cable reporting on the meeting was leaked by Wikileaks in February 2011. The cable noted that a recent report by Human Rights Watch suggested that Jalil had expressed 'reformist ideas about eliminating corruption within the Government of Libya' and had also noted his concerns about bringing Libya's security organisations within the rule of law – an implication that under the regime certain malpractices were being perpetrated.

This attitude has led many commentators to believe that he is an inherently fair person. However several question marks do hang over his views and beliefs. The Human Rights Watch report had suggested that this position was not actually based on a reformist agenda that might be based on democratic ideas. It was more likely to have been based on Jalil's own highly conservative approach to law. This is a viewpoint that probably arose from his early days in al-Bayda, and his own training in the analysis and interpretation of Sharia Law.

In August 2010 Jalil had taken what Human Rights Watch noted to be 'a strong stance against arbitrary arrests and prolonged detention without trial'. This language specifically referred to a group of over 200 people who had been seized and held by the regime. Theirs was to become a *cause celebre* that was to provide another element of the spark that would eventually see Gaddafi toppled from power.

Jalil's record on the internment of these individuals was to be followed up in November 2010 with another endorsement by Amnesty International, who also noted that 'Justice Minister Mustafa Abdul Jalil has publicly called for the release of these prisoners, but the Internal Security Agency, which holds them, refuses to comply.' Human Rights Watch backed up Amnesty International's recognition of Jalil's opposition in its submission to the 2010 Universal Periodic Review of the United Nations Human Rights Council.

Jalil however does have a track record as someone who sees justice through a quite narrow Islamic lens. In a high profile case in Libya in 2007, he confirmed the death sentence on a group of Bulgarian nurses who had been accused of deliberately infecting over 400 people with the HIV virus and also being responsible for the death of forty children. The prosecutors involved demanded the death penalty for what they alleged was an attempt to use the patients as guinea-pigs in a bid to find an HIV cure.

The medical people involved had been arrested at a children's hospital in Benghazi in 1999. The trial of the accused saw Gaddafi at one point suggest that they were operating on orders from the CIA and the Israeli secret service, Mossad. At their trial the accused called expert witnesses that explained that the infections had resulted from poor hygiene at the hospital.

After a high profile series of measures taken by the European Union to improve ties with the Gaddafi regime and a personal intervention by Nicolas Sarkozy and his then wife Cecilia, the accused were released in July 2007 into the hands of the Bulgarian authorities who immediately pardoned them. At the time Ms Benita Ferrero-Waldner, the European

Union's External Affairs Commissioner, hailed the release as 'a new page in the history of relations between the EU and Libya'. Four years later that new page had seen the man who had refused to allow the accused to receive clemency to be the de-facto recognised head of state of Libya and his predecessor on the run from the International Criminal Court.

The initial aim of the NTC was to be the 'political face of the revolution'. Seizing upon the initial advances made by the rebels as the uprisings threw the regime off balance, a statement was released by the NTC on 5 March saying that they were the 'only legitimate body representing the people of Libya and the Libyan state'. This was quite a claim for an organisation that had so hastily been assembled together from people with such a diverse set of opinions. The fractured nature of the alliance that had been created to oppose Gaddafi was to be sorely tested in the months to come. On its frailty the future of Libya might well hang in the balance.

At the outset however, the NTC did establish a structure that was to give it an increasing sense of purpose and allow foreign governments to start taking it seriously. Jalil was confirmed as the head of the NTC in its founding statement released on 5 March 2011. The newly appointed chairman was to go on record and call for the imposition of a no-fly zone four days later. The executive board of the NTC was created on 23 March 2011. This was four days after the military forces assembled to enforce the no-fly zone started their attacks on the regime's air defence network.

The Die is Cast
At the start of February the initial murmurings that had begun in January did not go away. People in Benghazi were beginning to find their voice, and it would be the social networking media of Facebook and Twitter that was to provide the means by which the vitally important narrative element that would help create the tipping point at which protests would boil over.

Of course, it is not just people expressing their grievances on Facebook and Twitter that creates a protest movement. Its people taking to the streets that provides the final sense that people are no longer prepared to grumble, they now want to act.

Learning lessons from the rapidly changing situations in Egypt and in other Middle Eastern countries a small but important group started to plan a 'day of rage' on 17 February 2011. This date had a specific significance in the eastern part of Libya as it was the anniversary of a previous uprising in Benghazi in 2006. What had started as a protest against the images of the Prophet Muhammad, which had been circulated in the western media, became a catalyst for wider grievances to be expressed. Quickly, via social networking sites, several thousand people signed up in support of the protest.

Fearing a full-scale rebellion might be about to erupt, the security services had opened fire five years earlier on unarmed civilians outside the Italian embassy. In the ensuing melee, security forces killed fourteen people who were protesting about the way in which one member of the Italian government had chosen to wear a T-shirt with the cartoon image of the Prophet Muhammad.

The protests had another catalyst five years later with the arrest of a lawyer, Fethi Tarbel, who was one of the instigators of the 'day of rage' protests. He had made his name campaigning for the relatives of around 1,000 people who had been allegedly killed in Abu Salim Prison in 1996. In recognition of his work on 30 May 2011, Tarbel was awarded the Ludovic-Trarieux International Human Rights Prize – the award given by lawyers to a lawyer who commands their respect for his or her achievements in the defence of human rights in the world.

His subsequent arrest on charges of 'spreading rumours that the prison was on fire in Tripoli' caused over 200 people to march on 16 February calling for his release. What started as a peaceful protest rapidly descended into an outbreak of violence. This was one of a number of catalysts that were to ignite the revolution.

These protestors had appeared to jump the gun on the 'day of rage'. Some commentators have suggested that this was a deliberate move to wrong-foot the authorities. If that was the case it worked, as the initial protests were met with a ruthless response. By the time the 'day of anger' dawned many people were already in hospital. Protestors calling for the release of Tarbel had tried to march on the headquarters of the Revolutionary Council in Benghazi and had ended up in Shajera Square were they had clashed with police. When freed on 20 February, Tarbel told Al Jazeera that the local security forces, 'firing from unmarked police cars', had killed 'dozens, perhaps hundreds' of people in Benghazi.

As Libyans buried their dead in Benghazi on 18 February, many rumours started to circulate about just how many people had died in the protests the day before. Estimates varied wildly. In one report published by the *Guardian* newspaper a local activist in Benghazi had reported that thirty-eight people had died in protests, noting that it was a massacre.

This was language that quickly chimed with emerging political fears of just how far Gaddafi might be prepared to go to defend the regime. But in such dynamic and fluid situations there are always those who may be prone to exaggeration. Obtaining a clear picture of what was going on in Libya was becoming increasingly difficult. With what was close to a total news blackout, even reliable outside sources, such as Human Rights Watch, were having to provide a view that might not be comprehensive.

Nevertheless, spontaneous protests arose in many locations around Libya. People on the streets of Tobruk, famed for its resistance in the Second World War, destroyed a statue of Colonel Gaddafi's Green Book chanting 'we want the regime to fall'.

Into this whirlpool of anecdote and rumours came other pieces of information that helped shape people's opinions. The Libyan security forces were often the subject of the rumours. They were, one rumour suggested, about to act against protestors in al-Bayda who had blocked the runway at the local airport to prevent the regime flying in mercenaries. Other troops were reported to have landed at Benghazi airport. In response to the growing anarchy the revolutionary committees issued a statement that promised a 'sharp and violent' response to anyone who dared to 'cross the regime's red lines'.

Gaddafi supporters were quickly rallied onto the streets of Tripoli and were shown on state television greeting their leader. The Khamis Brigade, specialised militia units commanded by one of Gaddafi's sons, were also quickly deployed and broke up a demonstration in Alzentan. Oliver Manning, a former British Ambassador to Libya, captured the situation when, writing in the *Guardian* on 20 February, he noted that 'Libya is the least transparent country in the Middle east at the best of times. Just now, with communications down, it is truly a mystery wrapped in an enigma.' It was clear that despite the lack of accurate reporting that the situation in Libya was rapidly becoming chaotic.

Watching from the sidelines, and apparently unable to intervene, the

European Union issued a statement urging the Libyan authorities to allow 'free expression' in North Africa and to 'listen to the protestors'. Colonel Gaddafi, however, was not in any mood to listen to people. He immediately imposed a news blackout. His tactic was to label the rebels as extremists and members of Al Qaeda.

Gaddafi's attempt to stereotype the revolutionaries as Islamic extremists did not carry any weight politically in London and Paris. In Washington, however, it might have caused some concerns to be raised. This may explain, alongside the fear of being dragged into another Iraq, the reluctance of the Obama Administration to become involved.

A civil war was about to engulf Libya. Just over six months later it would see Libya eject Gaddafi and his sons from power. It would give all Libyans a chance to create a new sense of national identity and to develop their own state that would fairly share out the wealth it could earn from its oil and gas reserves. Or would it?

As the protests gained traction and people left their jobs to join what was now a full-scale rebellion, the asymmetry in terms of the capabilities of the rebels and the Libyan Army would inevitably see the rebellion crushed under the weight of Gaddafi's tanks. That is, unless the rebels got some support from an outside source. Political leaders in London and Paris had listened to the protestors. Ignoring those who counselled caution, President Sarkozy and Prime Minister Cameron started to hit the international phone lines. Something had to be done. The question was what would the often dysfunctional international community agree to?

The Order of Battle of the Libyan Armed Forces
The Arab Spring was a complete shock to the international political system. It came literally out of nowhere. For Colonel Gaddafi it was, like many other dictators in the region, a shock. He was unprepared for having to mobilise his army to put down an insurrection. He was even more unprepared for having to deal with a threat from the international community to oppose his efforts to re-establish control of his country.

Having made the overtures to countries like the United Kingdom he must have been surprised that its leader was suddenly calling for his head. For Gaddafi, unused to having his authority to govern Libya challenged, it must have been a really difficult situation to grasp. The slowness of his response, a factor that was to punctuate everything that was to unfold, was indicative of the sudden and unexpected nature of the chaos that erupted in his own country.

From where he sat at the start of the rebellion Colonel Gaddafi must have thought he could ride out the storm. His Army was still relatively well equipped. At the start of the rebellion *Jane's Sentinel Security Assessment* (updated on 18 March 2011) assessed the Libyan Army as being made up of 45,000 people.

Its structure of eighteen infantry battalions, ten mechanised infantry battalions, ten armoured battalions and twenty-two artillery battalions, with several Special Forces groups and air defence capabilities, must have given the Libyan leader hope that he could put down the insurrection. That assessment, however, would be to belie the reality on the ground. In 1987 the weaknesses of the Libyan Army had been shown graphically as its own intervention in Chad had gone disastrously wrong, costing 4,000 Libyan soldiers their lives in a specifically challenging three months from January to March 1987.

International sanctions had also drained the Libyan Army of the spares needed to maintain its capability. On paper however the Libyan Army was assessed by *Jane's* to have 180 Russian-built T90S Main Battle Tanks (MBT), a notional force of around 1600 T54/55 MBT – of which around 500 were thought to be serviceable – and 170 T62 and 260 T72 MBT with seventy of the T62 held in reserve.

The army also had between 2,500 and 3,000 Armoured Personnel Carriers available that had been supplied by Libyan factories and external suppliers from Italy, the United Kingdom and former Warsaw Pact countries, although their serviceability was also in question. The total number of artillery and mortar pieces in service was also hard to estimate. *Jane's* assessment was that around 3,500 artillery pieces were available, many of these based on the Russian 82mm mortars.

Jane's also believed that the regime had retained 40 FROG-7 ballistic missiles in service. Many of the longer range SCUD missile that were originally part of the regime's ORBAT having been given up at the time of the rapprochement with the West. Add to this an array of anti-tank weapons that could have been useful had the Libyan armed forces gone into battle against another army. These, however, were to be of limited utility against a rebellion whose mechanised capability was to be largely based upon a number of hastily converted pick up trucks with hardly any armoured protection.

The ease with which the rebels were able to convert and field Toyota land cruisers in the role of mechanised infantry transports, provided a ready supply to replace any of those knocked out by any anti-armour capability. The tactics adopted by the rebels also did not help the Libyan Army, as they were inclined to 'shoot and scoot'. The Libyan Army ORBAT also included nearly 1,700 man-portable surface-to-air missiles and 200 ZSU-23-4 anti-aircraft weapons alongside a number of other variants.

On paper the Libyan Air Force looked impressive. At an assessed strength of 23,000 people comprising 10,000 regulars and 13,000 conscripts, the Libyan Air Force was capable of doing a lot of harm to the people of Benghazi. Its mix of MiG21, MiG-23 (NATO code name *Flogger*), Mirage F1, Su-24 (NATO code name *Fencer*) and Su-22 (NATO code name *Fitter*) provided an apparently comprehensive capability to help Gaddafi wage war from the air. Gaddafi also retained a relatively small helicopter force comprised of Mi-24D (NATO code name *Hind-D*) gunships which *Jane's* assessed at being twenty-two serviceable aircraft at the start of the campaign.

The MiG-23 provided the air defence capability for his Air Force. It was not to present a threat to NATO and coalition aircraft enforcing the no-fly zone. Had any MiG-23s actually engaged in air-to-air combat against the F-16 or Typhoon aircraft deployed in the air defence role it would have been a one-sided contest. On the limited number of occasions that Gaddafi's air force did fly in the run up to the imposition of the no-fly zone its impact on the ground from a military viewpoint was minimal. The few bombs that were dropped provided some helpful media images for those trying to make the case at the United Nations, but in practice the threat posed by the Libyan Air Force tended to be exaggerated. Very quickly a small number of those pilots tasked with attacking their own countrymen fled to Malta. They were not keen to be seen to be killing their compatriots.

Jane's assessment of the air defence weapons available to Gaddafi at the start of the campaign shows a mix of around 80 SA-2 (NATO code name *Guideline*), SA-3 (NATO code name *Goa*), SA-5 (NATO code name *Gammon*) and some Crotale (R-440) and SA-8 (NATO code name *Gecko*) missiles in the inventory. Many of these had originally been introduced into service in the early part of the 1970s and their serviceability must have been in doubt. For the NATO and coalition partners involved in establishing the no-fly area the threat from surface-to-air missile systems was never a major factor. On the rare occasions NATO and coalition aircraft came under threat it was mainly from Man Portable Air Defence (MANPAD) systems – some of which had been delivered to Gaddafi in the run-up to the war.

The Libyan Navy was hardly a force to concern the NATO and coalition partners involved in creating a blockade of Libyan ports. Theoretically it could deploy thirty vessels. Two warships of the *Koni*-class were the main stays of a fleet whose role in recent years had been relegated to patrolling the 1,770 kilometres of the Libyan coastline. The Frigates were backed up with eleven Fast Attack Craft (FAC) that, had they been serviceable, might have posed a threat to NATO warships and their replenishment vessels operating in the Mediterranean Sea.

Had any of the FAC actually emerged from harbour to conduct operations against the NATO navies in the area, the threat they posed would have been swiftly neutralised by the NATO air forces operating in the region. Such was the poor state of repair of the FAC that patrols in the Libyan coastal waters prior to the rebellion were conducted by the *Natya*-class minesweepers. These also posed little threat to NATO surface vessels.

At the time of the outbreak of the rebellion one of the two frigates was located in Benghazi. It was seized by the rebels early on. That left one Frigate based in Tripoli for the Libyan Navy. Any threat which that posed was quickly eliminated at the start of the enforcement of the no-fly zone. Throughout the war the Libyan Navy posed no surface threat to the NATO warships, other than an ad-hoc attempt to mine some of the harbours.

The Evacuation Program
Whilst the international community vacillated, the one thing they could agree upon was that they had to mobilise an effort to extract their nationals from what was clearly a disintegrating security situation. On 22 February

the British Foreign and Commonwealth Office had asked the Ministry of Defence to 'scope military options to support the civil and commercial efforts to extract British Nationals safely from Libya'. OPERATION DEFERENCE was to be undertaken by the RAF and the RN to evacuate British citizens from Libya.

This was to prove a difficult task. People working in the oil industry in Libya were dispersed over a wide geographic area. The media was quick to pick up on this and, always ready to criticise, latched onto one or two cases where people had been working in the desert and were using the internet to keep in touch with families at home wondering when they were going to be evacuated. With mobile phone and other telecommunications services being disrupted it made their sense of isolation all the more palpable. Their appeals for help, punctuated by the stories of hardship, lack of food and essential supplies, all added to the pressure that was building on the British Government. The feeling of an impotent response started to gather in many quarters.

In many of these kinds of situations the problems arise with unrealistic public expectations of what the military can actually achieve. To fly missions into the deepest parts of Libya to evacuate British nationals is hazardous at the best of times. How the Libyan Air Force and its air defence system might react to a slow moving Hercules aircraft flying into a remote part of south-east Libya to evacuate oilmen stranded by the conflict was difficult to predict. A humanitarian relief flight might so easily be accused of being an attempt to insert Special Forces into key areas of southern Libya ahead of a potential wider military operation. After all, had the Special Air Services (SAS) not forged their original identity in the very same deserts?

In practice however the reaction of the United Kingdom's armed forces was superb. Within days HMS *Cumberland,* having refuelled at Souda Bay in Crete, was ready to go into ports in Libya and commence evacuation operations. HMS *York* was also quickly diverted to the area, arriving on 26 February.

As things started to get really ugly many countries moved to commence evacuating their nationals from Libya. The evacuation of nationals from Benghazi to Malta was reminiscent of the images that emerged from OPERATION HIGHBROW as the Royal Navy moved people away from the fighting in the Lebanon to Cyprus in July 2006.

The irony for many of the crew onboard HMS *Cumberland* – or the mighty sausage as she was affectionately known – cannot have been lost on them. The SDSR had not been kind to the Royal Navy and HMS *Cumberland* was on her way home from her final mission, having been deployed in the Persian Gulf working alongside the Iraqis. She was, in helping in Libya, to get one last hurrah.

The Royal Air Force also got into the act flying Hercules aircraft deep into Libyan territory whilst being shadowed by E3-D Airborne Early Warning and Control System aircraft (AWACS) to provide alerts of any Libyan Air Force activity that might appear threatening. VC-10 aircraft were also deployed to provide air-to-air refuelling support. Three Hercules from 47 Squadron based at RAF Lyneham were quickly mobilised to Malta, from which they could stage into and out of Libya.

The first evacuation flight took place on 26 February from desert locations to the south of Benghazi and brought out 176 people, seventy-four of which were British citizens. A second flight, the next day, rescued 189 civilians, twenty-one of whom were British, from another desert location to the east of the country. This aircraft was engaged as it left a desert location with small arms fire. People on the ground that it had come to rescue apparently thought it was a Libyan Air Force detachment that had come to snatch them and hold them for ransom. As the bullets started flying, one of the pilots aboard the Hercules had a close shave with an incoming round. These were hazardous missions. The Hercules suffered minor battle damage. The aircraft, flown skilfully on minimal fuel reserves, landed successfully in Malta.

The operations were coordinated by a temporary headquarters that had been established by the Permanent Joint Headquarters deploying its high readiness Joint Force Headquarters (JFHQ) to Malta. The sixteen personnel that were deployed came from all of the armed services and represented a 'purple' team that was able to coordinate between the various groups involved in the evacuation task. The British Commander, Brigadier James Bashall, also chaired a multi-national Non-Combatant Evacuation Operation Co-Ordination Cell (NEOCC) located at the British High Commission in Valetta, Malta, that brought together eighteen nations involved in evacuating their citizens from the area.

As the evacuation operation gained momentum additional resources were made available. The government machine had now fully kicked into action and was responding to the apparent slow initial reaction to the plight of those that had appeared beyond the government's reach. Two warships, the Royal Fleet Auxiliary *Argus* and HMS *Westminster*, were also tasked to assist. Three Chinook helicopters were forward deployed to Luqa airport in Malta and the 3rd Battalion, the Royal Regiment of Scotland, was placed on shortened notice to move in the United Kingdom.

Fortunately, they were not required to become involved as the evacuation quickly completed its task. Yet again, at short notice, the British armed forces had worked alongside their international colleagues and carried out a brilliant response to a very challenging situation. OPERATION DEFERENCE was a complete success.

It also paved the way for the subsequent enforcement of the no-fly zone that was to emerge from the debates at the United Nations. The presence of the E-3D aircraft to supervise the evacuation of non-combatants had provided a unique opportunity for some early intelligence collection work to begin. The huge radar sensor on board the E-3D allowed a pattern of activity in Libyan air space to be assembled. This phase of the operations was referred to by Group Captain Chris Jones, the Commander of 907 Expeditionary Wing at RAF Akrotiri, as the 'understanding phase of operations'. This time spent building up the picture of air activity was to prove important once the transition to full combat operations was to start.

The Initial Skirmishes
The initial part of the conflict in Libya between the rebels and the Gaddafi loyalists developed as two distinct forms of warfare. The first was fixed, high intensity urban warfare based in Misrata and Zawiyah. The second was a very different form of warfare that saw manoeuvre in the rural areas of Libya along the coastal road and out into the southern areas of Libya around Zintan, Jabu, Yafran and Rujban. This was punctuated with the kind of urban warfare required to move into and capture the towns.

The uprisings in Libya spontaneously saw towns across Libya fall into rebel hands. This initial wave occurred along the kind of ethnic and societal boundaries that existed below the surface in Libya. Towns with constituencies loyal to Gaddafi remained quiet. Nearby towns, where the situation was very different, quickly proclaimed their independence from the regime in Tripoli. On the ground, the situation was unclear. The towns of al-Ghezaia, Tiji and Badr remained loyal.

In close proximity to these Gaddafi havens however, were a number of towns that quickly rejected the leadership of Colonel Gaddafi, including Wazen near the border with Tunisia, and Nalut, al-Majarbirah and Kabaw. It was Zawiyah, to the west of Tripoli, however, which became an initial focal point for the rebellion.

On 24 February as the formation of the NTC was being finalised, the people of Zawiyah rose up against the regime. The idea of an alternative government to the corrupt regime of Gaddafi clearly appealed to many Libyans. Loyalist forces in the town had fired upon a mosque where the rebels were mounting a sit-in. This caused a large number of people to take to the streets of Zawiyah ending up in the town's own Martyr's Square. These protests and others were a direct challenge to the authority of the regime. The forty-two year reign of Colonel Gaddafi was now in peril. It would be incumbent upon his military to bring the population back from the brink. As they attacked the rebels and tried to reassert the authority of the regime, so the images were broadcast across the world to a fearful audience.

Whilst a small number of Western political leaders may have been able to convince themselves that Gaddafi would see reason and leave the country before he was overthrown, most analysts feared that a different outcome would arise. This would be where the regime would dig in and seek to restore order to the streets of Libya, not matter how hard that task would be and what it would cost in human lives. The pictures of refugees fleeing the crisis into nearby Tunisia provided graphic evidence, yet again, of the capability of a dictator to flout the wishes of his people.

Confusion at the Heart of Government
Western political leaders watched on from the sidelines anxiously. Those that believed Gaddafi would go into retirement with good grace and accept his fate were proven wrong. As the armed response to the rebellion started to ratchet up the pressure on the rebels the British Prime Minister, in an announcement that seemed to shock Parliament, mentioned that he

was actively considering calling for the creation of a no-fly zone. On the 28 February 2011, he repeated an earlier call he had made for Gaddafi to step down and then added 'we do not in any way rule out the use of military assets'.

Some defence analysis at the time, mindful of the impact of the recent cutbacks announced in the SDSR, must have genuinely wondered what resources the Prime Minister had in mind when he said those words. As if to back up the point, he went on to state that, 'we must not tolerate this regime using military force against its own people. In that context I have asked the Ministry of Defence and the Chief of the Defence Staff to work with our allies on plans for a military no-fly zone'. The announcement seemed to catch the international community unawares. Cameron, it appeared, had decided that he was going to stamp his own authority on the position and others would be persuaded to get in line.

If Cameron had hoped that the announcement would rapidly gain a warm welcome across the world he was to be sadly disappointed. Leading actors in the Obama Administration were quick to distance themselves from the idea. Expressions of doubt over its effectiveness poured in from many quarters. Cameron appeared to hesitate, his rhetoric less certain. As the doubters placed their views on record suddenly the announcement appeared premature and ill-considered. Just what could a no-fly zone achieve?

It was an idea that quickly became characterised as something that had been cooked-up in Cameron's inner-circle. The United States Secretary of State, Hilary Clinton, seemed to capture the prevailing mood when she said that, 'military intervention by the military might be counter-productive'. She also noted that the 'Libyan opposition was anxious to be doing this by themselves on behalf of the Libyan people.' To her mind this meant that any external application of military power would be unwelcome.

Quickly, as if in damage-limitation territory, Cameron started to clarify what he had meant. Whilst making it clear the next day that they were 'keeping alive the option of a no-fly zone', the Prime Minister did move to distance himself from any suggestion that the rebels should be armed. In a statement expanding on his previous statement in the House of Commons the Prime Minister made it clear that: 'We should be making contact with them and getting a greater understanding of the opposition forces which are now in Benghazi, and in control of quite a lot of the country'. Adding, 'we are trying to step up our contact and get to know them better and know what their intentions are. I don't think we should go beyond that now'.

It appeared to some political commentators that Cameron was in retreat, backing away from his scheme to impose a no-fly zone. It was to be a temporary set-back. Paradoxically, the person whose actions were to give Cameron his let-out, and to bring the idea finally into implementation through an agreed United Nations resolution, was Gaddafi himself.

The next few days were to see a flurry of diplomatic activity aimed at deciding what the response of the international community should be to the violence in Libya. This part of the Arab Spring was somehow different. Whilst parallels with events in Yemen and Syria were apparent, Libya would somehow be treated differently. Order had been restored in Bahrain relatively quick by a move by the Saudi military. Elsewhere in Morocco and Algeria things were relatively quiet. In Egypt order had been restored as the Army asserted its position, and in Tunisia political wrangling had started over the direction the country would take.

On 2 March Gaddafi forces launched an attack on Zawiyah using air strikes, mortar and artillery fire. The attack launched by the regular army entered the town from two sides, trying to divide the lightly armed rebels in the area. Over the coming days Zawiyah was to be a location of some of the fiercest fighting throughout the civil war, as the situation inside the town dynamically unfolded with infantry, backed by twenty tanks, tried to secure the centre of the city.

This sense of confusion was not helped when on 4 March 2011 a Special Forces team escorting a diplomatic mission to make contact with the rebels, was captured in Libya. Fortunately they were seized by rebel forces who, having established their credentials, released the eight-man team. In what at the time appeared to be a terse statement issued by the Foreign Office, the British Foreign Secretary, William Hague, noted that a 'diplomatic team had been in Benghazi and had experienced difficulties'.

The feeling that the government was not fully joined-up on the approach to Libya was increasing. To be fair, it was their first experience at developing a narrative that would see an international consensus eventually develop. But for a few days there was a clear sense that despite the rhetoric about Gaddafi having to step down and leave Libya, no-one had much of a clue how that was going to be achieved.

The sense of confusion was also not helped with several Cabinet ministers offering apparently contradictory assessments of the situation. The United Kingdom Defence Secretary, Dr Liam Fox, even started to speculate about a 'de-facto partition of the country' with, presumably, Gaddafi holding onto Tripoli and the rest of the country being governed by rebels. Other ministers even speculated that Gaddafi could somehow be allowed to remain in Libya. At one point the idea that he would become a president without any specific powers was also being floated as a solution.

The wide-ranging nature of the debate emerging from within government served to illustrate the opinion that there was no clear leadership over the approach. Cameron's more inclusive approach to government, allowing for debate and ideas to be circulated, was not helpful. Days later, as he was to embark on getting a United Nations resolution adopted, the consensual politics in the United Kingdom had gone. Cameron now wanted a mandate to impose a no-fly zone.

Perhaps Dr Fox, aware of the severity of the impact of the SDSR, was voicing an opinion that suggested Libya would be able to sort out its own long-term solution without any form of intervention. But the differing views emerging from the government fed the notion that not everyone was singing from the same hymn sheet at the time.

Reports at the time from numerous sources had suggested that the diplomatic team had been inserted into Libya to make contact with the rebel forces and establish what, if any, help they required. But the mission was compromised early on. Despite the short-term embarrassment that followed, the mission did eventually lead to improved links that enabled Special Forces to provide discrete assistance to the rebels as the fighting intensified.

Presumably the mission was launched with the intention of looking at what aid might be needed in the short-term. The diplomatic language, of course, would also have hidden a covert side to the operation, which would have sought to make a swift assessment of the military capacity of the rebel forces and their ability to withstand an onslaught from the Libyan Army.

It is likely that what they discovered, in their brief period of being detained, painted a picture of a situation that was barely sustainable. Whilst the rebels had achieved some initial success as the Libyan Army was mobilised, it was highly likely that this was going to become a one-sided fight. For many European leaders the parallels with the war in the Balkans were hard to avoid. Despite Libya not being physically attached to Europe it was clearly on Europe's periphery. Insecurity on the southern border was of serious concern. The chance of a refugee influx across the Mediterranean Sea was a very real possibility. It was one that was too difficult to contemplate. The lights were burning late in many foreign offices in Europe as events unfolded in Libya.

This gradual pressure to get the international community to act created a number of important fault lines in NATO. Turkey, Germany and The Netherlands expressed the view that no intervention should occur. Indeed the German Chancellor, Angela Merkel, was so entrenched in her opposition that she made statements lauding what appeared to be political progress at getting Gaddafi to leave voluntarily. The move by the French Government to unilaterally recognise the NTC appeared to take most political leaders in Europe by surprise. The Netherlands Government was quick to distance itself, claiming that the NTC was not a state. Spain meanwhile had secretly dispatched an envoy to Benghazi to meet with the rebel leaders. This was the first recorded contact with the rebels on Libyan soil. Up until that point all informal contacts had been carried out in European and Arab capitals, such as Cairo.

On 11 March, in another pre-emptive announcement, the French Defence Minister, Gerard Longuet, declared that NATO countries had been authorised to plan for 'all possible scenarios' concerning a military intervention in Libya. His interview, broadcast on the publicly-owned France Inter radio station, made specific reference to using air raids to 'make runways unavailable'. The military aim of such actions being to ground the Libyan Air Force. Anyone familiar with the Falklands War would have offered advice to the French Defence Minister that might have straightened out his view on this.

Dropping bombs on runways to stop aircraft operating is not a particularly effective tactic. Any detailed analysis of this problem would have quickly concluded that a no-fly zone was the only effective way of stopping helicopter and fixed-wing operations. Airmen simply have too much agility in where they can take-off to knockout all possible runway configurations. Besides, to attack the runways, it is necessary to expose the aircraft involved to hostile ground fire.

Whilst Longuet's solution might have lacked finesse he did, however, make the important point that NATO had to lay down some ground rules before it could even contemplate military action. The presence of Arab states in the coalition was crucial, as was the absolute need to operate legally within the United Nations' framework. To act, a resolution would be required. Over the coming nights, that was to occupy the time of the United Nations Ambassadors in New York. Russia and China were to prove a challenge. Their view on the legality of military action against their friend Gaddafi was to pose an initial problem.

As the political situation meandered onwards, the Russian permanent representative to NATO even went on the record with some comments that tried to emphasise splits in NATO, and suggesting that the United Kingdom and France would not act alone on enforcing any resolution. He went on in the same interview on Russian television to suggest that 'if we call a spade a spade, even powerful armed forces like the ones of Britain and France are perhaps not particularly capable without the Americans'. Warming to his theme he went further, even suggesting that it was 'laughable to speak of any individual actions by the British or French on the territory of Libya without the outside support of America'.

Coming in the wake of the critical comments on the SDSR, for David Cameron such direct language by the Russians was not helpful. Cameron had been quite specific in his own comments on the SDSR that Britain was still able to protect its national interests. The Russian view seemed to differ with that markedly.

The Situation Deteriorates
Whilst the political leaders in Europe and America debated their options, the situation in Libya was going downhill quickly. Whilst media reporting with restricted information was available from open source satellite

imagery. The United Nations own technical teams were producing imagery through their United Nations Operational Satellite Applications Programme. A snapshot of the situation in Zawiyah was produced by UNOSAT on 22 March 2011 when they published a report showing detailed satellite images that had been analysed, portraying military activity in the town.

The date of the imagery was 8 March, two days before control of the town was regained by Gaddafi's forces. Reports coming out of the town at the time had suggested that up to fifty tanks were involved in an assault, accompanying around 120 light trucks. The analysis shows that approximately forty road blocks had been established by the rebels. The locations of pro-Gaddafi forces were also provided, showing around twelve tanks located to the south-east of the town, a small number to the north and a concentration on the eastern outskirts of the city. Other vehicle concentrations were also recorded to the west and north-west of the town.

The conflict in Misrata also started immediately after the NTC was formed. This was to be the start of a seventy-day campaign that had all the hallmarks of a smaller-scale Stalingrad or the Warsaw uprisings in the Second World War. It was classic urban warfare conducted street-to-street. As is often the case in such situations rebel forces like to quickly gain control of a number of symbolic locations, to announce their presence and to gain some initial momentum to their campaign. In Misrata it was to be the airport that was an initial objective. Over the course of 24 and 25 February, Gaddafi's forces battled with the rebels for control of the airport to the south-west of the city. Holding the airport offered the potential for flying in supplies, if it could be opened and declared secure.

The rebel's initial occupation of the city centre of Misrata also came under fire as Gaddafi forces battled to re-take it from the rebels at the start of March. To try and dislodge the rebels Gaddafi committed one of the elite elements of his army – the 32nd Brigade – to the battle for Misrata. The Brigade was led by Gaddafi's youngest son Khamis, who was to die later on in the campaign. On 12 March, the 32nd Brigade started an attack on Misrata coming to within 9 kilometres of the city centre. This attack stalled when a number of members of the army, including a high ranking officer, reportedly defected to the rebels.

Between 19 and 22 March, just at the point when the UN resolution started to be enforced, Gaddafi's tanks had re-taken control of Misrata. The daily news-feeds emerging from the town and from reporters who had managed to get close to its outskirts, showed the nature of the battle. This was hard street fighting, pitching untrained rebel forces against one of the top units in the Libyan military. What evolved over the coming weeks was a series of attacks and counter-attacks as the pendulum for control of the centre of Misrata moved one way and then the other.

Throughout this period the news media was fed with a diet of packages sourced from reporters who had hitched rides on various vessels that were entering the harbour of Misrata to extract the wounded. The pictures provided a graphic sense of the nature of urban warfare and highlighted the price being paid by the rebels for their apparent impudence in trying to dislodge the Gaddafi regime from their city. These images alone enabled the initial phase of the implementation of the United Nations resolution to maintain public support, even if Misrata was not Benghazi. Ironically, as far as NATO was concerned, the United Nations resolution which gave them a clear responsibility to build a protective shield over Benghazi swiftly evolved into a mission to help those in Misrata, whose plight seemed more desperate and more immediate.

The Swinging Pendulum in the East
Whilst the battles in Misrata resembled those in Stalingrad in the Second World War, the battle that was about to unfold along the coastal road from Benghazi, through Ajdabiya to Ras Lanuf, Bin Jawad and Sirte was very reminiscent of the North Africa campaigns of the same period.

But that was not a true reflection of a Libyan Army that was about to lay down its weapons and desert Gaddafi. There were simply too many vested self interests in play. The Libyan Army initially retreated from the area around Benghazi and, as is often the case, that initial withdrawal looked chaotic. False hopes were raised that the rebels could suddenly march on Tripoli. The reality of the situation was soon to become obvious, as their initial advance westwards ground to a halt. It was never going to be easy for lightly-equipped rebels to win an immediate victory.

The spontaneous way in which people from all walks of life in

Benghazi suddenly took to the streets and became armed was never going to develop the kind of military organisation that would immediately threaten Gaddafi. That a stalemate would eventually occur, in the absence of NATO being able to gain approval for the insertion of ground troops that would have a decisive effect upon the short-term military picture, was perhaps inevitable.

As the rebels started to push east out of Benghazi, in the immediate aftermath of the uprisings towards the end of February, their initial progress was swift, although chaotic. This was not a traditional line of advance through enemy held territory. This was a full-scale civil war that was developing. The battlefield was not easy to divide into who was on what side. Local tribal alliances and patronage networks helped Gaddafi maintain order in some areas. These however were not contiguous, allowing a front to be discriminated.

People in several of the towns along the initial route to Tripoli had risen up and taken over control of their towns. The oil port of Brega was an important strategic location that, by the beginning of March, had fallen into the hands of the rebels. On 2 March Gaddafi troops tried to recapture Brega. They were beaten back and retreated to Ras Lanuf. But the toll on the rebels had been high. The situation was complicated by the ways in which the rebels had gone to war, with many civilians leaving their day-jobs to take up arms.

Some fault lines had also emerged between those who had left their civilian jobs to take up arms and those that had defected from the military. Trying to decide on a command structure, and who was best placed to issue orders, provided a difficult test for the rebel forces. Many were distrustful of the people that had claimed to change sides. The rapidly assembled militia was in need of some structure and to know who was issuing the orders.

On 6 March a series of moves started by the regime loyalists, saw a concerted effort to re-take Ras Lanuf and Brega. The Gaddafi forces moved quickly forward as the rebels, lacking the discipline of an army, fell back in a state of disarray. On 10 March pro-Gaddafi forces re-took Ras Lanuf supported by a combined-arms operation, involving Libyan war planes and warships shelling the coastal area. Gaddafi's supporters were then able to move along the coast re-capturing most of Brega.

At this time reports also started to emerge suggesting that Gaddafi was receiving arms supplies from the Syrian – an accusation they denied vigorously. A website in Syria was the source of one of the accusations claiming that a ship which had left Syria, ostensibly to deliver humanitarian aid, had in fact contained missiles, night-vision and other battlefield equipment, as well as members of the Syrian Special Forces – the Mahir al-Asad.

In a typical, and somewhat cynical move, the regime arranged for each family in Brega to receive an *ex-gratia* payment of 500 dinars. A video released at the time by the regime showed an orderly queue of people waiting outside the Wahda Bank and a man carrying a wad of wrapped bank notes leaving the bank and, stating to the camera team that 'the situation was calm', and expressing defiant support for Mu'ammar Gaddafi.

Rebel forces were compelled to retreat to Ajdabiya, the last major town on the road to Benghazi. It appeared at this moment as if the campaign had swung in favour of the regime loyalists. The town of Ajdabiya was subjected to air attacks from the Libyan Air Force for three days. On 15 March the Gaddafi loyalists then mounted a flanking manoeuvre on the rebels defending the city whilst also mounting a rolling barrage and continuing air strikes.

At this moment the very survival of the revolution was in serious danger. It was at this point that the political manoeuvrings at the United Nations suddenly moved up a gear. Whilst the rebels had been on the offensive many political leaders had hoped that their momentum would carry them to Tripoli. Colonel Gaddafi, and his supporters, had other ideas. In their eyes Libya was not about to go down the road that had been charted in the past few weeks in Egypt and Tunisia. Libya was going to buck the trend and retain the government of Colonel Gaddafi. On 16 March, however, their attack towards Benghazi started to stall as the rebels, realising the gateway to Benghazi was open if Ajdabiya fell, dug in and fought a rear-guard action.

On 19 March the forces of Colonel Gaddafi were knocking on the door of Benghazi. The pendulum had suddenly swung in Gaddafi's favour. In Misrata and in the east of the country it appeared his military forces, whilst initially thrown off balance by the spontaneous nature of the rebellion, had finally started to get a grip of the situation.

Emboldened by the progress of his forces Gaddafi issued what historians will note was a hugely important speech. It was the defining moment for the international community to move from a fairly passive position to taking sides with the rebels. The threat of a bloodbath in Benghazi had yet again finally stirred European political leaders into collective action. It was not difficult to imagine many of them dusting off accounts of the Balkans War, looking for ideas as to what to do next. With the images of the massacres in Bosnia fresh in many of their minds inaction was no longer an option. Something had to be done.

The Initial Political Reactions
The initial political reaction to events in Tripoli had, perhaps understandably, been confused. Russia had moved to declare Gaddafi and his family *persona non grata* in Moscow and that he was 'not entitled to conduct financial transactions there'. President Nicolas Sarkozy had another agenda. As the situation in Libya deteriorated he called for the immediate imposition of a no-fly zone.

Whilst initially he failed to gain much support for this move he did persuade the Arab League to back the idea. Once he had their support he moved quickly at the G8 Summit in Paris on 14 and 15 March to consolidate the momentum he had achieved with the idea. Whilst Britain was generally supportive, the United States and Germany remained unconvinced. With the United States Defense Secretary Robert Gates going so far as to opine that, 'it remained unclear if it was a wise move'.

We may recall that it was David Cameron who was the first to suggest the implementation of a no-fly zone. His rhetoric caught many people, including some in his own party, off balance. It was roundly criticised in the media and the all-important reaction of the United States was lukewarm at best, some even suggesting that President Obama had snubbed the British initiative.

The British Prime Minister, perhaps fearful of being dragged into his own equivalent of Iraq, had noted that, 'Britain has no intention to get involved in another war in Libya'. It seemed that the British Prime Minister was making a reference to the Second World War and the attritional nature of the desert campaign.

Responding to this, the Chairman of the NTC, speaking to Al Arabiya television on 14 March noted that, 'I think the current language of the age is that which calls for subduing the peoples to the reign of their rulers by resorting to the use of force, bombs and all other forms of suppressive and coercive means. What is happening now in Libya to our brothers in Zuwarah, Misrata, and al-Zawiyah falls under the same category; namely, subduing people to the rule of a tyrant that has already imposed a dictatorship on them for more than forty years.'

The Chairman went on further, when questioned about the apparent lack of unity in the international community's response, to the call for implementing a no-fly zone. He noted that, 'we have made the international community aware of its responsibilities concerning the suppression, attacks and shelling in Libya'. In what however, was to be a telling point, he also added: 'We think the Security Council can skip international sovereignty and protect the civilians by all means necessary.' Coming from a trained lawyer with many years of experience, these were words that pulled few punches. They were quite literally a call to arms to defend the people of Libya.

The initial moves on the development of an international consensus for action had come from the French government. Prime Minister Fillon, in an interview on the France 2 television channel on 17 March, had made it clear that military action was imminent. Commenting in answer to a question, the Prime Minister observed that, 'It is France that has been at work for several days now trying to ensure that this resolution is adopted by the Security Council'. He went on to add that 'The President [Nicolas Sarkozy] had sent a letter to all of the Security Council members yesterday to urge them to adopt this resolution'.

The next day a French government spokesman speaking on RTL radio had backed up the position of the French Prime Minister, stating that air strikes would be carried out 'rapidly' and making it clear that French aircraft would play their role in defending the citizens of Libya from what was described as a 'massacre'.

The United Nations Resolutions
In order to legitimise any international action against Libya an initial draft resolution was passed to the Security Council, as the rebellion started to take shape. Its sponsors were France, the United Kingdom, Germany and the United States. It was adopted after a discussion lasting a day. The

debate resulted in United Nations Resolution 1970 being adopted on 26 February, nine days after the start of the peaceful protests in Libya.

The resolution was adopted unanimously by the Security Council, an unusual event of itself, given the often competing social and economic reasons why some members of the council chose to abstain or vote against a resolution. It was also a landmark event as it was the first time a country was referred to the International Criminal Court (ICC). In another unusual step, the then Libyan Ambassador to the United Nations, Abdurrahman Mohamed Shalgam, who had already left the service of the Gaddafi regime – defecting to the rebels – persuaded China, Russia and India to support the clause referring Libya to the ICC.

Russia however, insisted on the insertion of a provision in the wording of the resolution which made it clear that it precluded any military intervention in Libya. Russia was presumably trying to restrain the kind of military adventurism that had been so harmful in Iraq and Afghanistan, and protect its economic and defence ties with Libya. They need not have bothered. Any reading of the international atmosphere at the time would not have produced a list of many volunteers ready to sign up for another journey into the uncertain world of Arab tribal landscapes.

United Nations Security Council Resolution 1973 which was adopted on 17 March 2011 provided the legal top cover for the implementation of a no-fly zone over Libya. The resolution was adopted under Chapter VII of the United Nations Charter. Its content:

- Demanded an immediate establishment of a ceasefire and complete end to violence and all attacks against, and abuses of, civilians
- Imposed a no-fly zone over Libya
- Authorised all necessary means to protect civilians and civilian-populated areas, except for a 'foreign occupation force'
- Strengthened the arms embargo and action against mercenaries, by allowing for forcible inspections of ships and planes
- Imposed a ban on all Libyan-designated flights
- Imposed an asset freeze on assets owned by the Libyan authorities, and reaffirmed that such assets should be used for the benefit of the Libyan people

- Extended the travel ban and assets freeze imposed under United Nations Resolution 1970 to include an additional number of designated people
- Established a panel of experts to monitor and promote sanctions implementations

The political manoeuvring having now been completed, it was for the military forces, assembled across a diverse international coalition, to start work. With the passing of the United Nations resolution they did not take long to get started.

Two days after this resolution was passed, French airplanes entered Libyan airspace to enforce the no-fly zone. The battle for the future of Libya had started. It was one that yet again would test NATO's resolve and ingenuity in dealing with a quite different form of warfare.

For the RAF the coming weeks were to underline its raison d'etre. It was to seize the opportunity to underline how its ethos, of being agile and adaptable in its application of air power had changed, and how its doctrine of applying air power had developed. Given the cutbacks it had taken in the course of the SDSR process this was a heaven-sent opportunity to defend itself against any further cuts that might have to take place in the future. As the next few weeks were to unfold, the RAF was to use the opportunity to show-case its capabilities and to highlight the lessons it had learnt from past conflicts. The precision and accuracy with which it would carry out its mission would astonish many.

CHAPTER 4

The Initial Exchanges

Overview

Given the speed with which an international coalition had to be assembled, it was obvious that the initial command of the military activities should be handled by the United States. The atmosphere in America was, however, not particularly supportive, and measures were quickly put in place to hand over command to NATO. This created a number of difficulties, as not all of the NATO nations were supportive of the idea. Within days, however, an agreement had been thrashed out by NATO. They would lead an international coalition of countries that would enforce the UN resolution. OPERATION UNIFIED PROTECTOR was born. Colonel Gaddafi, once pariah and friend to the West, was about to start the last six and a half months of his life.

In rapid time NATO and its coalition partners had assembled a multi-national force to impose the United Nations Resolution 1973 upon the Gaddafi regime. Nearly 13,000 people from seventeen countries including the United States, the United Kingdom, France, Italy, Sweden, Turkey, Spain, Jordan and Qatar were now poised to be brought to war against the Libyan Armed forces.

Country	Air Force	Naval
United States	153	12
United Kingdom	28	3
France	29	6
Italy	12	4
Sweden	8	0
Belgium	6	1

Canada	11	1
Denmark	4	0
Norway	6	0
Spain	7	1
Turkey	7	6
Netherlands	7	1
Jordan	12	0
United Arab Emirates	12	0
Qatar	8	0
Romania	0	1
Bulgaria	0	1
Total(s)	310	37

**Table 1: The ORBAT of the Coalition Forces at the
Outbreak of War** [Source: The *Guardian*]

Table 1 provides a detailed breakdown of the commitment of aircraft and naval vessels obtained by the *Guardian* newspaper in the United Kingdom at the start of the campaign. Whilst the numbers deployed may have been slightly different, it nevertheless provides a good illustration of the importance of the United States commitment to the task in hand. Despite 'driving from the back seat', the United States commitment to the NATO and coalition effort was considerable, providing close to 50 per cent of the air power and a third of the naval power arrayed against the regime.

The coalition of the willing was also able to assemble their force contributions quickly. On 18 March the Danish Defence Minister, Gitte Lillelund Bech, announced that six F-16 fighters and a military transport aircraft were to be sent to an unnamed air base in southern Europe. Operations would commence 'from six o'clock tomorrow morning'. The Belgian's were not far behind, committing additional F-16s to the coalition military capacity, plus a minesweeper. Arab participation also quickly followed as the United Arab Emirates (UAE) Minister of Foreign Affairs issued a statement that it was sending six F-16 and six Mirage aircraft to participate in the patrols that would enforce the no-fly zone.

In addition to the air forces that started to arrive, warships were also gathering off the coast of Libya. The United States had sent four warships to the area. Bulgaria and Romania were quick to dispatch frigates, on what would be their first operational deployment in a NATO context. Romania's Supreme Council of National Defence (CSAT) had approved the deployment on 22 March. One month later the *Regele Ferdinand* left Romania to conduct maritime search and boarding operations in support of the embargo that sought to cut off Gaddafi from external help.

The French aircraft carrier *Charles de Gaulle* was also made ready for sea. It would arrive in the area of operations fairly quickly, starting operations on 20 March, escorted by the frigates *Dupleix* and *Aconit* and a replenishment tanker the *Meuse*. Gradually the military forces that would enact Cameron and Sarkozy's vision were assembling.

The first task for the coalition air forces at the start of the campaign was to attack Gaddafi's forces massing near Benghazi and also to neutralise the Libyan Air Defence systems. The onslaught of Tomahawk and Storm Shadow missiles launched from submarines and Tornado aircraft flown from RAF Marham, and French jets flown from nearby air bases, provided the initial impetus to the campaign. The coalition air power, backed up by its array of Intelligence, Surveillance, Target Acquisition and Recognition (ISTAR) assets, quickly stopped the regime tanks from any forward movement towards Benghazi.

The initial challenge for the coalition was that, despite fielding over 300 aircraft into theatre, only some of these were strike aircraft. This was to pose a constant problem for the NATO commanders as OPERATION UNIFIED PROTECTOR was to unfold.

In the early days of the campaign, as is the case in all contemporary wars, the target list was long. With insurrection having erupted across Libya there were many demands in the first few days for help, as the Libyan armed forces turned on the people of places like Misrata. The coalition's sortie generation rate for its strike packages was stretched in the first few days. Later on in the campaign, with the target list significantly reduced, additional air assets were deployed – by the RAF for example – to develop new intelligence for follow-up attacks. As the campaign moved along, the sortie generation rate was to become less of a problem.

For David Cameron the early exchanges in the military campaign achieved the initial result that was required. Having decided to protect the citizens of Benghazi that mission was accomplished in fairly quick time. The imposition of the no-fly zone quickly reduced the already dwindling capability of the Libyan Air Force.

That a real threat had existed could not be in doubt. Little more than two weeks earlier Libyan Air Force MIGs and Sukhoi fighters had tipped the balance in the fight for Ras Lanuf. When Gaddafi helicopter gunships joined the fray the rebels' resistance had fallen apart and they had withdrawn in total disarray. Gaddafi's rhetoric also hardly helped. His broadcast on Libyan television on 17 March had been quite clear. 'We are determined', he said, 'to restore Libya to what it was a month ago. This determination tolerates no hesitation.'

In trying to reach out to the citizens of Benghazi, Gaddafi spoke of the 'beautiful and beloved Benghazi' that 'a handful of vagabonds came from Afghanistan, from hungry and stricken Egypt, hungry Tunisia' to 'destroy your country'. In words that must have sent a chill down the spine of many in Benghazi supporting the rebels, he went onto say, 'we are coming' and that 'we will have no mercy on them'.

In response the radio operated by the rebels issued a reply, daring the Libyan Army to enter Benghazi. With patriotic songs playing in the background the commentator urged the people of Benghazi to 'rise now against the tyrant'. Making reference to what had already been achieved, the broadcaster went on to note that, the 'hour of victory had come' and that 'after the blessed *Intifada* [uprising] of 17 February there is no more room for terror, fear and exclusion'.

Noting the difficulties of their military situation the broadcaster said that 'the insurgents cannot reverse their course despite the [superior] hardware and equipment of the despot'. Issuing a call to arms for the residents of Benghazi, the broadcaster went on to say, 'this is because they are armed with the faith of God, and they have already scored brilliant victories'. The scene was set for a battle in Benghazi. Had it occurred it would have been a bloody affair.

Whilst the capability of the Libyan Air Force was never likely to challenge the Royal Air Force or its NATO colleagues in any air-to-air combat situation, a single Libyan Air Force aircraft penetrating the shield around a NATO AWACS aircraft directing the airspace over Libya, could have had catastrophic effects for the alliance.

The multi-national nature of the crews on board the AWACS aircraft might well have revealed some home truths about contributions to the NATO campaign that a number of governments would have wished to have kept off the media radar. That kind of catastrophe had to be avoided at all costs.

The projection of air power over Libya had two initial objectives. One, to suppress the Libyan air defences. The second was to maintain the safety of the ISTAR platforms that had been deployed in the area. These were to provide airborne command and control of the missions entering Libyan air space, and deliver near-real-time intelligence to enable fleeting targets to be attacked.

This initial application of air power saw a variety of missions being developed by NATO planners. These covered:

- Targeting specific command and control sites inside Libya that were used by the regime to maintain their air defence systems and major ammunition and staging areas – where military forces might be concentrated.
- Flying, what in the military jargon are called, 'overwatch' or armed reconnaissance missions. These are largely aimed at placing airborne strike assets over areas – or boxes – from which they can launch attacks against ground forces that emerge as targets. ISTAR assets such as the Sentinel platform would provide cues onto the targets they detect, directing in Typhoon or Tornado aircraft.

One over-riding characteristic emerges from an analysis of the Libyan campaign – the precise nature of the attacks carried out by NATO and its coalition partners. The attacks conducted by the RAF epitomised this emphasis on precision. By combining the weapons effects that could be created by the varying forms of Paveway bombs that were used in the campaign with the very versatile Brimstone missile, the RAF were able to minimise the risks to civilians near to the targets. The ubiquitous cockpit videos that now punctuate all military campaigns as part of the war of words and images, reveal just how precise the attacks were in terms of achieving that goal.

The development of tactics during the conflict also showed the versatility of contemporary air power. The combination of the Typhoon and Tornado – each with its own weapon fit – would prove to be innovative. Initially tasked into theatre in the role of an air-to-air fighter to impose the no-fly zone, the Typhoon was quickly re-rolled into a ground-attack variant.

Operating the Typhoon and Tornado together in formations of two and four aircraft provided additional flexibility with respect to emerging targets. The variations of the Paveway bomb aboard the Typhoon, coupled with the slightly different configurations on the Tornados, allowed NATO and coalition planners to configure armed reconnaissance packages that could respond to any form of emerging target. This was air power being applied with great versatility and flexibility – responding to events as they occurred on the ground.

It is tempting to see the RAF deployment in Libya through the somewhat narrow lens of the strike aircraft deployed into theatre. The Tornados shouldered the initial burden, being joined by a number of Typhoons that were configured to operate in a ground-attack role after the campaign gained momentum. But that would be to deny the important, time-critical role, played by the Sentinel R1, Nimrod R1 and Sentry E-3D ISTAR assets, whose task was to build the situational awareness and make decisions about which targets to prosecute.

To direct the strike aircraft to one of any number of targets requires the deployment of a number of ISTAR assets. Some of those operate at the strategic level. Their performance is sensitive and subject to a great deal of media speculation. Suffice it to say that RAF photo-interpreters would have been kept busy analysing imagery obtained from such 'national' assets from the start of the campaign. Their goal would have been to identify key installations associated with Gaddafi's military machine. This would then be entered into a target list that would have been handed off to NATO planners. Their task was then to match the airborne and naval strike assets at their disposal to deliver a variety of effects on each of the targets selected.

Operational assets, deployed in the airspace over Libya, included the RAF Sentinel R1 aircraft normally based at RAF Waddington. The Sentinel platform was originally conceived as a platform that would sit behind the Forward Edge of the Battle Area (FEBA). It would operate in a stand-off role to monitor a Warsaw Pact incursion into what was then West Germany.

Despite the end of the Cold War it was clear from the role played by Joint Surveillance and Target Attack Radar System (JSTARS) in Iraq in 1991 that stand-off radar-based sensor systems were to have a continuing role in the new world order, or disorder, that was to emerge at the start of the twenty-first century. The introduction into service of the Sentinel R1 platform was to give the RAF its own variant of the JSTARS capability. In Afghanistan and Libya it was to earn its colours and prove its value in cueing strike aircraft to emergent targets.

Within twenty-four hours of the start of the Libyan air campaign a single Sentinel R1 aircraft, operating from RAF Akrotiri, was operating over the skies of Libya. On board, image analysts were to watch their screens and detect 'pop up' targets throughout the seven and a half months that the air campaign was to last.

The image analysts had to learn how to detect targets from building up patterns of behaviour from which abnormal activity stuck out. They could then inform the RAF Sentry E3-D aircraft operating in the area managing the battlespace. Their task was to evaluate the information, decide upon priorities and then direct the strike aircraft into an area to conduct a detailed analysis of the designated target area, before unleashing an appropriate weapon given the context of the situation. On many occasions weapons were not launched against targets because of the close proximity of civilians.

Into this mix of ISTAR assets the Nimrod R1 was also deployed to collect strategic insights by intercepting communications and radar signals emanating from pro-Gaddafi forces during their operations. The Nimrod platform had been proven in the Kosovo campaign as a versatile command platform in its own right. Operating over the Adriatic Sea the operators aboard the Nimrod platform had been able to monitor the fast changing Electronic Warfare (EW) threat environment posed to inbound strike packages operating from airbases in Italy and off the aircraft carriers operating in the area.

This was quite a role change for the Nimrod R1, which had originally been purchased to collect sensitive intelligence on radar and communications systems operated by the Warsaw Pact countries in the Cold War. In that role it was a strategic intelligence collection asset.

In Kosovo the Nimrod R1 had shown its versatility as a tactical platform. Helping inbound strike packages to be aware of what was a dynamically-evolving radar environment. That flexibility and agility was again to be proven off the coast of Libya. The combination of the Sentry E-3D, the Sentinel R1 and the Nimrod R1 was to provide those tasked with attacking pro-Gaddafi elements with crucial and timely intelligence that allowed the campaign to be conducted with the kind of precision that previous NATO commanders would have been deeply envious.

As the campaign evolved pro-Gaddafi elements tried to hide in areas where they were shielded by local people. By doing this they were trying to exploit NATO's over-riding concern about civilian casualties. If these could be avoided it was hoped that Gaddafi could be isolated from his people.

Gaddafi's Strategic Surprise
The nature of the air and naval attacks was a major surprise to Gaddafi. It would seem that as Colonel Gaddafi had been able to reconcile his regime with the West through offering to give up his WMD program that he thought it was unnecessary to invest in updating his air defence systems. He obviously did not imagine that the circumstances would arise when his new-found friends in the West would decide that he needed to be replaced.

Clearly the Arab Spring and its rapid impact upon the people of Libya had completely surprised Gaddafi. He could not believe his former subservient people would wish to overthrow him; after all he was their great benefactor. In a commentary aired weeks before the rebellion gained ground, Gaddafi had boldly declared that his people loved him. In his last moments, in a desperate appeal for his life, he can be heard asking his captors, 'what have I done to you?'

For Colonel Gaddafi the next few weeks were to provide him, quite literally, with the strategic shock of his life. For David Cameron and Nicolas Sarkozy the Gaddafi shock was to be their benefit. Launching a war against a country with a well equipped air defence system carries huge risks. The images of airman captured and tortured in Iraq in the first Gulf War in 1991 are still fresh in the minds of many in senior command levels in the Ministry of Defence. Any military operation carries inherent risks. For David Cameron the idea that members of the Royal Air Force might be captured and tortured in Libya and displayed on television must have been a recurring moment of concern.

The political landscape may have changed since 1991, but the threat of airman being shot down and paraded in front of the world's media still has the ability to erode support for what might be advertised as a moral campaign. Fortunately for Cameron and Sarkozy the environment in which the combat aircraft they had committed to the campaign quickly became permissive.

The Libyan air defence system was literally taken off the air within hours. The intelligence assets deployed by the United States, the United Kingdom and France in the run up to the conflict had done their initial tasking well. The key nodes of the Libyan Air Defence system had been quickly mapped and target profiles developed that enabled the first wave of strikes to be very effective.

The Initial Target Portfolio
The air defence capability that could be fielded by the Libyans proved no match for the initial military onslaught. Early on, American and British warships and submarines fired 110 Tomahawk cruise missiles against fixed targets. With these elements disabled, the enduring threat to the coalition aircraft that operated over Libya came from the kind of man-portable surface-to-air missiles so effectively used by the Mujahidin against the Russians in Afghanistan. The Russian Air Force paid a heavy price for underestimating the ability of irregular fighters to master the apparent complexities of the Stinger missile. This was not to be repeated by the NATO forces in Libya.

That Libya had been delivered the very latest Russian surface-to-air missile systems became apparent in the aftermath of the war, as empty boxes were discovered in a warehouse in Tripoli. However their lack of use in the campaign is a slightly more puzzling element to the way the war in Libya panned out. The reasons why Gaddafi's forces did not make extensive use of the SA-28 missiles supplied by Russia is not immediately clear.

As Libya's main supplier of military equipment the outcome of the war for the Russians can only be described as a disaster. Senior officials in the Kremlin moved quickly to ensure damage limitation, commenting that the Libyan regime was using 'outdated air defence systems'. For the Russians the Libyan campaign was not a great shop window for the weapon systems they had supplied to Gaddafi.

Coming in the wake of the military strike carried out with impunity by the Israeli Air Force against the Syrian nuclear reactor, in the face of what was supposed to be the most modern air defence system deployed by an Arab country supplied by the Russians, only serves to illustrate the technical imbalance that currently exists between NATO and Russia. It is a point that David Cameron and his advisors will not have failed to appreciate.

The degree of embarrassment for the Russians was so significant it left them appealing to the incoming leadership in Tripoli to 'honour existing contracts'. The reaction of the NTC to this was to instigate a 'review' of all contracts that have been signed to ensure that they have not been subject to any corrupt payments, noting that some of the prices paid do not seem to be 'competitive'. The implications are significant.

Opening Fire
On the 19 March 2011, nineteen aircraft of the French Air Force entered Libyan air space. Their tasking was two-fold; to collect reconnaissance on potential military targets and to prevent any pro-regime military assets conducting operations against the people of Benghazi. In the evening Italian aircraft also joined the mission, before dusk fell, when the initial wave of assaults from United States and British assets joined the campaign.

In order to enforce the no-fly zone and to ensure that the aircraft could operate in what in defence circles is referred to as a 'permissive environment', the first targets that would be attacked would inevitably be the Libyan air defence systems.

The air defence system is made up of a number of components. These include missiles, control centres and any communications infrastructure that linked the various elements into an integrated capability. This first wave of attacks was to be conducted by Tomahawk Land Attack Missiles (TLAM) and the stand-off cruise missiles launched from Tornado GR4s – the Storm Shadow. On the first night of the campaign four RAF Tornados were to fly a mission that saw a number of Storm Shadow missiles fired at strategic locations around Tripoli.

Given the short notice on which the operation was launched this would have been a difficult mission as there had been only a limited time window in which to collect a range of intelligence on the configuration of the Libyan systems. The lights would have been burning late in the various ministries of defence involved in the mission, trying to look back over a range of publications to find any insights into the nature of the threat posed by the Libyan air defence system.

A large number of questions would have been on the mind of those preparing to enter Libyan air space. How many surface-to-air missiles systems does the regime have? Which radar systems do they operate? What frequency bands do they occupy? Are there any special features of the radars that make them difficult to jam?

These questions, and others, would have sat alongside the concerns that would have existed over the extent to which the Libyans would have been able to use MANPADS against any aircraft entering their air space. As it turned out the extent of the threat from the Libyan air defence system was limited. The political leaders need to appreciate the huge advantage this gave them in prosecuting this campaign. It might not be the same in another theatre of war.

Overnight four Tornado GR4 ground attack aircraft left their base at Marham to mount attacks against key nodes in the air defence system. They flew 3,000 miles to the target, initially at the lower altitudes of 15,000 feet due to their fuel weight and weapons load. This was the longest bombing mission recorded since the Black Buck missions flown during Falklands conflict. It was a mission that was to be repeated several times in the coming months of the campaign.

To accomplish the mission the Tornados were refuelled by VC-10 and Tristar aircraft and were also supported by E-3D Sentry, Nimrod R1 (with its sophisticated electronic listening capabilities) and Sentinel R1 surveillance aircraft. This was an operation that had been put together really quickly. An operation that would have taken many weeks to plan was assembled in hours. The E-3D aircraft provided the 'eyes' of the operation and the Nimrod R1 aircraft provided its 'ears'. This helped the RAF maintain situational awareness in the areas which were considered to be dangerous.

In less than eighteen hours the RAF had taken a political instruction to 'do something' over Libya and put that into action. At 03.00 hours on Friday 18 March, RAF personnel were informed by senior officials that they 'had to act fast in order to get an operation underway'. By 08.00 hours, the aircraft were ready to go, awaiting the final confirmation from the Prime Minister. This arrived at 20.00 hours on Saturday 19 March, at which point the aircraft left on their first bombing raids from Marham, and the tanker aircraft that supported them left RAF Brize Norton.

The French Air Force Acts First

Using their geographic advantage, the French military had stolen a march on the RAF and arrived first over Libyan air space. However the RAF was hot on its heels and was about to deliver the first of a series of blows to the Libyan air defence system that would quickly render it useless. This first mission was also to define the nature of the pivotal role played by the RAF throughout the war. Numerically the French would end up flying the most missions in the period until Tripoli was seized by the rebels. However it was the RAF that achieved the most effect.

A few nights after the mission commenced on the 23 March, two Rafale B aircraft of EC-1/91 took off from Saint-Dizier armed with two of the French equivalent of the Storm Shadow – the Scalp-EG missiles. As they climbed out on a heading for Libya they were joined by two Mirage 2000D aircraft from Nancy airbase. Each of these aircraft had a single Scalp-EG. The package was then also joined by two further Rafale M aircraft that had been launched from the French aircraft carrier *Charles de Gaulle* also carrying a single missile.

This single missile deployment was necessary as aircraft returning to the aircraft carrier cannot land in an asymmetric configuration, so they have to operate with a single, underbelly, missile configuration. If they had launched with two under-wing missiles, a hang-up on launch or a single missile being deployed, would create an asymmetric configuration that would mean the aircraft having to divert.

The package was inbound to the Libyan Al Jufrah airbase located 500 kilometres to the south-west of Benghazi. Clearly disabling that air base was important if the people of Benghazi were to be protected. The base was home for some TU-22 and Mig-25 aircraft that were housed in sand berms and aircraft shelters – although their serviceability might have been in doubt. As the aircraft closed to their launch point a computer malfunction prevented one of the Mirage 2000D from launching its missile. Seven missiles were launched against the airfield that night. It was a target that NATO was to return to on 13 June in a follow up attack.

On the night of 27 and 28 March, another mission was launched by the French Air Force and Navy. This time two Rafale B of the EC-1/91 and two Rafale M from the 12F Flotilla, each armed with a single Scalp missile, attacked a remote command and control centre located in the deep south of Libya.

This, and a small number of other attacks, saw the French Air Force and Navy use 15 Scalp-EG missiles – four fired by Rafale M, ten by Rafale B and a single one from a Mirage 2000D, on a variety of hard targets in Libya. The stand-off capability available from the Scalp-EG had allowed targets as far as 400 kilometres from the launch point to be attacked. Given the geography of Libya, that enabled nearly 50 per cent of the country to be attacked from an aircraft that was operating off the coastline.

The RAF Gears Up to Operations
The speed with which the RAF was to be able to commit its forces showed its huge versatility in being able to assemble a range of assets in such short order to mount the attacks. The speed with which the mission planning was done being reflected in the comments made by those in the RAF charged with conducting the mission. The praise heaped upon the people involved showed just how much effort it had required. All the stops had indeed been pulled out. Once again the professionalism of the United Kingdom's armed forces had answered a political call to arms.

The Tornados carried the Storm Shadow missile system which is a versatile weapon system that can attack in a stand-off mode. This avoids the need for the aircraft to fly into hostile territory. The Storm Shadows maximum range is reputed to be 155 miles (250 kilometres). This offers versatility when it comes to attacking command and control centres that may have been based deep inside an adversary's territory, well behind the front line of surface-to-air missiles that provide a shield over a country's airspace.

Once launched, the Storm Shadow missile acts like a cruise missile, comparing the terrain and inputs from the Global Positioning System (GPS) navigation system to fly a highly accurate path to the designated target. In the final attack phase the nose cone is jettisoned, allowing a highly accurate infrared camera to do the final pattern matching on the approach to the target, to ensure a precise delivery of the warhead. In order for it to penetrate the concrete that inevitably covers a command bunker, a two-stage warhead detonation sequence occurs. The first, smaller charge, penetrates the concrete, before enabling the second larger charge to then detonate inside the bunker.

Commenting on the raids mounted by the RN and the RAF, David Cameron noted: 'Tonight, British forces are in action in Libya. They are part of an international coalition that has come together to enforce the will of the United Nations and to support the Libyan people.' Making sure he emphasised the legality of the actions being undertaken, the Prime Minister went on to add, 'It is legal because we have the backing of the United Nations Security Council and also of the Arab League and many others'.

He was clearly making sure that the international consensus for action that he and President Sarkozy had secured was front and centre in the arguments being made about the initiation of the campaign. David Cameron now had his war. How it would unfold would, to some extent, define his premiership.

Collateral Damage

The campaign had got off to a decisive start. But, as ever with military campaigns, once in contact with the enemy things can go awry. The situation on the ground in Libya was 'fluid', according to reports being broadcast by the media. In a dynamic environment, where equipment can be seized and turned against an adversary quickly, the situation on every street corner can be quite different. The urban and rural environments were equally chaotic. For NATO this was a very different operating environment. Not the kind of warfare envisaged in the Cold War where a distinct FEBA would exist between NATO forces and the Warsaw Pact countries. This was warfare 'amongst the people', as General Sir Rupert Smith had characterised the new forms of war in the twenty-first century in his book, *The Utility of War*.

Against this backdrop, in the early stages of the campaign, it is perhaps understandable how tanks were considered to be weapons of the Libyan Army and therefore legitimate targets. On 6 April the coalition air forces had engaged and destroyed what appeared to be a Libyan tank operating against rebels between the towns of Brega and Ajdabiya. This tank had in fact been captured by rebel fighters who had turned it on the Libyan Army. With communications between the rebel forces and NATO being 'patchy' at best, there was little chance that such an event could have been avoided. Even in Iraq and Afghanistan where communications were supposed to be much better, blue-on-blue engagements had sadly occurred. On this day a blue-on-grey event occurred – where a coalition warplane destroyed a tank, killing five of the rebels who had seized it hours earlier.

Making a statement on the event, and another one that had occurred around the same time, Rear Admiral Russ Harding, the British deputy commander of NATO's Libya operation, said, 'alliance jets had conducted 318 sorties and struck twenty-three targets across Libya in the past forty-eight hours'. He added that, 'it would appear that two of our strikes may have resulted in [rebel] deaths'. The deputy commander pointedly refused to apologise for the incidents, in language that some commentators regarded as insensitive. Reacting to the fallout from this event the NATO Secretary General, Anders Fogh Ramussen, commented saying that 'this was an unfortunate incident', adding that he 'strongly regretted the loss of life'. He also noted however how fluid the situation was on the ground but emphasized that NATO was operating in a way that sought to 'avoid civilian casualties'.

For NATO, thrown into a mission that was quite different to that which had characterized its missions in Afghanistan, new lessons would have to be learnt quickly. The subsequent measures to improve communications with the rebels, and the definition of areas in a number of towns where rebel forces operations were restricted, provides a testament to the additional measures introduced after these two events to avoid further bloodshed. One such measure involved the rebel forces painting their vehicles a peach colour and the United Kingdom Foreign Office donating 500 satellite phones to the rebels to improve their command and control arrangements.

The Defence of Misrata
The nature of this defence becomes apparent from an analysis of the data presented by the *Guardian* newspaper and presented in their *Datablog*. On 12 April, the data blog records twelve NATO attacks in the Misrata area on tanks and armoured vehicles. On that day only five other strikes were recorded against targets in Sirte. The 14th of April saw four more attacks in Misrata, whilst NATO air attacks focused for that day on Sirte. On 17 April, NATO targeted four command and control centres in Misrata.

NATO returned to Misrata on 18 April, conducting a range of attacks in the city. The *Guardian* records twenty-six strikes in Misrata over the coming days. On 22 April, Gaddafi forces started to withdraw from the city centre of Misrata. The focused effort from NATO in the city had clearly had an effect. On 23 April, as the Gaddafi units abandoned the city centre, NATO mounted its single most significant day of attacks in Misrata carrying out sixteen missions.

In what was to be a pivotal moment in the campaign, coalition air strikes conducted against the regime loyalists on 26 April prevented them re-taking the port in Misrata. During the day NATO conducted fourteen attacks on Gaddafi forces operating in the area. One of these was directed at a surface-to-air missile site and the remaining thirteen against the improvised military vehicles that are often referred to as 'technicals' – based on a four-by-four vehicle.

On 2 May NATO targeted twelve ammunition dumps in the Misrata area and on the third a further six attacks took place. Three of these were on tanks operating in the area, and three against further ammunition sites. Over the next two weeks NATO kept up the pressure in Misrata conducting sixty-three attacks against a variety of targets. This was the period in which the rebels were able to establish control over the main areas in Misrata. With help from NATO the city had endured its siege and come through. It was to be an important turning point in the conflict. One from which Gaddafi's forces would not readily recover.

The Campaign Narrative
The Ministry of Defence name for the campaign in Libya is OPERATION ELLAMY. One of the notable elements of the early part of the operation was the frequency with which briefings were given to the media. On the Sunday morning of the first day of operations the Ministry of Defence (MoD) fielded Major General John Lorimer in the role of the Chief of the Defence Staff's Strategic Communications Officer. This was an interesting development, and clearly highlights some learning within the MoD about ensuring that the messages that needed to be put out in the public domain were organised and working to a single strategic narrative. The language that became a consistent theme of the briefings that were to follow, showed a constancy that was less easy to observe in previous campaigns.

David Cameron clearly wanted the messages kept succinct and to the point. This was a new departure for the MoD who had shied away from giving this kind of regular briefing in the face of what had become a hostile press during the Iraq War and the subsequent counter-insurgency campaigns. At the outset the MoD clearly took the view that it was the right thing to do to provide daily updates to a voracious press.

The age-old adage of 'tell them once and them tell then again' applied. The themes of the legality of the action, and the need to protect the citizens of Benghazi, were hard-wired into each briefing. As the campaign unfolded however, and the inevitable mission creep started to develop, it became quite difficult to hold to those themes.

As the mission developed, and immediate threat to the people of Benghazi quickly evaporated, the attempts by the rebel forces to then strike out to the west to capture towns and cities en route to liberate Tripoli shifted the requirements on the missions being flown by the Royal Air Force and their coalition partners. The mission subtly morphed into one that now had a new aim, the replacement of Colonel Gaddafi as leader of Libya. This was no longer a mission to protect the citizens of Benghazi from the wrath of Gaddafi. It was to achieve regime change. As far as many members of the international community were concerned this was not what they had signed up to at the start. Frictions were then to arise that, as the pace of progress faltered, would throw the previously organised strategic narrative into disarray.

The Campaign Unfolds

Within days of the start of the campaign the RAF threw its newest fighter aircraft into the fray. Royal Air Force Typhoons were flown in action for the first time on 21 March. This was day two of the campaign. Their mission was to help enforce the no-fly zone. It was a mission for which they were very well suited, having been originally designed and developed to provide air defence cover over the United Kingdom against what at the time was the threat from the combined might of the Warsaw Pact air forces during the Cold War. The Typhoons were deployed forward from their bases in the United Kingdom at RAF Coningsby and RAF Leuchars to Gioia del Colle airbase in southern Italy.

The commitment of the Typhoons was also important for another reason. The Libyan campaign was to become a shop window in which countries like India had shortlisted both the Typhoon and its French rival the Rafael fighter for its own modernisation program. With the Saudi's also deciding not to purchase F-15 aircraft, the potential for sales for the manufacturers of these two aircraft types was too good to miss. The close cooperation between France and the United Kingdom over the operations in Libya covered a very different and intense rivalry in the international defence market place. How the two air forces emerged from the Libyan campaign might well determine who secures significant export orders.

Events on 22 March were to start a pattern that was to define the early stage of the campaign. The MoD briefing by Major General Lorimer made the usual points about the legality of the campaign whilst also noting 'we are still conducting detailed assessment of the effects of military action against specific targets'. He also added that, 'it would not be wise to disclose to Colonel Gaddafi precisely how well we believe we have performed in degrading his command and control network and his integrated air defence system'. His reticence on commentating on how effective the raids had been was to change twenty-four hours later.

Such was the speed at which the Libyan air force was driven from the skies that on day three of the campaign the RAF's commander of the operations over Libya was able to declare that the Libyan air force 'no longer exists as a fighting force'. Air Vice Marshall Bagwell went further, declaring that, 'its integrated air defence system and command and control networks are severely degraded to the point that we can operate over [Libyan] air space with impunity'.

The certainty of his comments would have arisen from the analysis work conducted from the signals that would have been picked up by the Nimrod R1 intelligence aircraft operating off the coast of Libya. It was one of two remaining Nimrod platforms that the RAF operated. In an ironic twist that gave David Cameron yet another advantage in the prosecution of this war, the retirement of these two platforms had been delayed long enough for them to perform their last mission.

To confirm that the Libyan air defence system no longer posed a systematic threat to the RAF and coalition aircraft patrolling the no-fly zone. Once that mission had been completed, the final two remaining Nimrod airframes were retired at a ceremony at RAF Waddington. Whilst that capability will, for a short-term, be unavailable to the RAF in the form that the Nimrod airframe provided, it will return in the form of the Rivet Joint aircraft and their sensor suites that are being purchased as part of a new equipment program.

The declaration that the Libyan air defence systems had been 'neutered' was a decisive point in the campaign. It enabled the RAF to focus its attention on how to apply air power to assist the rebels in their aims to move out from their newly acquired bastion of Benghazi towards Tripoli. It was to be a period of erratic progress that was to define one of the major lessons to emerge from the campaign. When a well organised and professional military force has to cooperate with what is essentially a hastily thrown together and untrained indigenous militia, previous doctrine has to be quickly adapted.

The view from 22 March was that the air forces which had committed resources to the operations over Libya had started to mobilise and arrive. This had an almost immediate effect on the threat to the people of Benghazi. In his briefing Major General Lorimer was able to note, 'last Friday, you will recall that regime troops were on the outskirts of

Benghazi, the second largest city in Libya and home to more than 670,000 civilians. Colonel Gaddafi vowed that his men would be going from house to house, room to room, to burn out the opposition.' Amplifying the language for dramatic effect, he further stated that, 'Libyan troops were reportedly committing atrocities in outlying areas of the city'. The implication was clear, without the intervention by the United Nations a massacre would unfold.

The 23rd of March was also to see an initial batch of Tornado GR4 dispatched to Gioia del Colle air base. This allowed the RAF to conduct both air and ground missions alongside seven other countries who at the time were also mounting operations to patrol the no-fly zone. That evening four Tornados flew from Gioia del Colle airbase on reconnaissance missions over Libya.

The 23rd also saw the introduction of the NATO-led naval mission that was to impose an arms embargo on Libya. OPERATION UNIFIED PROTECTOR started operations patrolling the Libyan coastline based on a multi-national naval force in which units of the Royal Navy were engaged.

A stock-take of progress was provided on 25 March by Major General Lorimer at a briefing held at the Ministry of Defence headquarters in London. Starting the briefing by noting that, 'Colonel Gaddafi continues to flout the will of the international community and is continuing to mount deadly and indiscriminate attacks on his own people', Lorimer stated that, 'our operations have saved many lives'. This was also the point at which it was announced that responsibility would pass from the United States to NATO for mounting the operations over Libya. The United States had enough on its hands withdrawing its troops from Iraq and maintaining pressure on the Taliban in Afghanistan to take on the main load for operations in Libya.

Whilst the United States filled the initial gap, it made it clear it wanted NATO to take over the task. NATO duly obliged when the Secretary General, Anders Fogh Ramussen, issued a declaration on 25 March that it was ready to take command of operations concerned with the no-fly zone imposed as part of United Nations Security Council Resolution (UNSCR) 1973. This was also the moment when the United Arab Emirates also decided to commit twelve aircraft to the campaign, becoming the second Arab nation to participate after Qatar.

The underlying political message from the US being that this is Europe's back yard and if it wants to do something about Gaddafi it is their responsibility. David Cameron not only had his war, he had to conduct it alongside the French, his new and closely-engaged political and military friend. This was to be a new test of an emerging relationship with France. The entente cordiale was about to move to a whole new level. No longer was it to be defined by a friendly understanding between political powers which had little practical meaning. It was to redefine how Europe would shape its military future.

The 25th of March was the day that the Brimstone missile system made its debut in OPERATION ELLAMY. The missile system is a high-precision weapon system that has a warhead that specifically helps reduce collateral damage. In the course of the campaign this capability was to be used with impressive effect against demanding and mobile targets. It was to be the start of a very successful campaign for this missile which had already proven itself in the skies above Afghanistan. The first attacks using the Brimstone were launched by Tornados that attacked a number of regime armoured vehicles threatening the civilian population of Ajdabiya, a town 150 kilometres to the south of Benghazi on the road to Tripoli.

By 26 March the future nature of the campaign was already becoming clear. Tornado aircraft engaged and destroyed three armoured vehicles in Misrata and a further three in Ajdabiya. By this time the uprising against Gaddafi had become entrenched along the coastline. This complicated the situation as UNSCR 1973 was quite specific about Benghazi. But the people of Libya, sensing that a unique opportunity to overthrow the regime had arrived with the support of NATO, began to take up arms across a wide range of areas on the ground.

At this moment Gaddafi's control of Tripoli and a number of other towns along the coast meant that the uprisings created a heterogeneous military landscape, made up of a number of areas where rebels sought support and other towns and cities that remained firmly in Gaddafi's control. This fractured military landscape was to create enormous challenges for NATO and for the RAF. Engaging targets that were inside population centres always had the potential to go badly wrong. It is a testament to the nature of the effort put in by the RAF that so few accidents occurred during the campaign.

NATO therefore had to operate along a non-linear front – one where the rebels hold on some positions after rapid advances was, at best, tenuous. When Gaddafi's forces did commit against the rebels they easily overmatched them on the ground. Without the presence of NATO the rebels would have been easily crushed. The lessons from the parallel revolt in Syria provide ample evidence of what would have happened.

The briefings conducted by Major-General Lorimer also settled down to a routine pattern. Statements would be made on the day's events and, where it was thought helpful in getting the narrative across, short videos would be shown. Often these would last for less than one minute and show the kind of precise attack upon a military target that underscored the message that NATO was doing all it could to minimise civilian casualties.

Of course in trying to disentangle the complex and dynamic nature of the situation on the ground, in the various towns like Misrata that had risen up, the contributions of sensor platforms like the Sentinel R1 aircraft flown by 5 Squadron based at Waddington was crucial. Like the Nimrod R1 this platform had also been sacrificed in the SDSR. The operations in Libya were to be its first main test as a piece of equipment and its last.

The Sentinel R1 aircraft was a radar equipped ISTAR platform that was bought as a result of research work that had been carried out in the Cold War. Its purpose was to fly close to what was called the Forward Edge of the Battlefield Area and track Warsaw Pact troop concentrations massing along the border between what was then East and West Germany. By tracking these massed formations, the British Army would be able to use its longer range artillery units to attack the follow-on forces that would accompany the first wave of attacks mounted across the border onto the German Plain and blunt their momentum.

In Libya the situation was radically different. There were no large scale formations employed by Gaddafi's forces, no single frontal point. Suitable targets had to be detected and engaged when they posed a threat to the civilian population. Detecting these targets against the complex urban backdrops in which they were deployed required advanced image interpretation skills.

The RAF maintains such a group of people that are trained to look for individual objects and associated patterns of behaviour that might be indicative of the presence of specific military vehicles in an area. Sometimes this is likened to detecting or finding the proverbial needle in a haystack. This only becomes possible as, over the duration of a mission, the patterns of behaviour become clear, allowing background activities to be discounted. Sometimes the detection of the target comes after an area becomes of interest as what might be termed normal activity in an area suddenly changes. Tanks, for instance, can have quite a deterrent effect upon local traffic. Once the changed pattern is detected the target to be engaged can be located by focusing in on specific areas in greater detail. If other sources of intelligence also point to activity in a specific area then the fusion of these can provide high-level products which make target detection simpler.

By 31 March the tone of the daily briefings emerging from the UK MoD had almost become routine. The initial hectic activity to mount operations had started to settle down almost into the mundane. In the daily briefing Major-General Lorimer spoke of RAF Tornados conducting 'further patrols over Libya yesterday', launching missiles against military assets of pro-Gaddafi forces that were operating in the Misrata area. In the course of the operations Major-General Lorimer confirmed that, 'Paveway IV and Brimstone missiles' had been used to engage 'three main battle tanks, two armoured vehicles and a surface-to-air missile site'.

The contribution of the Royal Navy was also briefly confirmed, supporting OPERATION UNIFIED PROTECTOR with HMS *Cumberland* patrolling in international waters off Libya, conducting sea denial and surveillance activities to monitor shipping in the area. Major-General Lorimer was to also confirm that HMS *Cumberland* launched her Lynx helicopter on a number of surface search operations. For the Royal Navy the initial contribution of TLAM to the suppression of the Libyan air defence system had quickly become a mission aimed at creating an embargo to prevent the shipment of arms or supplies to the Gaddafi regime in contravention of UNSCR 1973. Whilst during this part of the campaign the Royal Navy focused its ISTAR effort on the sea, in time it was to broaden its activities as the radar systems on the Sea King helicopters aboard HMS *Ocean* were to provide important observations on land movements

Given the speed with which the military operations achieved their first objectives of creating a permissive environment in which the aircraft of the RAF and its coalition partners could operate, it is difficult to identify a specific point at which the campaign became bogged down. The point at which the Press started to use the dreaded 'stalemate' word, with its inevitable impact upon the politicians involved. It would appear that today's generation of political leaders have an unrealistic expectation of what the military forces of their countries can achieve. To maintain what is often a fragile consensus for military action, the imperative is for progress to be achieved and maintained.

Yet progress in the campaign did stall. It was the inevitable result of a combination of factors that were for the first time appearing in Libya. None of those involved in writing military doctrine had quite imagined a campaign like it. The complexities of how to manage that campaign had to be worked out 'in contact'. That was to take time. Time the politicians reluctantly had to concede to the military. The next few months were to prove testing for the alliance as progress appeared to slow to a snails pace.

CHAPTER 5

Stalemate

The Rhythms of the Campaign

Military campaigns often start in a blaze of publicity. As the media tires of the daily grind of warfare they move onto other subjects. The military operations in Libya had plenty to contend with for media coverage. The enduring impact of the European financial crisis was rarely away from the front page and television headlines. A war that does not involve British troops being deployed on the ground seems a little unreal and fails to grab much attention. For David Cameron this would, at first, also be an advantage. However, as OPERATION UNIFIED PROTECTOR approached its first important milestone, 100 days into the campaign, the mood changed and questions started to be asked.

The permissive environment created for the military operations conducted by NATO almost creates a kind of sanitary warfare, in which aircraft can pick up and dispose of adversary's tanks, artillery pieces and missiles at will. Warfare that grabs the attention of the media is supposed to be risky. People are supposed to die and be mourned. The kind of warfare NATO embarked upon in Libya does not have that immediate media interest.

Of course, as little moments in the campaign arise, the media are only too happy to return to the coverage. The events that saw Tripoli fall clearly provided a point where the media would increase its coverage. The death of Gaddafi and its confusing circumstances brought another bout of intense media scrutiny. But they were brief periods amongst many days when the war in Libya struggled to get the headline writers' attention.

When a war appears to adopt a monotonous grind of daily bombings and attacks, it can easily fall off the radar screen. Media disinterest suddenly becomes a campaign that is stuck or bogged down in the desert.

Metaphors abound at this moment as do references to past campaigns where amateur historians amongst the ranks of journalists can submit a piece that shows an intellectual argument as to why the whole campaign is fatally flawed. Coming as it did in the wake of the controversial SDSR in the United Kingdom, it was perhaps inevitable that political leaders and former members of the Armed Forces would use this apparent stalemate to raise their concerns. Resource constraints after SDSR were always going to have an impact on the tempo of operations. To apply air power in complex and confusing situations, where the main driver is to prevent civilian casualties, takes time. Unless they are prepared to invest more significantly in airframes, political leaders will have to learn to be patient.

OPERATION UNIFIED PROTECTOR Unfolds

On 1 April an update was presented by the UK MoD on the past week's military strikes. Targets had been attacked by the RAF and the RN. They included underground bunkers that stored ammunition for the Libyan Army. For any campaign to make progress against a reasonably well equipped foe there needs to be a phase of attrition. This will always occur when the leader of the state being attacked thinks that his forces can outlast the coalition strikes against them. The dictator leading the regime will bet that the coalition will come up against something that will inherently test its political fragility, such as a large number of civilian deaths as a result of collateral damage.

After all, the argument would have gone, if you go to war to protect citizens how can you possibly justify occasions when bombs fall short or missiles go astray? Unfortunately for Gaddafi on this occasion those bets were not to pay off. The effort put into avoiding civilian casualties was huge and a by-product of genuine lessons learnt from the military interventions in Iraq and Afghanistan.

For the NATO forces, attacking ammunition stores clearly became a focal point in the mission. One of the problems they faced in mounting the attacks was to locate the facilities in the first place. With the overall mission being established so quickly there had been little preparation time in which a comprehensive target list could have been developed. Fortunately ammunition bunkers rarely tend to be based in the middle of cities. Even dictators like Colonel Gaddafi have some sense about the risks posed. However, even when they are located in rural areas and on the outskirts of urban areas, they still need to be discovered using ISTAR assets. Mobile ammunition centres can appear inside cities, as staging posts appear where military forces assemble, re-fuel and re-arm. Taking aim at them would require very careful consideration of the potential for collateral damage.

The detection of fixed ammunition bunkers requires the commitment of some dedicated ISTAR platforms. Some may have been disguised. Some will have been at a fixed location for many years, visited by weapons inspectors, their positions well known. Others however are more difficult to detect directly. Indirect methods are required that look for indicators that a site may have a specific military purpose. Patterns of behaviour have to be developed that show the kind of routine coming-and-going of supply trucks to and from the sites.

Platforms like the Predator and Reaper unmanned aircraft that are able to dwell over such targets for long durations of time, are crucial in helping build such patterns of behaviour. Their ability to persist over an area contrasts with the rather rapid over-flights associated with fast jets. They can collect the background data on the target and allow its possible role as an ammunition bunker to be identified.

On 24 March Tactical Land Attack Missile (TLAM) missiles launched by both the United States Navy and the RN targeted a site north of the town of Sabha, which was thought to house forty underground bunkers that stored a range of munitions. RAF Tornados using Storm Shadow missiles attacked part of the same facility to the north-west of the site. After the attack the nature of the explosions in the area confirmed that it had clearly been an ammunition storage facility. The aim of the attack was to disrupt the supply of ammunition to the Gaddafi forces operating in Zintan and Misrata.

By 6 April the progress made had been sufficiently consolidated to allow William Hague to declare that the military mission had 'prevented a huge loss of life and a humanitarian catastrophe'. But he also spoke of the Gaddafi regime's continuing ability to mount attacks against the civilians in towns such as Brega, Misrata and Zintan. In the update that he delivered to the House of Commons, Mr Hague noted that thirty-four countries had now joined the coalition and that in the previous week a total of 701 sorties had been flown, and that 276 of these involved an element of engagement with the Libyan armed forces.

With the citizens of other towns in Libya coming under an extended air umbrella, the focus of the mission had already started to creep. It was now inevitable that NATO would have to try and help the rebels remove Colonel Gaddafi. Already the United Kingdom was one of thirty-six countries that were also delivering humanitarian aid to the citizens of a number of Libyan towns. The fate of the people in Misrata was also starting to become a concern as media broadcasts showed injured people being evacuated by a Turkish hospital ship that was running into and out of the port, sometimes whilst gunfire was erupting very close by.

As the campaign developed it was also inevitable that the RAF would have to split its time between two forms of targets. These were those that emerged in real-time, the so-called emergent or time-sensitive targets, and those that were located in fixed positions. Each presented slightly different challenges for those developing the target lists. For the fixed targets, many of which were hardened, the Storm Shadow missile provided an option along with the possibility of a RN TLAM attack.

For the emergent targets the issues were slightly different. These required the Tornados and Typhoons to maintain an overwatch capability and be refuelled to maintain time on station. That was to cause a number of former Admirals to use these tactics to criticise the early retirement of HMS *Ark Royal* which had provided a platform for Harrier aircraft to carry out this form of attack during the campaign in the Balkans.

The issue was how to maintain the political consensus, for it was at that point when various nations across Africa started to break ranks and seek a political compromise with Gaddafi. The next few weeks were to create strains in the coalition, as the South African President tried to develop a road map that would bring the crisis to an end. Yet again Gaddafi failed to appreciate the potential benefits that a long drawn out political process might have given him as a lever with which the place pressure on the coalition.

On the same day, the MoD briefing noted that on 5 April RAF Tornado GR4 aircraft flew from Gioia del Colle to carry out overwatch and armed reconnaissance missions over Libya. During these activities a number of Paveway IV and Brimstone missiles had been launched. This attack resulted in the destruction of six armoured fighting vehicles and six battle tanks. The RAF also announced on the same day that four of its Typhoon aircraft would be converted from their air defence role to a ground attack configuration. At this point the RAF had sixteen ground attack aircraft operating under NATO command with an additional four fast jets allocated to police the no-fly zone.

In a briefing on 7 April, provided by the deputy commander of NATO's operations in Libya, Rear Admiral Russell Harding, a change in tactics by the regime forces was noted. The Admiral commented on how the Libyan government forces were now 'blending in with road traffic and using civilian life as a shield for their advance'. He said that this had enabled the regime elements to regain the initiative, allowing them to move back towards Ajdabiya and pose a renewed threat to Benghazi to the north. This was one of a number of occasions where NATO had to adapt to what was an ever-changing pendulum of force dispositions that occurred when the regime was able to over-match rebel forces forcing them to withdraw.

On 11 April the RAF attacked seven main battle tanks used by the Gaddafi regime forces in two separate missions. In Ajdabiya the Tornados located and destroyed two tanks inside the city which had turned their guns on rebel fighters. The other five destroyed that day where located near Misrata and were being prepared to be loaded onto tank transporters. The MoD footage of the attack again showed the precision with which the Brimstone missiles found and destroyed their targets, even leaving nearby buildings relatively undamaged and the tank transporters apparently undamaged.

At sea on 11 April, HMS *Liverpool* took over the maritime contribution from the United Kingdom alongside HMS *Brocklesby*, allowing HMS *Cumberland* to return home, ironically to be decommissioned. Yet again another piece of military hardware left the battlefield of Libya to be withdrawn from service. For HMS *Liverpool*, and its commander and crew, the coming few weeks were to pose a diverse range of challenges. Not least of which was responding to being fired on by a Libyan shore battery. This was the first time a RN warship had been engaged in combat since the Falkland Islands. Had anyone aboard HMS *Liverpool* harboured doubts about the willingness of the Libyan armed forces to defend the regime in Tripoli they would have been rapidly dispelled by the orange glow on the radar screens of the incoming fire. HMS *Liverpool* was in a war zone and on 3 May, just off the coast of Brega, as far as the captain and crew were concerned, it has just gone live.

In the following days NATO was to mount a series of ad-hoc attacks against emergent targets, such as main battle tanks as well as a number of fixed targets. On 13 April, in a mission update, Major-General Lorimer stated that, 'most of the fighting in Libya remains focused firstly around the siege of Misrata'.

The General was to go on to note what he also termed the 'rather fluid situation in the region of Brega and Ajdabiya'. He also reported that out of sixty-one armoured vehicles and air defence assets that were targeted over the previous weekend, twenty of these were attacked by the RAF in the areas of Brega, Misrata and Ajdabiya. At that point the RAF had attacked around 100 tanks, armoured vehicles, artillery and surface-to-air missile sites as well as many other fixed targets.

The mixture of weapon systems which the Typhoons and Tornados carried made them a popular choice for those planning operations. The combination of the Paveway, Storm Shadow and Brimstone missiles proved themselves in the operations as a versatile set of weapon systems. At this point the RAF was conducting around 25 per cent of the ground attack missions. Whilst a great compliment to the service, it was also not a fair distribution of the workload.

In between attacking emergent targets the RAF also continued its aim to suppress important parts of the command and control networks. On 19 April a number of communications sites were attacked by RAF Tornado and Typhoon jets, which were to strike seven times in as many minutes with precision, again illustrated by the cockpit videos taken during the missions.

Unfulfilled Expectations
It is axiomatic that military campaigns can often promise swift results but can then fail to deliver. With the world's media often conducting a feeding frenzy at the start of a war, with main broadcasters taken from the relative

safety of the studio and placed in the front line, the seriousness of the situation is somehow enhanced. The coverage is intensive, reporters appear scattered over the battlefield, the war is given graphic coverage with warnings to the audience that some of the scenes they are about to see may be distressing. It is almost guaranteed to keep some hooked to the screens.

This is all a far cry from past wars. The second-by-second reporting, delivered twenty-four hours a day, creating a very different level of expectation, sets a public mood. That mood is fickle and passing. The national sense of urgency about the Second World War, that belief that everyone was at risk, is so difficult to achieve when the fighting is set over the horizon and far away. As the broadcasters tire of covering the same scenes of battle, a sense of repetitiveness starts to sink in and the front line newscasters return to the United Kingdom to resume their coverage of other more pressing matters about the economy, education or health issues. The war slides into the background, its routine condemning it to a temporary obscurity. But when civilians are caught in the cross-fire, as they inevitably are, the clamour from the public is for the military to take more care. Their expectations are that with the kind of precision weaponry that is available today the military should be able to avoid killing civilians.

Sadly, despite the kind of advantages that NATO inevitably can field in terms of sensor systems, it remains a truism that simple measures taken by an adversary can create confusion. When targets are presented travelling along a road in the open, away from any civilians, they can be engaged with relative impunity if the right weapon configuration is selected.

If however, showing complete disregard for life, the adversary chooses to place military hardware near to schools, hospitals and other centres of population, it is a fact that on occasions civilians will die in the cross-fire. At this point the media will re-engage, often eager to develop a critical line about a specific incident, questioning the morals and ethics of those that could have conducted the operation. They fail to appreciate, and take little interest in, the complexities of warfare. They just want the story, something that gets them headlines.

The Libyan Stalemate
After the initial phase of the campaign came to a close the battlespace in

which NATO was operating became clearer. The original dividing lines were restored, helping NATO avoid collateral damage. In the early phases as the battlefield shifted chaotically there were cases when the rebel forces had moved so far forward that they had become difficult to mark out from units of Gaddafi's military. The chances of an accidental attack being undertaken against rebel fighters grew rapidly. The days of the linear battlefield, captured by the Cold War term the Forward Edge of the Battle Area, were consigned to history. In contemporary warfare there is no such thing as the front or the rear echelons or units. The battlefield becomes a confused area where the demarcation between allies and adversaries changes almost hour-by-hour.

One specific example of this problem came in Misrata. It had been amongst the first cities to rise up against the Gaddafi regime. But it was remote and cut off; sitting behind what would have been conventionally named the forward area of operations for Gaddafi's units. Misrata rapidly became a scene of intense door-to-door and street-to-street fighting. In this confused and dynamic situation NATO commanders chose to play it safe. They ordered the rebels to avoid crossing certain imaginary red-lines drawn at various boundaries in the city. Frustration grew amongst the rebels who sensed that they had the upper hand and were ready to fight.

Leaders of the rebel Black Brigade and the Swehdi Brigades claimed that they felt 'constrained from launching pre-emptive assaults'. Illustrating a mounting sense of frustration with what was seen as a cautious policy developed by NATO, one commander from the Libyan rebel Black Brigade specifically cited a belief that if they had been given permission to cross a specific red line that they could have captured Tarhuga within two hours.

On the ground there was a perception that Gaddafi's forces were tiring in the fight and that one last push would see them vacate the area. Their optimism was to be misplaced. The battle of control for Misrata, which was seen to be such a strategically vital enclave, would last for the majority of the campaign and cost hundreds of people their lives.

The signs of faltering progress came early on in the Libyan campaign. As the military effort reached the crucial mark of 100 days writers were quick to highlight the early confident remarks from some politicians in the United Kingdom. For people like George Osborne this was their first war at the Treasury. It was unwise to suggest that wars can be fought on a budget. In military expenditure terms £250 million is not a lot of cash. At the same time the significance of the passing of 100 days seemed to have an effect upon the political leaders with the Italian Foreign Minister calling for a halt to bombing to avoid civilian casualties. This was an argument that was to prove largely specious and based on a somewhat stereotypical response to warfare. But it did highlight a growing unease within the coalition.

The regime had been expected to crumble quickly in the face of overwhelming firepower. As with many dictators their values and beliefs systems tend to be very self-centered. They do not concern themselves with the lives of their supporters. They can sacrifice their lives. The rules for the dictators are different. Their survival is paramount.

As for the military forces the strain was already appearing. The initial campaign had gained authorisation to continue for another ninety days, military leaders such as Air Chief Marshall Sir Simon Bryant – the second most senior officer in the Royal Air Force – had already gone on record to express his concerns. Once aircrew and their support teams completed their first tour it would not be long before they would be heading back to Sicily to start another.

This kind of operational intensity, with all of its implications for family life, was not supposed to be how it works. Military people were supposed to get a period of rest and recuperation after serving in a theatre of war, followed by a work-up period before deploying again. One four month tour a year was a target to achieve, with the military stretched some argued to breaking point, it would appear that the Prime Minister's words on restoring the military covenant appeared hollow.

That the military have an ethos based on doing their best to continue with the mission at all costs is a testament to their resilience and fortitude. But when aging equipment starts to play-up even their ingenuity can be tested. The example of the Royal Air Force's fleet of VC-10 aircraft is one that attracted some media coverage in a BBC report on the first 100 days of the campaign.

These airborne tankers had been purchased at the height of the Cold War to provide an airborne refuelling capability for Royal Air Force Air Defence variant Tornados operating out over the North Sea, intercepting and if necessary engaging, Russian bombers probing the United Kingdom's air space. Had the Cold War turned hot it is highly likely that despite their efforts to remain stealthy that their survival times would not have been able to be measured in days. They would have been a primary target for Russian fighter jets accompanying the bombers.

Over Afghanistan, in the immediate aftermath of 11 September, they distinguished themselves refuelling fighter jets launched from aircraft carriers operating in the Indian Ocean, allowing the jets to increase their duration over Afghanistan and be able to attack what are known as 'emergent targets'. This is a vitally important capability for any COIN (counter-insurgency) campaign. It allows the fighter jets to be available as the adversary's emerge from their hiding places to move. Over Libya the venerable VC-10s were again to remind anyone caring to pay attention just how important it is for military operations to have a gas-tank in the sky. The British, French, American, Canadian and Italian aircrews would all agree with that sentiment.

For many observers the point at which the campaign had lasted for 100 days was a point to reflect upon progress. This landmark occurred on Sunday, 26 June 2011. Political leaders who had staked a lot in the campaign in the first place seemed to sense the need to reassure. David Cameron's language was typical when he said 'time is on our side, it is not on Gaddafi's side'. This was an interesting use of language given the predilection of modern war leaders to want to see the military achieve objectives quickly, worried about how a prolonged war would play out in the court of public opinion.

Despite the apparent slowness of the military build up, progress had been forthcoming on other fronts. Writing in the *Financial Times* James Blitz, Michael Peel and Anna Fifield acknowledged that, 'NATO has gone some way towards achieving the central mandate it received from the United Nations Security Council to stop Colonel Gaddafi murdering his own people'. They also noted that the broadly-based coalition had remained 'largely intact'.

However the doubts about whether the military intervention, as far as it went, would create the conditions whereby Gaddafi would step down were also recognised. He was not alone in holding reservations about the direction of the campaign at this point. Gaddafi, it appeared, may be able to hang on. The political noises that were starting to appear even suggesting that some compromise deal could be found to leave him in power. The coalition may have still been intact but so, to a large extent, was Gaddafi's regime. Early defections, such as those of several senior figures in the regime, had stopped. Gaddafi's power base was hardly ebbing away.

Quoting a senior, but yet unnamed military source in the United Kingdom, whose view was that Gaddafi was 'on the way out', the reporters from the *Financial Times* also wondered if this was mere hubris. The situation on the ground did not appear to back up that assertion. If anything Gaddafi's appearances on television were becoming more theatrical as he posed for the cameras and drove around Tripoli amongst his friends and supporters whipping the crowds up into a frenzy. The *Financial Times* reporters were taking a slightly more objective view. After all, they also argued, one way or another it had been a bad week for the coalition as NATO conceded it had accidentally killed nine civilians in an attack on Tripoli.

This was NATO's first public admission of a collateral damage event. As if to pick up on the concerns at the time, as the campaign moved towards its 100 day point, a candidate for the Egyptian presidency, Amr Moussa, expressed his concerns about the mission and if it would achieve the aim of getting Colonel Gaddafi to leave Libya willingly. At this point military historians will recall a similar set of concerns occurring in the Kosovo mission undertaken by NATO. It too seemed to enter a phase where a lack of military progress appeared to start a round of political unease.

Being a war time leader is not so easy, as David Cameron was finding out. The Libyan situation for him was personal. Afghanistan was a situation he inherited from a weak Labour government that had little idea how to wage war. As a Tory, with all the images of Margaret Thatcher's leadership in the Falklands War, Cameron was somehow supposed to win. That is what the Tories did when they went to war. The coming weeks would test his mettle as the campaign appeared to metaphorically get stuck in the sand and his military leaders would start to express their own reservations on the outcome publicly.

Towards the end of June the overall commander of NATO operations in Libya, Canada's Lieutenant General Charles Bouchard, expressed a very upbeat assessment of progress in the campaign when he said that the alliance had 'destroyed Colonel Gaddafi's ability to conduct offensive operations'. Whilst that may have been an important point in the campaign, it was not decisive. Through the early part of July the impetus seemed to move away from NATO as the alliance appeared to lose focus.

One of the challenges for NATO at this time, as in any military campaign, was how to retain the initiative? For NATO commanders this was a difficult time. They did not have a lot of options. A land campaign had been explicitly ruled out by United Nations Resolution 1973. Targeting electricity supplies, as had been done in the Kosovo campaign when Serbia power stations were attacked, was going to disrupt the lives of local people when the summer was at its height. This was hardly a way to create a good impression with those that you are hoping will finally rise up and eject Gaddafi from power.

There was also the underlying worry that NATO and its coalition partners had set out to achieve a short-term victory in Libya whilst only committing a limited number of forces. War rarely succeeds if political leaders are unable to take it seriously. In the United States there was little appetite for the idea of replacing Gaddafi, despite the noises about the events in Lockerbie and the outrage at the release of the one person convicted of that crime on compassionate grounds.

This situation was compounded by the rather ad hoc nature of the rebels and their highly improvised approach to the campaign. It all seemed a little chaotic. When the forces fielded by the rebels met the disciplined forces under the control of the Gaddafi regime the outcome often saw the rebels beat a tactical retreat. Without NATO bombers in the air to provide the top cover to their activities the rebels would have been hopelessly outgunned. The graphic images of the situation in Syria provide all the evidence, if it were needed, of what would have happened if NATO had not intervened.

That the campaign was going to stall was, with the benefit of hindsight, inevitable. Gaddafi's intransigence was always likely to be an issue. For Gaddafi, however, to fail to use this period of uncertainty in the campaign was one of a number of major opportunities he would lose to draw out the conflict and test NATO and its coalitions partners resolve.

As the NATO campaign appeared to grind to a halt, the media started to widen the debate in its coverage. This was not helped by politicians who suddenly saw the swift war dragging on. One article written by Jonathan Stele in the *Guardian* on 26 July has the headline, 'Libya's stalemate shows it's time to tempt Gaddafi out, not blast him out'. It was a sentiment that echoed the private thoughts of many international political leaders at the time, even if they were not prepared to publically confront the topic. For David Cameron it must have been a worrying time.

Such statements in the press are often accompanied by a very detailed appraisal of the political manoeuvrings that are going on in the background. The shuttle diplomacy that now inevitably accompanies all wars had stuttered into life as the mediator appointed by the United Nations, Abdul Elah al-Khatib, moved from capital to capital trying to develop a consensus on a way forward. For some nervous politicians in the United Kingdom it was a time when the debate was allowed to range across a number of solutions. This was aggravated at the time by the sense of mission creep that had set in by the start of July. NATO was running low on targets. Its attacks were also moving beyond the defence of Benghazi.

Whilst in the early stages of the campaign most observers understood the need to suppress the Libyan air defence systems to ensure NATO could control the skies. Once that initial wave of attacks was completed the rationale for NATO to keep attacking across the country instead of anything that approached Benghazi seemed odd. If the aim was to protect the people of Benghazi why attack other strongholds of the regime?

The fact is that mission creep did start to occur at this point. Targets that had little utility with respect to protecting targets in Benghazi were attacked as they popped up on the radar screens of NATO's intelligence collection assets. For the non military minded this was not how to fight this kind of limited intervention. For those with a little more understanding of the ways that campaigns evolve, this was all about shaping the battlefield.

The other factor that came into play was the move by the rebels out from Benghazi towards Tripoli. Their initial efforts were somewhat chaotic. Brief bursts of activity along the main highway to Tripoli found ill-prepared Gaddafi forces falling back. The rebels appeared to be on a roll. The situation was illusionary. With echoes of the battles of the Second World War, as the rebels advanced so they found their supply lines becoming extended. Axis and Allied commanders had experienced similar difficulties along this very same piece of land seventy years previously. It is axiomatic that despite advances in technology that some elements of warfare stay the same. Logistics is one of those. Fuel, ammunition and food supplies still have to reach the fighting men as they advance. In Libya the supply lines rapidly became extended.

The rebels had rushed forward sensing that Gaddafi's downfall was imminent. In fact his military commanders were simply retreating to allow the natural impact of over-extended supply lines to create an opportunity for a counter-attack. NATO commanders could only watch from the sidelines, attacking Gaddafi loyalists if they broke cover, to try and help the rebels maintain their advance. Once that progress was halted, and went into reverse, the decision to deploy military advisors on the ground to help coordinate the rebels' activity was inevitable. Another little, but important, step had been taken along the route that redefined the mission.

With hindsight it is clear that the initial expectations that once military power was brought to bear by NATO that the Gaddafi regime would split became rapidly discredited. Gaddafi was going nowhere fast. His calculation was that if he could draw this out and create the stalemate effect, NATO itself would tire of the war and its united approach would splinter. This was a game of who blinks first, and it appeared in early July as if the coalition's collectives eyes had begun to flutter.

One complicating factor was the speed with which the international prosecutor, Luis Moreno Ocampo, had moved to secure an arrest warrant for Gaddafi. Within days of the NATO operation starting Ocampo had sought and obtained a warrant from the ICC. Any talk of keeping Gaddafi in place was now at odds with the desire to see him legally transported to The Hague to answer the allegations against him over his treatment of his people. The problem was that once an arrest warrant had been issued it could not easily be withdrawn without someone losing face. Libya was also not a legal signatory to the statute that created the ICC, further complicating how Gaddafi might be treated in the future.

The theme of a campaign mired in the desert spread. The word stalemate became part of the daily fare of media reporting. The malaise about the campaign seemed to allow journalists to speculate about the future potential of the military instrument of power well beyond the borders of Libya. Richard Norton-Taylor writing in the *Guardian* on 26 July actually went so far as to ask the question, 'can NATO actually win any of its wars'? For anyone interested in the subject it was a very fair question to ask.

His arguments were clear-cut, noting that by some estimates NATO has spent billions in trying to counter an insurgency in Afghanistan. His opening line stated, 'the armed forces of the world's mightiest military alliance, NATO, have failed twice now to win a war'. His commentary, written against a confusing political backdrop and a stalemated military campaign in Libya, seemed to suggest that NATO was on the verge of giving up. He placed the cost of the war in Libya at the time in excess of £120 million.

The language was accompanied with the unwritten implication that this cost was growing on a day-to-day basis, which at a time of national austerity was a major burden to carry for what appeared to be an uncertain outcome. The piece hinted, in the classic language of the media, that the political moves being made were looking for a rapid exit strategy, one cobbled together on the fly.

Cameron, he pointed out, had only just returned from a visit to Afghanistan were he defended the apparent lack of progress with the point that 'you cannot drop democracy from 14,000 feet'. Ironically, as the situation in Libya deteriorated the United Kingdom Prime Minister was to 'join Nicolas Sarkozy in trying to do just that'. A matter of a month later NATO was to achieve a breakthrough in the campaign that was to see the rebels seize Tripoli. It was not a victory. The war had not been won, but an objective – albeit an unwritten one – had been achieved. Cameron had got his regime change by stealth. It is a situation that is unlikely to happen again.

The problem with his language, and this is common to many people that fail to appreciate the challenges that now face the military, is that pretty much everyone who understand asymmetric warfare knows that the language of defeat, winning and victory no longer apply to military interventions. It is a dated lexicon.

It is time that the so-called defence elements of the press caught up

A Tornado GR4 awaits another mission over Libya. (*Crown Copyright*)

A Tornado GR4 leaving RAF Marham on a Storm Shadow mission over Libya. (*Crown Copyright*)

An Enhanced Paveway III bomb. (*Crown Copyright*)

A British Army Apache helicopter lifts off from HMS Ocean during Operation UNIFIED PROTECTOR. (*Crown Copyright*)

The Sea King Airborne ISTAR Helicopters on board HMS Ocean during Operation UNIFIED PROTECTOR. (*Crown Copyright*)

A RAF Sentinel R1 aircraft flying over its home city of Lincoln. (*Crown Copyright*)

Two Tornado GR4s preparing to leave for a mission over Libya. (*Crown Copyright*)

A Typhoon operating over Libya. (*Crown Copyright*)

The flight deck of a VC-10 about to take off for a mission during Operation UNIFIED PROTECTOR. (*Crown Copyright*)

A pair of RAF Typhoons waiting to participate in Operation UNIFIED PROTECTOR. (*Crown Copyright*)

A RAF Tornado GR4 on the ground showing the mix of Paveway and Brimstone missiles. (*Crown Copyright*)

A RAF pilot from 3 Squadron emerges after the last flight over Libya. (*Crown Copyright*)

A USAF AWACS aircraft on the ground during Operation UNIFIED PROTECTOR. (*US DoD*)

A US warship undertakes a Replenishment at Sea (RAS) during operations to enforce the trade embargo off Libya. (*US DoD*)

A pilot getting ready to fly an RAF Typhoon over Libya. (*Crown Copyright*)

A RAF Typhoon leaves the United Kingdom to enforce the no-fly zone around Libya. (*Crown Copyright*)

with this simple fact that military commanders now appreciate. Wars are no longer winnable. All the military instrument of power can do is to shape the political, military and economic space to create favourable conditions in which a political solution can emerge. It was Von Clausewitz in his notable work *On War*, first published by his wife in 1832, that first noted that wars are 'politics by another means'. But he was also to provide other insights that also retain their relevance today. His thought that, 'politics is the womb in which war develops', is unlikely ever to be challenged.

As the campaign carried on into August the lack of media coverage helped the military commanders in charge. Once off the radar screen of the media they could conduct the kind of shaping operations that would build to a decisive point. All campaigns are based upon trying to achieve a series of decisive points. The situation in Libya however, called for some additional manoeuvring. It was time for a limited deployment of boots on the ground in the form of 'military advisors', a euphemism for the deployment of Special Forces and other specialists, to help coordinate the response of the rebels.

The tensions in the NATO alliance and the onus on the rebels to make progress started to come to a head in the middle of August. Media reporting now headlined that the NATO alliance had underestimated the strength of support for Colonel Gaddafi. Reporting even suggested that certain tribes in the Libya societal landscape had joined the fray to help Gaddafi.

That a number of tribes remained loyal to Gaddafi was hardly surprising. He had been able, through the kind of patronage networks with which all military commanders engaged in COIN operations are very familiar, to retain that loyalty. He bought their loyalty. However when that largess is not longer able to be extended, the apparent support can appear wafer thin.

Reading the often dynamic nature of the societal landscape is a crucial skill that military commanders now have to master. During the kind of stalemate situation that prevailed in Libya throughout July and into early August it would have been hard for any kind of intelligence assessment to have been clear as to how the tribal loyalties might evolve. Human beings are well known to reach certain tipping points in their mindsets when they believe that 'enough is enough'.

The Momentum Runs into the Sand

It is very hard to say when the air campaign over Libya lost momentum but around the end of April and into early May the day-to-day tempo of operations appeared to lose NATO the initiative it had originally gained. Appearances however can be deceptive. Whilst the RAF and the RN continued the attacks on an increasingly wider target set, gradual changes on the ground were being put in place to help the rebels become more coordinated. The RAF and the RN conducted what can now be thought of as shaping operations. This is classic military prose that defines the period in a campaign where it takes time to gradually wear down the opposition through attacking forces as and when they appear.

This is where one of the consequences of the SDSR can be seen. The reduction in the total number of aircraft available to the RAF meant that the operational commitment to Libya and Afghanistan was challenging. Had SDSR not seen elements of the Tornado fleet retired early, the RAF may well have been able to speed up the time at which Gaddafi's forces were diminished to such an extent that they could not longer defend Tripoli. The sortie generation rate that arose from the assets deployed into the NATO operation was a constant source of frustration for the campaign commanders. They clearly would have liked to have had more assets.

But overall, when the target set that was available was being constantly eroded by precision attacks, it was just a question of time before things would change dramatically. Whilst some commentators liked to resort to describing this as a stalemate, in practise it was anything but that – Libyan defence forces were suffering a constant array of attacks and were having a great deal of their freedom of manoeuvre diminished by day and by night.

The impact of the efforts of the RAF and their coalition colleagues together with the effectiveness of the naval blockade was eventually going to create pressure on the Gaddafi regime elements. The issue was that the political leaders started to use this form of language too early in the campaign, setting expectations that a tipping point was almost there and Gaddafi's days were numbered. With other members of the coalition simply unable to provide greater resources to commit to the air campaign, the burden fell on the RAF to undertaken more than its share of attacks. It was a challenge to which, in the famous traditions of the service, it would rise.

From 18 April onwards the main focus of the attacks carried out by the RAF gradually moved towards emergent targets. On 23 April the RAF attacked three armoured personnel carriers destroyed near Misrata and, perhaps more importantly, a surface-to-surface missile facility that was located near the same city. On the same day eight rocket launchers were seriously damaged and eight support vehicles were destroyed.

At the time, the rate of consumption of the various missiles used by the RAF was starting to cause some concern. Within a month, speculation in the press was to cause the UK MoD to deny that it was in any danger of running out of the Brimstone missiles and had been in discussion with the supplier over converting some of a previous production standard missile to replace those used in the campaign. NATO issued a similar statement at the same time.

The issue of the rate of use of the Brimstone however raises an interesting question. Despite it obvious success in the campaign, is it the most effective way to deal with the range of targets that now routinely present themselves on contemporary battlefields?

Having spent over $1 billion developing the missile system since its development started in 1996, in the wake of the First Gulf War, the issue would be whether or not its basic elements could be adapted to encompass an even wider set of potential targets? Any development would have to build upon the existing elements rather than starting again on a new and potentially risky project.

The classic Toyota land cruiser vehicles that were being adapted by the regime and rebels to carry weapons, allowed the pro-Gaddafi elements to field a large number of potential targets. One lesson for future campaigns, especially in asymmetric warfare situations, is that any combat estimate process (which of course did not occur in this operation) would not only have to address the numbers of armoured vehicles available to an adversary but also how quickly they could adapt so-called 'technicals' as improvised weapon platforms.

This would add another important factor to the combat estimate that would make planning future wars difficult. If each 'technical' requires a single Brimstone missile to destroy it the cost-ratio of the Brimstone to the technical seems entirely unbalanced. At a reported £35,000 to £45,000 per missile to destroy a 'technical' it could be argued that a cheaper form of weapon system is required in the future.

In one of the more significant developments in the air campaign RAF Tornado GR4 attacked FROG-7 surface-to-surface ballistic missiles that were located near Gaddafi's birth place of Sirte on 5 May. In what was to be a rapid turnaround from another (unnamed) target, two Tornado GR4 aircraft were cued onto the location of the missiles. The video taken from the Litening III video pods showed many secondary explosions.

Developments in the West
Despite what can now be seen to be gradual progress being made in the east as rebels advanced slowly towards Tripoli, bypassing some of the Gaddafi strongholds of Sirte and Ben Walid, the real break through in the campaign was to come from the south-west. Rebels in the Nafusa Mountains launched a major offensive against Gaddafi forces holding the town of Ghazaya. This phase of the campaign was important, as Gaddafi forces in the town were able to use its location to shell the supply routes used by the rebels across the border from Tunisia. To gain some operational manoeuvre-room the rebels needed to remove Gaddafi's forces from Ghazaya and the nearby town of Al Jawsh. Despite briefly entering the town, using tanks captured from the Gaddafi loyalists, the rebels were unable to secure it and therefore reluctantly withdrew back into the mountains.

The Nafusa Mountain range lays just over 100 kilometres to the south -west of Tripoli. Throughout June and early July the rebels had used the terrain in the area to build up their military supplies. It is likely that their activities were also aided by the presence of some military advisors, although this was not confirmed in reporting that appeared at the time.

Whilst that progress had been slow, it had created an opportunity to use the terrain of the area and the increasing operational stretch that was being placed on the Gaddafi forces to create a new flank – one that was closer to the centre of power of the regime. It was to be from the west that the decisive phase of the battle for the liberation of Libya was to emerge. Whilst all the media attention had been directed at the advance from the east, it was from the west that the second front would finally emerge that would squeeze Gaddafi into Tripoli and ultimately out of power.

CHAPTER 6

The Breakthrough

Observations on the War

One of the difficulties of contemporary warfare *amongst the people*, to refer to General Sir Rupert Smith's now well worn phrase, is that it makes detailed analysis of the campaign difficult. In the past the notion of a battlefield was quite simple. The red and blue forces faced off across a line that delineated each others' boundaries of occupation. In the middle was the FEBA.

In Libya, as had been the case in Afghanistan and Iraq, as the conflict developed such neat divisions of who occupied what space were not to arise. The urban battlespace was especially confusing and caused issues for the employment of air power in various cities and towns that had joined the rebellion.

The duration of the battles in Misrata and Brega were to provide a graphic testament to the limitation of air power in complex and rapidly changing urban environments. In Libya, important population centres such as Brega, Zlitan and Zawiya were to hold out against the rebels for long durations as the conflict unfolded. Bani Walid and Sirte also proved difficult to finally capture. Defining where the FEBA was in such situations is a task that is nigh-on impossible. Each population centre has to be treated as its own little micro-war zone.

This complexity of war *amongst the people* poses problems for the ways in which military forces are employed. The risks of collateral damage are significantly enhanced in such a fluid and dynamic battlefield. In the course of the campaign the NATO-led coalition would conduct over 26,000 sorties. Between 31 March and 18 September, 23,055 of those sorties would be flown at an average daily rate of 134. Of those 8,582 were strike missions, an average of fifty a day. Not all of those saw weapons released against targets.

Looking across the NATO dataset it is apparent that in July a significant shift in the targeting occurred from the viewpoint of the range of cities and towns targeted. This was the crucial point at which the NATO approach to the battlespace shifted from its initial target set towards a more attritional approach designed to wear down the enemy. This is the point at which the media started to express its emerging collective view that the campaign had become stalemated.

That perception may also have been helped by the untimely death of one of the rebel's military leaders, General Abdel Fatah Younis. He had been one of the most important defections from the Gaddafi regime. He persuaded the Benghazi Interior Ministry Brigade to switch sides at a critical point in the initial stages of the confrontation with the rebels. His high profile television appearances, in which he visited the rebel forces around Benghazi, clearly irritated the regime members in Tripoli. General Younis was labelled a traitor and opportunist. His death, in suspicious circumstances, on 28 July, was to disrupt the command and control chain of the rebels. It also removed a highly experienced military person from the services of the NTC.

A few days earlier Britain had followed France in recognising the NTC as the 'sole governmental authority'. Any possible deal with Gaddafi was now firmly off the table. The mission was now formally to change the regime in Tripoli. The loss of its main military leader was a hammer blow from which the NTC would recover with the help of a number of military advisors that had been deployed by the French and British.

This was to be a really important moment; from that point on the NATO-led coalition would be able to coordinate with the activities of the rebels on the ground. Whilst it would not fully solve some of the difficulties of working in complex urban environments, it would greatly help the aim of reducing casualties, either to the rebels or to civilians.

The Targets Emerge
Table 1 shows the break-down by month of the total targets attacked by the NATO-led coalition. The rate of attacks, bearing in mind that August was not a complete month, and that October saw the end of the campaign, shows a high rate of sustainment of attacks by NATO on a monthly basis. The peak in August occurred at the time that Tripoli fell.

Month	Total Targets Attacked
April	373
May	618
June	575
July	666
August	680
September	533
October	66
Total	3,511

**Table 1: Total number of Targets Attacked by
NATO-led Coalition**

In practice this notion of a stalemate propagated by the media, and a set of nervous political leaders, was not a correct assessment. All military campaigns have periods when commanders need to assess the situation and decide how best to achieve their objectives. The mission creep that was apparent in May, as a wider target set became engaged, created some difficulties for the coalition. The small drop in targets engaged in June may well be a reflection of a political fragility in the coalition about changing the nature of the mission from one of protecting a specific set of citizens to one of regime change.

As the campaign developed so the need to use air power across the whole theatre to protect Libyan citizens from the pro-regime fighters became apparent. Whilst the Russians, amongst many other states, tried to call foul at this point and say that NATO was breaking its mandate, the original arguments about focusing the effort on protecting the people of Benghazi had been specious at best.

The idea of a stalemate was in fact a work of fiction. It was simply a reflection of their own impatience with the rate of progress and the kind of false expectations of progress that had arisen from previous military ventures in Iraq (in both 1991 and 2003) and in Afghanistan. For media people, the 100 day anniversary of the beginning of the war will always produce a spate of reporting and opinions as to the level of progress achieved. That point passed towards the end of June. NATO's activities in July therefore came under an even greater degree of scrutiny as the political debate about the objectives of the campaign, were re-ignited.

The geographic pattern of attacks in July is interesting. The month starts with attacks all over Libya. Names of towns and cities that had barely featured in reporting before suddenly emerge. In the early part of July daily reporting by NATO introduces a new set of towns and cities that are now being attacked with greater vigour. Yafran, Bir al Ghanam, Gharyan, Okba, Dur al Turkiya, and Al Khums are relatively new names on the target list.

During the early part of July it could appear to the casual observer that NATO was widening its target set. However, as time moved on, the pattern of attacks in July shifted. What had been a list of towns and cities that was nearly twenty was wound down to a focus of six crucial areas. These were Tripoli, Brega, Waddan, Misrata, Zintan and Zlitan. The military focus on these towns and cities was to prove crucial. It was to shape the way the final battle would evolve.

NATO and its coalition partners were not engaged in some thoughtless attritional battle designed simply to wear down Gaddafi's forces. It was engaged in a carefully orchestrated campaign. The reporting provided by the United Kingdom's Ministry of Defence that provided a commentary on the campaign, highlights the very selective nature of the targeting that was carried out. The table presented in Appendix A provides a detailed breakdown on the targets engaged as a result of going through all of the UK MoD reporting.

NATO was engaged on a specific campaign that would take time to come to fruition; using its limited resources to good effect to prepare the ground for what would be an inevitable tipping point. This would be the point where the main resistance of the pro-Gaddafi regime would disintegrate around Tripoli and, hopefully, create the conditions whereby the conflict would quickly close. As it turned out, the liberation of Tripoli was only to signal the start of the final stage of the campaign – as the resistance put up by the Gaddafi loyalists folded into towards his traditional tribal and family strongholds of Sirte and Bani Walid.

Helped by undercover operatives that had established contact with people inside Tripoli who were prepared to start their own rebellion, the moves were being made that would eventually lead to Tripoli falling. It was just that in July this was not apparent. As with many tipping points in wars it was not totally obvious, apart to a small cadre of NATO commanders, that the end game had just kicked in.

Physical and Cognitive Manoeuvre

Modern battlefields are not just a physical space in which combatants manoeuvre. There is a hugely important element of *cognitive manoeuvre* that also plays a role. The Gaddafi regime showed a high degree of agility in maintaining its broadcasts to its supporters. Its television station continued to broadcast from Syria; providing a daily feed of information designed to maintain the fear of change that many former regime supporters must have felt in Libya.

Throughout the campaign Gaddafi used the media to broadcast his message of defiance to NATO and the rebel forces opposing him. Despite falling into the inevitable hyperbole on many occasions, his appearances in the media, both of television and through radio, would have provided some comfort to his supporters. Gaddafi's repeated calls for people to rise up and throw out the colonialists – a derogatory term that he tried to apply to those in the NATO alliance highlighting their historical dominion over Libya – his messages largely went unheeded. The lack of reaction to Gaddafi's repeated call to arms showed just how distant he had become from his people. It was clear that the vast majority of them wanted the regime to fall. That however was not a unanimous view.

One thing that strikes anyone analysing the data that has emerged through open sources, is the willingness and ingenuity of the Libyan Armed forces to continue the fight. In this chapter one pattern clearly emerges from a detailed look at the data. The Libyan armed forces did not crumble into a disorderly rabble in the face of NATO's onslaught. The kind of widespread defections that many may have expected from the army, mirroring the kind of images that were seen in Iraq in 1991, did not happen.

Despite the one-sidedness of the campaign, with NATO to some extent holding all the aces, the Libyan armed forces continued their resistance. Their loyalty to the regime remained intact. This is not a good sign for the future. It would appear that the links between the pro-Gaddafi forces and the regime remained intact right up to the end.

It heightens the chances that some will resort to on-going violence against the new government in Tripoli. Whilst the former regime loyalists refuse to enter the political process, and they have some central figure such as Saif al-Islam around which to forge a resistance movement, the situation will remain uncertain. It would also appear that money is unlikely to be a major issue if a Libyan insurgency was to develop. These are exactly the same conditions that existed in Iraq. Money, weapons, a leadership in exile (in Iraq's case former Baathists) and a group of people who feel displaced by the political change that has occurred, are elements of a cocktail around which an insurgency may develop.

Research work into a phenomenon known as Social Dominance Theory (SDT), conducted by Roger Petersen, a professor of political science at the Massachusetts Institute of Technology who investigated Nazi leadership through the Second World War and Russian dominance in the Cold War, shows how a group of individuals that feel displaced can resort to violence.

SDT highlights the reactions of groups of people to major political change. When new political structures emerge in a country that has established governance, such new structures will displace some individuals. Their original status in society is replaced by being associated in some way with the previous regime. SDT shows that fear and rumour associated with the new structures and perceived loss of status can create a violent backlash as fear, resentment at lost power and status, and hatred of a new political structure that seems to have relegated them to some inferior position in society, creates the conditions in which an insurgency can develop.

These issues, combined with the mistakes made in Iraq as the Army and governance structures were disbanded, helped contribute to the emergence of the insurgency. These are important lessons to learn for Libya going forward. Reconciliation with all those in Libya needs to be the key theme of the coming weeks and months. From their initial public statements this is something the NTC has recognised.

For some commentators the fall of Tripoli and the death of Colonel Gaddafi have allowed them to draw a line under the war. They can say, without the fanfare afforded to the same situation in Iraq, mission over. This has been a low key end to a war. Libya may have a transitional government, but for anyone to suggest that it cannot slide into the kind of horrific situation that was witnessed in Iraq would be to more than tempt fate.

The Air Campaign

Despite impressions to the contrary that may have been gained through some of the reporting in the media, the average attack rate each day across the campaign was remarkably consistent. Information derived from the *Guardian* data set, which reflects a sample of the full data, reveals some interesting patterns. From 11 April to the end of the month the average daily attack total was eighteen. This pattern was almost to be repeated month-on-month with the following figures: nineteen in May and June, nineteen and twenty-one in July and August and seventeen in September. By the end of the campaign the RAF would have flown more than 3,000 missions with over 2,100 of those as strike sorties which resulted in the successful engagement of around 640 targets.

The constant rate of missions across the campaign provides a clear indication that a limiting factor in the mission was the total aircraft committed to the attacks. NATO's strike rate, its ability to lay down bombs on targets, was a constant, but mild, frustration to the NATO commanders involved. It does raise an important question. Had they been able to field more strike aircraft would the campaign have come to a conclusion more quickly?

It is difficult to model that outcome with any degree of accuracy. But it is very likely the answer would have been no. In these complex situations just having more aircraft in the sky does not necessarily bring about a quicker resolution. If anything the danger was that the campaign would have inherently accepted more risk of collateral damage. NATO's patient approach to the campaign, whilst potentially frustrating its political leaders did pay off in a remarkably low death toll of civilians.

The meticulous approach to the launching of strikes and the numerous occasions that attacks were called off despite a target being identified, clearly will become a feature of future campaigns. If you have the ability to deliver precise effect in the kinetic space it is worthwhile taking every care not to create a backlash in the non-kinetic or soft space – where populations support can rapidly evaporate in the aftermath of an attack that caused many civilian casualties. The issues of civilian deaths punctuated many conversations between General David Petraeus and President Karzai in Kabul through his tenure as leader of International Security Assistance Force (ISAF).

In Libya the insurrection occurred across large areas of the country. But the area to the east of the country was relatively homogeneous as most people joined the rebellion quickly. Across the rest of Libya, the picture quickly became less homogeneous. The societal landscape in Libya in the west created a very heterogeneous environment in which individual cities either stayed calm and supported the regime or joined the rebellion.

This geographic distribution partly explains the main locations of the attacks that were conducted in the course of the campaign. The early focus on helping the people in Misrata was understandable given the media coverage of the onslaught they were facing from the regime.

RAF Operations in the Campaign
The RAF's campaign had got off to a good start when all forty bunkers at Sebha had been targeted by Storm Shadow missiles flown on Tornados from RAF Marham on 24 March. This was a base from which the regime was supplying arms to their fighters in Zintan and Misrata.

RAF Tornado formations operating with the Storm Shadow missiles were launched on three occasions from RAF Marham to attack specific hardened targets in Libya. In total twelve Storm Shadows were launched in three separate missions each of which comprised a 3,000 mile round trip. They are the longest air attack missions ever flown by the RAF from the United Kingdom.

In April the RAF also agreed to re-role four RAF Typhoon aircraft to allow them to operate either in the combat air patrol or ground attack roles. At this time NATO was keen to re-balance the force that had been deployed by its coalition partners. Within hours the Typhoons had conducted their first successful ground attack sortie, proving the versatility of this new aircraft. All of the aircraft deployed were conducting lengthy missions, not just the ISTAR assets.

On 13 April commentating on the nature of the flying operations the UK MoD spokesman, Major-general Lorimer, said that 'these aircraft are all conducting very prolonged missions on a daily basis. RAF aircraft are flying around 15 per cent of the NATO sorties, but have been accumulating 25 per cent of the hours flown'.

The RAF campaign in May was notable by some of the attacks it prosecuted. On 5 May the RAF attacked and destroyed twenty FROG and SCUD ballistic missile canisters at Sirte. If the regime had intended to hold these back as a terror weapon to be used as the conflict unfolded to coerce the population, that option was removed. At this point in the campaign NATO had flown 5,300 sorties in total with around half of them in a strike role since NATO had assumed command of OPERATION UNIFIED PROTECTOR on 31 March.

By 14 May this figure had reached 6,000 sorties in total. In ten days since the FROG missiles were attacked NATO had flown another 700 sorties. On 18 May the UK MoD noted that the RAF and the RN had damaged or destroyed over 300 regime targets since the start of the operations to enforce UN Resolution 1973. The attack on regime warships anchored at Al Khums on 20 May was another first for the RAF using precision weapons. Synchronised strikes, by other coalition partner's air forces, in Tripoli also saw other regime warships and patrol boats destroyed. This was the day that any residual threat from the Libyan Navy was removed.

Another notable first for the RAF campaign occurred on 25 May when a joint strike by Typhoon and Tornado aircraft saw nine Paveway bombs released in an attack on a regime storage facility at Tiji. The release of four Enhanced Paveway II bombs by the Typhoon in a single attack was the first time the Typhoon had carried out such an attack. The five Paveway IV bombs released by the Tornado in the same strike formation was another first. In Zlitan on 30 May the RAF successfully engaged and destroyed five Heavy Equipment Transporters (HET). They were carrying five MBT. In a follow up attack the following day the RAF destroyed another three HET.

On 31 May the RAF received its first Paveway III 2,000 pounds 'bunker busting' bombs. It would give the RAF an additional capability to strike hardened targets. This completed the weapons inventory for the

RAF which now included Enhanced Paveway II (EPII), Enhanced Paveway III (EP III), Paveway IV and the Brimstone missile system.

The evolution of the Paveway bombs provided the RAF with a versatile suite of weapons with which to engage both fixed and mobile targets in all weathers. The development of the Enhanced Paveway series of weapons had arisen from the lessons drawn from the Kosovo campaign. The need to be able to attack a variety of fixed and mobile armoured targets in all weathers was a key conclusion to emerge from the Kosovo experience. Whilst attacks on the dug-in MBT in Kosovo and the local terrain were to prove a challenge, the different circumstances in Libya were to highlight the benefits of having the enhanced Paveway suite.

The addition of the Global Positioning System Aided International Navigation System (GAINS) also improved the accuracy of delivery – something that was crucial if civilian casualties were to be avoided. The EP II was equipped with a 450 kilogram general purpose warhead. The EPIII had a larger warhead at 900 kilograms that was of a penetrator class. Operating either under laser designation or under autonomous control from the GAINS systems, the two bombs had shown similar improvements in accuracy over the systems fielded in Kosovo.

The work horses of the Libyan campaign however were to be the Paveway IV and Brimstone missiles. The increased accuracy of the Paveway IV bomb enabled its warhead size to be significantly reduced to 225 kilograms – with consequent reduction in any potential collateral damage. The 'late arm' facility on the Paveway IV provided additional safeguards in using the weapon. It was also designed to have increased resilience to jamming (of the Global Positioning System signals on which it depends). Its lower profile also reduced drag and its explosive warhead was made of safer compounds.

In May the RAF had engaged targets in Brega, Sirte, Misrata, Tiji, Waddan, Tripoli and Zlitan. From a geographic viewpoint, in May the RAF was roaming across the skies of Libya in and around the main coastal highway, interdicting and attacking emergent targets as well as fixed sites; although the ratio reported by the UK MoD placed an emphasis on the attacks on emergent targets.

The reporting produced by the UK MoD in June suggests that for the

RAF it was a quiet month, with only eight reports produced to cover the military targets attacked. On 7 June the UK MoD confirmed that the RAF had flown over 500 missions up until that point and released over 300 precision weapons. The MoD noted that on a single strike sortie, RAF aircrews may have released one weapon against a target before travelling across Libya to release another on a very different form of target.

The overall lack of reporting, coupled with the close proximity of the 100th day of operations on 27 June may have led some in the United Kingdom media to speculate that the RAF was running out of targets. June saw the introduction of the Apache helicopters operating off the coast of Libya aboard HMS *Ocean*. The attack on a ZSU-23-4 gun dish on 12 June, a feared weapon of the Cold War, was to be their first mission.

On 7 August Apaches were launched from HMS *Ocean* on a mission that saw them penetrate deep into Libyan air space to conduct an attack on a troop concentration at Al Watiyah, 64 kilometres south of the coast at Zuwarah. RN Sea King helicopters flew with the Apaches to detect any threats to the mission using its Searchwater radar to help augment the information derived from the other ISTAR assets in the area. In the course of the attack Hellfire missiles and cannon fire saw one headquarters and military vehicles destroyed. Four other vehicles were also assessed to have been seriously damaged once video from the mission had been analysed.

The cockpit imagery released after a Tornado and Typhoon had attacked a weapon storage facility in Gariyat on 14 June, shows a spectacular explosion indicating the large quantity of munitions that were located at the site.

In July the operational tempo of the reporting emerging from the UK MoD increased, as twenty-three reports were generated. The diversity of the targets attacked is clearly shown in Appendix A. The RAF was continuing to be deployed by NATO war planners across a diverse range of targets. On 18 July the RAF deployed four Tornado aircraft to Gioia del Colle air base in Italy. One was seen arriving with its Reconnaissance Airborne Pod for Tornado (RAPTOR) pod fitted.

These were primarily going to be deployed in the reconnaissance role. It was clear at this point that NATO required some additional ISTAR assets and the RAPTOR pod on the Tornado has long been recognised as a much-prized asset in such conflicts. Its capabilities include the ability to transmit imagery directly to a ground station for immediate processing or to record the data for post-flight analysis. In the cockpit of the Tornado the images are also displayed. Its ability to stand-off and image targets at a safe distance provided NATO planners with an additional platform to use in Libya. The high quality motion-free imagery was to prove its value as pro-Gaddafi loyalists adapted their tactics.

Data from the RAPTOR and Sentinel R1 aircraft were to be processed by members of the RAF Tactical IMINT Wing (TIW) that had been deployed into theatre from RAF Marham. Based in what is amply named the Tactical Air Reconnaissance Deployable Intelligence System (TARDIS), highly trained and experienced RAF Image Intelligence (IMINT) interpreters worked on the data looking for targets of interest. During OPERATION UNIFIED PROTECTOR a special emphasis was placed on locating targets of opportunity, fuel queues, vehicle checkpoints and active engagements. This combination of sensor systems provided a flexible response to pro-Gaddafi regime efforts to disguise, camouflage and hide their military assets close to specific centres of civilian activity.

The RAPTOR sensor system allows images to be taken in the electro-optical and infra-red parts of the electro-magnetic spectrum. Its capability, couple with the back-up ground staff and image analysts and interpreters, provided a boost to the generation of intelligence information at a crucial point in the campaign, as the Gaddafi loyalists were adapting their tactics and trying to hide their military hardware amongst the civilian population.

With the potential for collateral damage, which had largely been avoided until that point in the conflict, the need for additional Tornados became obvious. They could look into the complex urban environments and detect threats that may have been hidden from the normal ISTAR assets that had been able to detect targets in open and rural areas relatively easily. The thirteen Paveways released on 23 July against the Bab al-Aziziya command complex, which breached the outer walls, was the largest single use of the Paveway weapon system cited in the UK MoD reporting.

If the reporting produced by the UK MoD is any sort of guide as to what was happening on the ground, August was the busiest month of the entire conflict for the RAF. The geographic distribution of the targets still ranged across Libya with targets in Tripoli, Bani Walid, Waddan, Sirte and Hun. On 16 August eleven Paveway bombs were used to attack a command post in Hun and on the next day the RAF attacked and destroyed a tug boat evacuating pro-regime fighters from Al Zawiyah. In further attacks additional SCUD and FROG-7 ballistic missile systems were also destroyed.

On 1 September the RAF undertook what even by its standards must have been an unusual mission. A C-17 was loaded with over 280 million Libyan dinars which had been printed in the United Kingdom for onward delivery to the Central Bank of Libya in Benghazi. It was released by the UN on 29 August. William Hague noted that the money was to be used to pay the wages of many in the Libyan public sector who had been unpaid for several months. The timing of this mission, coming as it did towards the end of Ramadan, was clearly carefully orchestrated. Yet again lessons from the wars in Iraq and Afghanistan were being put to work.

Ironically on the same day the RAF delivered this money to the rebels, Gaddafi issued one of his last calls for action. In a statement that was to last ten minutes he claimed that 'NATO will collapse'. Patently his interpretation of the political and military situation facing his regime remained flawed. The end game was approaching quickly.

In September and October the gradual narrowing of the geographic focus of the campaign becomes clear in the UK MoD reporting. RAF attacks are clearly focused upon Sirte and Bani Walid, engaging a range of target types as the war draws to a conclusion. The last Storm Shadow mission also occurred on 8 September when a military vehicle compound was attacked at Sebha. On 15 September the very first salvo firing of the Brimstone missile system occurred with twelve missiles being fired, destroying seven or eight military vehicles. In October with the overall tempo of the campaign now winding down, the RAF attacked targets in Bani Walid and Sirte on one occasion releasing seven Paveway bombs to attack a missile depot – which was extensively damaged. On 31 October the NATO-led coalition halted its strike missions over Libya. The war was over.

The Concept of Operations for the RAF
NATO planners allocated certain areas of Libya to specific elements under

their command. This would vary over a period of time. For the RAF this enabled them to launch aircraft onto an armed reconnaissance mission in designated areas. For fixed targets that were already known, an attack against those could be planned before take-off from the airbases in Italy or in the United Kingdom.

It is worthwhile taking the time at this point to highlight how the various airborne assets worked together to reduce the risks to civilians, and addressed what in the military vernacular are often referred to *pop up* or *emergent* targets.

For emerging targets a different concept of operations was developed. Like with all of the attacks, the coordination of the airspace over Libya was provided by the E-3D Sentry aircraft operated by the RAF and the NATO equivalent platforms. A typical duration for one of its missions would be nine hours during OPERATION UNIFIED PROTECTOR. The mission for the eighteen-person crew would be to oversee the delivery of the planned air missions and to watch over any attempts to violate the no-fly zone.

At least one AWACS was on station during raids entering Libyan airspace, drawing on a combined force of NATO E-3A and RAF E-3D aircraft. Using techniques pioneered in Kosovo, this enabled the AWACS to inform the inbound attack aircraft of any other nation's aeroplanes operating in the area. Management of the airspace over a country such as Libya is essential if missions are to be conducted in an orderly way.

To ensure effective prosecution of emerging targets the Sentinel R1 aircraft would be designated an initial area to search when it arrived on station. Its sensor system could provide indicators of suspicious activity on the ground. During the campaign the operators on board the Sentinel became skilled at recognising unusual patterns of behaviour.

The sensor system provides an ability to monitor cars and vehicles moving along specific roads in an orderly pattern. Where the natural background of traffic has been removed by conflict, the targets on the move would raise suspicions. Any areas of unusual activity would be notified to the E-3D Sentry and handed off to the Tornados and Typhoons waiting for emergent targets. Once over the area designated the Tornado, for example, was able to use imagery derived from its LITENING precision targeting pod to pick up and identify potential targets of interest and any civilians in the vicinity. For the RAF the concept of operation is described doctrinally as SCAN, CUE and FOCUS.

OPERATION ELLAMY provided a combat validation of the development of cross-cueing work that had been undertaken experimentally for many years. This was research and development work emerging from the laboratories into operations. This enabled all of the capabilities of the dedicated ISR (Intelligence, Surveillance and Recognition) sensors and combat ISTAR to be combined in innovative ways. It paid huge dividends for the duration of the campaign.

OPERATION UNIFIED PROTECTOR

Military campaigns of this nature often focus initially upon an adversary's command and control capabilities. In April thirty targets reported by NATO were attacked. The majority of these, a total of twenty-three noted in the *Guardian* dataset, were located in Tripoli and Sirte. A further three were in Misrata. These initial attacks clearly destroyed the majority of the bunkers that NATO wished to remove as only four more sites were attacked in the course of the rest of the campaign, with two of these located in Bani Walid and one in Sebha.

Month	Command and Control Centres Destroyed
April	17
May	62
June	71
July	79
August	84
September	60
October	9
Totals	382

Table 2: Command and Control Centres Reported Destroyed by NATO

Whilst the hardened bunkers represented one dimension of the regime's command and control facilities the other elements are found in the mobile headquarters. Table 2 provides an indication of the numbers of command and control centres reportedly destroyed by NATO in the course of the campaign. Whilst not an absolute set of figures it does provide a remarkable insight into the resistance put up by the pro-regime forces.

In June the fighting in Brega, a city that was still a source of resistance by the pro-regime loyalists, twenty-three of the total of sixty-two command centres were destroyed. For NATO in June dislocating the resistance in Brega was a key issue and trying to destroy what were often mobile command centres established quickly at ad hoc locations was important. In July that total dropped to seven as the resistance in Brega finally crumbled.

The picture of the attacks on command centres in Tripoli in July, however, is revealing. It shows NATO starting to shape the battlespace for the end game that was about to emerge. Despite the widespread view in the media and in some political circles at the time that the campaign had become stalemated, the truth on the ground was somewhat different.

Of the seventy-nine command centres engaged in July, forty-two of these were located in Tripoli. The days on which the targets are engaged is spread out across the month. There is no defined peak. On several days five centres were destroyed across Tripoli. The focus on disrupting the ability of the defenders of Tripoli to resist what was about to descend from the mountains is a clear example of the way NATO was shaping the battlespace whilst the media talked of a stalemate.

The reduction in the figure to twenty-five of the total of eighty-four in August is a reflection of the success achieved by NATO in July in Tripoli. The pattern of attacks on the command centres also shows a residual series of attacks in Tripoli at the start of August followed by a pause in the middle of the month as the advance on Tripoli occurred, with some residual attacks towards the end of the month presumably aimed at removing any ad hoc command centres that still survived as the regime's control of the capital dissipated.

In the course of August the figures reported by NATO showed how the targeting of command centres had branched out across Libya. In

August the remaining fifty-nine command centres that were attacked were spread over ten other major towns and cities. NATO was clearly branching out in August attacking the regime's ability to sustain its operations through trying to dislocate its command and control capability. Given the increasing difficulty of locating MBT and other targets to attack, it appeared NATO shifted its priorities towards regime nodes that were still operating as part of a network to enable pro-Gaddafi fighters to resist the rebels.

For NATO to still be targeting sixty command and control centres in September, at a point where the regime had been displaced in Tripoli, are hugely important. Thirty-five of these were located in Sirte, according to NATO reporting, with eight destroyed on 16 September. The leadership of the pro-Gaddafi forces was still able to muster and mobilise it forces right up to the point where the NTC declared Libya as having been liberated.

The nature of the resistance that developed in Sirte and Bani Walid in the closing days of the campaign – whilst hopeless and futile – still showed the mobilising power of the regime and its social contacts. The length of time it took the NTC and their armed forces to bring the resistance in Sirte and Bani Walid to an end provides a clear indication of the difficulties ahead.

Initial Targeting Priorities

The initial phase of attacks in April had to focus on two important groups of targets. The first of these were those that were of immediate relevance to the threat to Benghazi. The second group comprised those that might attack aircraft and ships enforcing UN Resolution 1973. At the start of the campaign, understandably, for NATO they were perhaps of equal priority from a military viewpoint.

The database provided by the *Guardian* newspaper did not start recording data until the 11 April. So there is a slight gap in the data on targets that were of priority in the first few weeks of the campaign. The reporting provided by the RAF, which is documented in detail in Appendix A, shows that their early engagements were focused upon Misrata, Brega and Adjabiya. On the 5 April, as the reporting commences by the RAF, twelve targets were engaged and destroyed in a single day in Misrata.

The attacks carried out throughout April saw close to twenty MBT destroyed by the RAF, and NATO claiming twenty-eight MBT destroyed in Misrata alone, close to half of the sixty-four MBT destroyed in the month. The Tornado strike on the 8 August was a specifically successful mission, as it caught five MBT about to be loaded onto their low loaders. The attack by Brimstone missile was precise and deadly. It was the precursor of many more successful attacks using the Brimstone missile.

Month	Sites Destroyed
April	131
May	197
June	18
July	17
August	23
September	19
October	4
Total	409

**Table 3: Total numbers of Ammunition Sites
Destroyed per Month**

Another obvious priority for the coalition was the ammunition supply dumps maintained by the regime. If they were attacked and destroyed the regime would be unable to use them against the rebels or to coerce the civilian population. Table 3 shows the monthly totals of attacks reported by NATO. The surge in April and May is understandable. The follow-on attacks from June onwards reflect a long-term requirement to attack any storage facilities that were developed, either in fixed or mobile locations, using ISTAR assets.

One revealing insight from the April figures is that there were no reported attacks against ammunition sites in Misrata in the figures. Either the regime had not trusted the local people in Misrata to have a weapons storage dump in their area, a view that was to be borne out by the resistance that quickly erupted in the city, or that NATO chose to avoid attacking the sites because of their close proximity to population centres. The side effects of an attack on an ammunition site can be quite dramatic. However, as intelligence sources were developed, fifteen ammunition sites around Misrata were to be attacked in May, suggesting these may have been mobile sites created by the regime during the initial hostilities, and subsequently detected by NATO ISTAR and attacked.

In May the attacks on ammunition sites widened geographically as fifty-seven sites in Sirte and Tripoli were attacked out of the total number of 197. Hun, a city in the middle of Libya to the south of Sirte, was the subject of a series of attacks on ammunition sites in May. On 7 May twelve sites were attacked and on the 8th a further twenty-six sites were also destroyed. Of the total of 197 sites destroyed in May, 169 of them were engaged before 14 May. NATO was clearly in a hurry to eliminate the ammunition stockpiles available to the regime.

By 14 May, which was just under sixty days into a campaign that would last officially for 228 days (i.e. circa 25 per cent of the total duration), 300 of the final total of 409 ammunition sites had been engaged and destroyed. From the middle of May onwards the attacks on the ammunition sites were to reduce dramatically. The pattern of attacks that followed suggests that targets were either fixed and well known or emerged as the Gaddafi forces were driven back towards their last strongholds in Bani Walid and Sirte. The three ammunition sites destroyed in Bani Walid on 10 October were the last of that type to be reported by NATO.

Of the 131 ammunition sites attacked in April 103 (nearly 80 per cent) were located in Tripoli and Sirte. Of the remaining twenty-eight Mizdah hosted twenty-three sites. The ammunition site attacks in April focused upon three major centres. All of which Gaddafi believed would be loyal to the regime.

Alongside the command bunkers, the early focus on the air defence systems, which were quickly neutralised, is not represented in the

Guardian data, which only starts on 11 April. The small scale of reporting of attacks in the *Guardian* data on surface-to-air missiles sites provides an insight into the effectiveness of the initial attacks directed at its capability. After the 11 May only twenty-four surface-to-air targets were attacked and the six of those engaged in June suggests that it had taken time for some of the intelligence collected over Tripoli to be analysed to reveal the targets. At this point the focus on the bunkers and ammunition storage facilities was reducing, suggesting at this point the IMINT analysts working for NATO were able to start to look around for other fixed sites to attack.

The city of Sirte was an important geographic and political point for the campaign. Whilst it was the subject of daily raids throughout the conflict its importance waxed and waned until the final battle occurred in its streets. Gaddafi died in his home town. From a relative lull in June and July, when NATO was focused on Brega and Zlitan, Sirte became the focus of an onslaught towards the end of August as 151 targets were engaged and destroyed in a matter of ten days. That rate of an average of fifteen targets being destroyed per day in a single city was amongst the higher rates of attacks in the campaign. Two specific days came to epitomise the focus on Sirte at the time.

The 25 and 26 of August stand out in the month as specific days when thirty and nineteen targets were attacked in the city – the majority of these being designated in the NATO reporting as 'other vehicles'. What is very interesting in the analysis of the data is how few Libyan tanks NATO destroyed in Sirte. As Gaddafi decided to make his final stand there it would seem reasonable for him to order the massing of any firepower that he could assemble to defend the city.

It is a testament to the ISTAR and NATO firepower that was available, that when any tanks started to move the threat they posed was quickly neutralised. Across the campaign the Libyan Army suffered a regular level of attrition of its tank capability with sixty-four being destroyed in April and fifty-eight in June. The total losses to emerge from the NATO reporting, gathered by the *Guardian* newspaper (see Table 4), showed 270 of the Libyan Army MBT being destroyed in the campaign.

132

Month	Tanks Destroyed
April	64
May	42
June	58
July	43
August	37
September	24
October	2
Total	270

**Table 4: Reported Destruction of Libyan MBT
by Month**

In August, when NATO attacked 151 targets, only four tanks were destroyed in Sirte. In September, as the rest of Libya fell to the NTC, the NATO-led coalition attacked and destroyed 288 targets in what became a daily focus on the city. In that period fourteen tanks were destroyed in Sirte out of a total of twenty-four that had been put out of action in the month. On one day, 6 September, six tanks were destroyed in Sirte. That total was only to be surpassed in the campaign by the loss of twelve tanks on 12 April in Misrata, and the worst single day in terms of tanks destroyed on 10 June when fourteen were lost to NATO attacks in Brega. At the end of the campaign the Gaddafi regime supporters had lost over 50 per cent of what *Jane's* had assessed at the start of the campaign was their serviceable fleet of MBT.

Bani Walid was also a pro-regime stronghold that held out to the end. Its profile of attacks shows that the first time it was attacked was on 29 July. In August, through to the end of the military operations, Bani Walid was attacked on a further twenty-eight days and eighty-eight additional targets were destroyed. After the fall of Tripoli the air power at the disposal of the NATO-led coalition quickly focused its efforts on Sirte and Bani Walid, with some residual attacks on Sebha in the south of the country.

As the campaign drew to a close the collapse of the regime's authority is reflected in the ever-reducing scope of the attacks conducted by NATO.

From the viewpoint of the Libyan Army the GRAD rocket launchers were probably one of the most important weapons other than the MBT. Table 5 provides an indication of the targets engaged by NATO and shows a continuing level of threat from these weapons throughout the campaign. The multiple launch systems were mobile and could reign down firepower on a rebel position or convoy to devastating effect. It was a weapon the rebels feared. They had no defence against a barrage launched by Gaddafi loyalists other than to hide. In the course of the campaign 220 of these rocket launchers were to be destroyed by NATO.

Month	Rocket Launchers Destroyed
April	29
May	37
June	24
July	42
August	54
September	31
October	3
Total	220

Table 5: Rocket Launchers Destroyed by Month

On 13 April, of the twenty-nine rocket launchers that were destroyed were attacked in Misrata, with 24 April seeing seven systems destroyed in a single day by the RAF. In May, thirteen were destroyed in Misrata out of the total of thirty-seven. Also in May a wider geographic range of attacks against rocket launchers was reported by NATO covering seven towns and cities. In Brega twelve rocket launchers were also destroyed in the month. May had therefore seen twenty-five of the thirty-seven rocket launchers attacked destroyed in two locations. The remainder were spread out across the country. That pattern was to some extent repeated in June with rocket launchers being attacked in six separate locations and eleven of those being destroyed in Misrata.

The continuing nature of the dire situation in Misrata is reflected in the thirteen rocket launchers that were attacked in July. That NATO also attacked six launchers in Brega on 31 July – an area that might by that point to have been thought to be secure – shows the chaotic nature and non-linear nature of the battlefield. It must have seemed on occasions that each town and city had to be won by the rebels from the regime in fierce fighting. In part this is a reflection of the weakness of the rebels but it also highlights some of the limitations of air power. To attack and neutralise a target it has to be observed. As the campaign wore on, the ability of the Libyan Army to hide their rocket launchers did create additional problems for NATO.

Month	APC	AAG	SPG	OAV	OV	Totals
April	6	3	15	7	40	71
May	7	5	46	10	53	121
June	17	27	82	32	96	254
July	1	42	1	183	64	291
August	0	31	2	79	138	250
September	0	86	2	118	11	217
October	0	0	0	21	23	44
Totals	31	194	148	450	425	1248

**Table 6: Analysis of Other Military Assets
Reported as Destroyed**

Lastly, in terms of the detailed analysis of the NATO released data, Table 6 provides an analysis of the attacks conducted by the coalition on mobile military assets deployed by the pro-regime forces. Aside from the Air to Air Guns (AAG) and the Self Propelled Guns (SPG) in the second and third columns of the Table, the Other Armoured Vehicles (OAV) and Other Vehicles (OV) that were engaged and destroyed by NATO barely constitute a recognised piece of military hardware. For this reason the data is presented in a single table. One concern arises from the NATO reporting which notes the destruction of only thirty-one Armoured Personnel Carriers (APC). Given the assessment of how many serviceable APC that the pro-regime forces were assessed as being able to deploy at the start of the campaign (assessed by *Jane's* to be of the order of 2,500 vehicles) this final total seems remarkably low. It introduces a slight word of caution into the analysis of the data.

However, in war, military forces that are fighting for their very existence do tend to be innovative. Just like the rebels use of the now infamous Toyota Land Cruiser (TLC), or technical as they are more generically known, and other similar variants of motor vehicles to provide them with a ready-made platform for various types of weapons, so the pro-regime loyalists adopted a similar approach. Future editions of major publications by the leading open source intelligence provider *Jane's* of a country's military prowess and capabilities will have to include indications of how many TLC are in the country.

Looking at Table 6 some interesting developments emerge. The increase in the attacks on the OAV and OV from June onwards suggests that NATO had adopted a stance that any vehicle that was apparently armed, even if it was not armoured, was a legitimate target if it was threatening or could threaten the local population.

The sheer scale of the attacks on OAV and OV over the course of the campaign is an indicator of the ease with which the pro-regime loyalists put them into service. The slight time lag for the OAV may be an indicator of NATO being pre-occupied with destroying MBT at the start of the campaign. But the figure of 183 OAV destroyed in July stands out. Of these 102 of them were destroyed in one location, Brega. Given its close proximity to Benghazi and Ajdabiya – the locations most under the immediate threat of attack from Gaddafi's forces at the outset of the campaign – that pro-regime loyalists were still fighting in Brega in July is noteworthy.

Clearly by this point in time their tactics had shifted. They had mobilised the ubiquitous TLC as military assets, as the MBT that had been originally in the town had either been withdrawn or destroyed. Given NATO's superiority in ISTAR, had any MBT been withdrawn from Brega along the coastal road they would surely have been quickly engaged and destroyed.

The fact that NATO was still engaging and destroying MBT in Brega up until the end of June shows how the pro-regime loyalists were able to conserve and hide what for them would have been hugely important assets. MBT in Brega still posed a threat throughout July and into August. The last reported engagement in Brega by NATO was on 22 August when a multi-rocket launcher system was destroyed. In July and August a further twenty MBT had been destroyed in Brega. The total of forty-two in the campaign was to be 16 per cent of the final total reported by NATO. Given the large area of Libya this concentration of MBT showed how important it was to the regime.

Between the start of the campaign and the end of 22 June of the 164 MBT destroyed by NATO had been targeted in Brega. It would appear that despite the town's physical proximity to Benghazi that the regime was intent on not giving any ground. Brega was to all intents and purposes isolated as the rebels had dashed past along the coastal road intent on reaching Tripoli.

This was not the only town where pro-regime elements adopted tactics designed to maintain the threat from MBT. In Misrata the regime also maintained a threat up until the last MBT that NATO reported as being engaged was destroyed on 15 July. In the battle for Misrata sixty-seven MBT were destroyed in the campaign, with twenty-eight in April, eighteen and seventeen in May and June and four in July as the battle for the town was gradually coming to an end. The pro-regime resistance in Misrata proved stubborn and the rebels found it hard to get to a final point where the town was liberated. NATO aircraft had to conduct an additional forty-three raids on targets in Misrata over the final month, destroying a range of targets including Multi-Rocket Launched System (MLRS), MRLS, OAV, OV and AAG and some missile systems.

Despite progress in the rest of the campaign the situation in Misrata was difficult. The battle for the city had gone on for nearly six months and had cost a considerable number of lives. For those inclined on the back of the Libyan campaign to offer views on the flexibility of air power, they should take care. The situation on the ground and the nature of the targeting in Brega and Misrata bear further detailed study before too many far-reaching conclusions are drawn. In the end Tripoli fell quite quickly once the breakthrough occurred. For the people of Brega and Misrata, however, the Libyan campaign was a long and very bloody affair.

If there is to be a focal point of analysis from which to draw lessons from the Libyan campaign, the temptation to look at Tripoli should be avoided. It did not bear witness to the scale of devastation and destruction caused elsewhere. For the people of Brega and Misrata the road to normality will be a long one.

The Final Dénouement

Once Tripoli had fallen it was only a question of time before the NTC would be in the position to declare Libya as liberated. Its announcement on 23 October tried to draw a line under the revolution. What had started on the 17 February was now at an end. It had taken 228 days to replace a dictator that had ruled Libya for over forty years.

The final run in to the end game however was to prove troublesome. The last stand made by the Gaddafi loyalists in Sirte and Bani Walid had tested the military capabilities of the NTC and its armed forces. As Libya moves forward it needs to think carefully about its future military needs.

Once Tripoli had fallen on 21 August there were many that thought this marked the end of the battle for the future of Libya. That they proved wrong in that assessment is already a matter of record. Amongst the wild crowds that celebrated their liberation in the streets of Tripoli on that evening there can have been few that saw the military effort reaching out for another two months. Those that supported Gaddafi were not going to go quietly. The loss of Tripoli was not the final end game. That would come in the regime strongholds of Bani Walid and Sirte.

NATO's targeting shift in the immediate aftermath of the liberation of Tripoli is apparent from its reporting. From 22 August until the end of the month, out of 244 attacks launched by NATO 149 of those were directed at military targets in Sirte. This amounts to 61 per cent of the military strike effort deployed by NATO. Of that set the main targets were OV, with eighty-five being destroyed. Thirteen command and control centres were also engaged alongside twelve sites related to surface-to-air missile threats. Only four MBT were engaged in Sirte in the latter part of August. In September the focus on Sirte remained as NATO raids attacked 298 targets in the city; this was 56 per cent of the military strike effort expended by NATO in the month.

As the military campaign in Libya started to wind down pro-rebel fighters captured the strategic town of Ash-Shuwayrif on 12 September 2011. It was hailed as a really important and peaceful victory as it cut the main road from the Gaddhafi stronghold of Sabha in the south to Tripoli, therefore preventing supplies moving along the road to the rebels that were holding out in Bani Walid and in Sirte. The seizure of Ash-Shuwayrif provided the NTC with an important first step into the vast areas of the south of Libya in an effort to bring security to a region that is largely uninhabited.

In the course of September the NATO-led coalition reported that it had destroyed thirty-five command and control centres, seventy-seven OAV, eighty-two sites related to surface-to-air missile threats, twelve MBT and seventeen MLRS. As NATO's effort on Sirte reached a climax, twenty-nine OAV were destroyed in a single day on 24 September. Throughout the month, bar the last day, NATO warplanes had come back every day to attack targets.

Attacks on Waddan in September accounted for the second highest allocation at 100 of the total of 533 targets. Therefore two targets, Sirte and Waddan, took 75 per cent of NATO's strike effort in September. Clearly after the fall of Tripoli the battlespace was narrowing. In September whilst the focus was on Sirte and Waddan, the cities and towns of Hun and Sabha would also be targeted by NATO warplanes. In October the NATO reporting shows that the targets in Bani Walid that were engaged comprised mainly of OAV and OV with a small number of command and control centres.

The Naval Activity off the Coast of Libya
The naval activity throughout the campaign in Libya had remained largely unseen. From the outset it had provided a vital part of the capability to evacuate non-combatants that had been caught up in the fighting. Once UN Resolution 1973 came into effect the operations of the various

coalition navies deployed off the Libyan coastline focused on conducting vessel search and board operations to ensure that the regime was unable to smuggle arms into Libya.

Throughout the period from 31 April to the 18 September NATO reported that 2,639 vessels had been hailed at sea and that 289 had been boarded and searched. The navy's busiest days were on 30 June and 8 July when eight and seven vessels were boarded on the same day. The NATO coalition maintained a naval fleet that on average comprised eighteen vessels in the area and peaked in the middle of May at twenty-one ships.

At the time of writing no reports had appeared in open sources suggesting that any weapons had been found in the course of these missions, although a number of ships were refused permission to enter Libyan territorial waters. Whilst the naval fleets did not enjoy the same profile as the air force strike forces, the maritime domain contributed significantly to the outcome of the conflict.

For HMS *Liverpool* and her crew, the time on station off the coast of Libya had proven eventful. The first engagement with Libyan forces on 3 May was not the end of her story. On 12 May *Liverpool* returned fire for the first time, engaging a pro-Gaddafi position that had opened fire on the warship in the vicinity of Zlitan. The warship's Lynx helicopter had been airborne at the time and was able to call in the fire mission on the target. This was not to be the last time the naval gun aboard the warship was to be used. Its use of star shells to illuminate targets trying to move at night, proved particularly effective in deterring military activity.

Intelligence sources continued to suggest that the pro-Gaddafi forces were intent on mounting some sort of spectacular attack against one of the coalition warships operating in the area. HMS *Liverpool* and her sister ships in the naval task force operated just far enough out to sea to ensure they had sufficient warning time of an incoming attack. Libyan Special Forces were known to pose a surface threat, launching an attack from rubber inflatable craft.

By creating a complex maritime screen through which any smugglers wishing to supply arms into Libya would have to pass, they imposed the blockade that had been envisioned at the outset of the campaign. If the regime was to obtain weapons from outside it would have to do it overland, and that was a hazardous venture.

CHAPTER 7

Libya Post Gaddafi

The dark spectre of Iraq hangs over Libya like the sword of Damocles. The potential for the security situation in Libya to stabilise under the leadership of the NTC, and then disintegrate as factional in-fighting breaks out, is a major worry for the international community. Whilst significant progress has been made in the six months following the war, there are disturbing signs of rivalries that keep surfacing in sudden outbreaks of violence. The threat by local people in Benghazi to break away from Libya and form their own state, is one of a number of worrying developments. It is far too early to make a final judgement on this, but some of the deeply ingrained issues that form fault lines in Libyan society, do need to be addressed. With the fall of Gaddafi a page may well have been turned in Libyan history books. It has taken over forty years for that to occur. If another is not to turn quickly, indicating that Libya is not on a path to stability, several things have to be done. For the NTC the next few months are going to be very busy.

At the point where they liberated Tripoli it has been easy for the NTC to hold the line that they were all working towards a common goal – the removal of Colonel Gaddafi from power. To some extent, that was the easy part. Creating a functioning government, after years of people being excluded from power, is not going to be straightforward.

As Libya settles down to deciding how that government will marry up the needs of being Islamic whilst respecting the human rights of all people in the state, major theological and political challenges lie in wait. It is clear from the protests on the streets of Benghazi calling for the implementation of Sharia Law on 29 October, that not everyone shares the vision laid out by the Chairman of the NTC. This is one of a number of issues the NTC face as they try and create the conditions for Libya to move forward as a stable member of the community of international nations.

What comes now is all about building a new nation state that can play a part as an integrated member of the international community, losing its erstwhile tag as a pariah state. For NATO, and its formulation of future military doctrine, how this pans out is crucial. If it is a success and Libya evolves into a stable state, then there will be many who can take some satisfaction from the way the campaign was conducted.

If it is a failure, and an insurgency develops in Libya, the consequences for Europe could be profound. If Al Qaeda were able to exploit such a situation the security landscape in Europe would look distinctly different. The prospects for more acts of terrorism in Europe, undertaken by people and resources smuggled across the Mediterranean Sea, would not look good. It for this reason alone that what happens in Libya now, post-Gaddafi, is so important.

Some of the initial indicators are not promising. Reports originating from Al-Ahar Television in Doha on 30 October suggesting that Gaddafi forces are still on the ground in areas of Bani Walid, do not bode well for the future. Despite the claims of a successful campaign there are still things to be tidied up in Libya. The privately owned Algerian newspaper *Echourouk El Youmi* carried an article on 28 September citing the extent to which black market arms are available in Libya. The way Gaddafi was killed has also cast a shadow over the successful completion of the campaign.

In developing a government for Libya the NTC is going to have to try and reach out across a number of tribal fault lines to heal the wounds created by the campaign. For the NTC, predominately drawn from the eastern side of Libya, this is going to be a difficult period. The chances to get things wrong and to alienate part of the population are evident.

The important role played by the rebels in the west who had come from the Nafusa mountains will need to be recognised, as will the ideas of the people of Misrata who suffered so much as the hands of the regime. Their initial reaction to the NTC, and scathing views of its competency, exposed fault lines that still have the potential to destabilise Libya. Commanders in Misrata were at pains in August to point out that they did not take commands from the NTC.

Creating an integrated society and reconciling that with former members of the regime is going to be difficult, as Petersen's work on SDT shows. The former regime supporters may well be inclined to fight on, creating the basis for an insurgency to bring violence and chaos to Libya. When Nick Meo from the *Daily Telegraph* visited Bani Walid at the end of October he found a confused population. Their resistance in the last days of the OPERATION UNIFIED PROTECTOR considering the overwhelming odds against them was a matter of tribal honour. With Gaddafi gone their future looks increasingly bleak.

Reports of looting in Bani Walid, whilst unconfirmed, provide just the kind of backdrop against which the kind of resentment Pedersen speaks of in his work that fuels social breakdown. The speed with which the NTC is able to deploy police back onto the streets of Libyan cities and to enforce the rule of law will be very important.

This is not the only security matter on the agenda for the NTC. Reconstituting the Libyan Navy, whose capability was all but destroyed by the coalition in the course of the conflict, is a hugely important task if people traffickers are not to exploit the obvious security gaps that now exist along the Libyan coastline.

The route from the shoreline in Libya, or its western neighbour Tunisia, to the immigration staging post of Lampedusa Island is around 200-300 kilometres. The actual figure depends on the precise launch point used on the coast. That it remains active as a major people smuggling route for economic migrants to try and reach Europe cannot be in doubt. For the European Union, already concerned at the levels of economic migrants trying to reach its shores, increasing the level of security patrols off the coast of Tunisia and Libya will be a priority. It will also hope to disrupt any attempts by organisations affiliated to Al Qaeda that may try to infiltrate terrorists into Europe across the same route.

Libya: A Descent into Chaos?

History shows that for an insurgency to gain some traction in a region there must be a number of elements in place. First amongst these is some form of sanctuary from which attacks can be launched. In Iraq this was the border regions with Syria and Iran. These porous areas allowed factions involved in the insurgency to establish rat-runs through which potential suicide bombers, weapons and money could be moved. In Afghanistan it has long been recognised that the Taliban enjoy the sanctuary of the remote mountains of the Federally Administered Tribal Areas (FATA). For the remnants of the Gaddafi regime the potential locations from which they could mount an insurgency are limited by a number of major geographic barriers.

To the south of Libya the borders with Mali and Niger are long and would prove difficult to secure. But, in contrast to the relative closeness of the insurgent entry points into Iraq and Afghanistan, anyone trying to reach major urban areas in Libya, such as those associated with the economically vital oil industry, would face an arduous journey of over 1,600 kilometres across uneven and difficult terrain before getting to any reliable form of road system on which they could then move onto their final destination.

Whilst for a dedicated member of the former regime this may prove surmountable, the natural geographic barrier created by areas such as the Idhān Murzūq to the south of the strategically important town of Sabhā and the Plateau du Djado in northern Niger, may help provide a *cordon sanitaire* to the south of Libya that only the local nomads, the Tuareg, can move through. Their patterns of movement are highly unpredictable and whilst they have past affiliations with the Gaddafi regime it seems unlikely that they can establish the kind of regular supply lines into southern Libya that parallel the channels into Iraq and Afghanistan.

The fact that 21,000 Nigerian citizens (the large majority of whom are Tuareg's) have returned to Niger, many of whom have weapons, will be a major potential source of instability in the north of the country. It highlights the kind of base that Gaddafi loyalists could use to conduct operations across the border through the Agadez region. The reports are not derived from unreliable sources. It is based on reporting originating from the *Nigerdiaspora* website in French published on 10 September 2011 under the headline, 'Massive return of migrants from Libya: The authorities are worried over security in the north'. That regional instabilities may now arise is another cause for concern.

To the east across the border in Chad the situation does not get any better. The Tibesti Plateau provides another natural barrier with several mountains rising above 3,000 metres. Local escarpments also hinder the movement of supplies through these areas. So, despite the relatively open terrain and difficult to secure borders, the southern part of Libya may prove a challenging route for any insurgents trying to move in and out of Libya.

Given the lengths of the routes involved they would also be subjected to regular surveillance by drones that will no doubt be deployed along the border areas. Any movement of four-by-four vehicles in the area is unlikely to go unnoticed. For those travelling in the vehicles, death may arrive swiftly and somewhat unexpectedly.

It is therefore to the south-east along the Algeria border that the Libyan government must look to ensure it has a secure situation. This is the area where AQIM has been known to operate as it moves supplies and people across the border with Mali. Algeria has its own persistent insurgency that manoeuvres in the foothills of the border region with Libya. This could provide a platform from which they could launch attacks into the population centres in the west of Libya.

As if to underpin this concern Al Qaeda's North African branch claimed to have conducted an attack on the military academy in Tipaza, west of Algiers, on 26 August. The attack followed the format of what is now regarded as a standard modus operandi for a suicide attack, two bombers detonating devices within a short time period of each other to ensure the second explosion kills people brought to the scene to assist with the recovery of the injured from the first attack. The attack cost thirty-six people their lives with more than thirty-five people injured.

The concern for the transition in Libya is that of AQIM moving their assets north and away from their traditional operating areas in Niger, Mauritania and Mali. If it were possible for AQIM to be able to establish a significant footprint in Algeria close to the Libyan border, then that might become the kind of platform from which an insurgency in Libya could be encouraged and developed. This happened in Iraq where Syria was the major source of recruits and equipment needed to maintain the insurgency.

The nomadic Tuareg that roam over the areas to the south-west of Libya and whose loyalties to the Gaddafi regime have already been proven could also provide support and shelter for those seeking to move into Libya. Despite the past relationships, *Le Figaro* reported on 9 September 2011, in an article entitled 'Loyal supporter recounts flight of Al-Gaddafi Clan', that significant leaders in the Tuareg community have called for a cessation of armed activity.

The contrast of an AQIM-established base in Libya and Algeria with the chaotic situation for Al Qaeda in Somalia and Pakistan is apparent. Al Qaeda's centre of gravity may be moving and splintering into two major groups. One, AQIM, seeks to dominate the Maghreb. The other, AQAP, seeks to dominate the Arabian Peninsula.

The tribal dynamics of Tripoli are also a source of potential friction for the NTC. The majority of people in Tripoli are affiliated to the Masrata tribe. They include people from a number of prominent families in the city, such as the Suni, Qadi and al-Bashi. If elements of these decide to support an insurgency it would add another dimension to the challenges facing Libya in the immediate future.

To create such a rat-run from the south-eastern border region with Libya would require a series of safe houses to be established along the routes into Tripoli in the Fezzan region of Libya in the south and central area. Given the geographic significance of Sabhā, ensuring the survival of regime loyalists in that town is vital. It could easily become the prime assembly point of an insurgency. The basic elements required for an insurgency to develop and be maintained could readily fall into place.

If Libya descends into the kind of ethnic and tribal conflict that beset Iraq, a very different conclusion will be drawn. The early signs are positive, although the remnants of the regime are likely to try and conduct a number of operations designed to reduce international political confidence in the NTC.

Reported attacks conducted by pro-Gaddafi elements on 12 September against the oil refinery near Ras Lanuf, which the pro-Gaddafi Syrian television channel Al-Ra'y television claimed resulted in the death of seventeen people, provides an indication of the challenges involved in countering potential insurgents. They can blend into the background and appear suddenly in areas which the rebel forces may have thought they had cleared of Gaddafi supporters. The attack on the oil refinery came just after the NTC had issued a statement saying it had resumed limited production. For the NTC securing the oil production facilities is crucial, as this is at the heart of the Libyan economy.

In another worrying development Lieutenant General Mas'ud Abd-al-

Hafiz, the former commander of the Libyan army units in the central and southern region of Libya in the Gaddafi regime, proclaimed his intent to create a new state called the Fezzan Republic in the area of Sirte, Bani Walid, Sabhā and A-Burayqah. Claiming he had the support of a number of friendly African states, the general stated that the new republic would be led by one of Colonel Gaddafi's sons and that Gaddafi would be the country's symbolic president. This statement has all the hallmarks of an attempt to establish a shadow government that would drive and shape the insurgency.

Additional reporting on the resistance being mounted at one of the final bastions of the regime in Bani Walid may also prove to be exaggerated. One thing is clear the immediate transition of power will prove difficult. Whenever power vacuums arise there are those who can prove adept at exploiting them. This is particularly true of people who have little respect for the conventions of international law. Highlighting the urgency with which NATO views the situation, the Secretary General, Anders Fogh Ramussen, noted that Islamic extremists would 'try and exploit' any weaknesses as Libya was being re-built after over forty years of Gaddafi's rule.

One of the unsaid elements of the Secretary General's comments may have been a worry about the activities of members of the LIFG and how they might align with any insurgency. The LIFG have been at the centre of previous unsuccessful uprisings in Libya using local support bases in Darnah and Benghazi. Many of those previously aligned with the LIFG clearly joined forces with the rebels as their power base developed. Where they intend to take the political construct that will emerge in Libya is an important question. The signs are mixed.

Reports emerging on 12 September 2011, published by an Algerian newspaper spoke of 'activists close to the Al Qaeda branch in Libya' having been 'conducting consultations' with what was referred to as the general command of Al Qaeda in Afghanistan and Pakistan. The report suggested that final preparations were being made for an announcement of the formation of a new group aligned more closely with the international objectives of Al Qaeda. If this is true it would be a worrying development for the incoming Libyan government. For now it seems likely that this may originate from a small group that has little actual power that is over-stating its capabilities. Time will tell if that prognosis is correct.

The joyous nature of the celebrations on the streets of Tripoli seems a world away from the kind of horrors witnessed on the streets of Iraq. But if the NTC and any new Libyan government were not to be seen to have made any progress in tackling the deep-seated issues in the economy in Libya, then the potential for an insurgency to gain traction may well change.

Ironically this was the same set of arguments used by Colonel Gaddafi at the start of the protests when he accused those who started the revolution as being Islamic extremists. It would appear that despite their differences NATO and Colonel Gaddafi share a common concern that Libya might descend into chaos.

In the same interview the NATO Secretary General was also concerned about reports emerging of infighting between members of the NTC. Any evidence of disagreements is bound to give succour to those who wish to oppose the creation of a new Libyan state. Any secular or ethnic divisions that exist beneath the surface of the NTC may suddenly create the conditions in which an insurgency can gain hold.

A Political Vision for Libya
The speech of the Chairman of the NTC on 13 September to cheering crowds in Tripoli therefore was crucial, as it laid out his vision of the future and how Libya would balance its commitment to being an Islamic state with Sharia Law providing the main basis for its legal systems and still allow secularism. It was a comprehensive speech that reached out across many of the potential fault lines that exist in Libya.

From a global perspective the transition from Gaddafi's rule, and the parallel journeys being made in Tunisia, Egypt and Iraq, will shape the security landscape over the next decade. It is to be hoped that Mr Mustafa Abdul Jalil achieves his aims. There will be some who will find it hard to agree to all of the elements he included in his speech.

The speech by the Chairman of the NTC outlined a democracy that treads a careful path between a monotheistic state and one that is based on a secular approach. For the kind of basic human rights to be established in Libya, a point which went to the heart of the intervention in the first instance, the NTC has to be seen to deliver on a secular state. Given the primacy of Sharia Law as a given treading, this path is going to be difficult. At its heart, in the interpretation of some of the schools of Islam, it is simply not possible to operate a state in the way that the NTC Chairman outlined in his speech. That said he did also lay out some other important elements of a democracy with which the West can identify, highlighting specifically the role of women in running the state noting that 'women will have a place in Libya's future'.

As these countries transition to their own unique form of democracy the world is literally entering a new era. One in which the narrow vision of an Islamic state, with no tolerance of other religions, as envisaged by Al Qaeda, challenges the results of the Arab Spring. This is a fight for the future of Islam. It is one whose outcome is far from certain.

The Concerns over Missing Weapons

One of the major factors that contributed to that outbreak of anarchy in Iraq was the readily available supplies of explosives and small arms. For Libya, in the immediate period following the deposing of the Gaddafi regime, this issue of the availability of weapons is a crucial concern.

Of all the issues faced by the new government of Libya the security situation in the country is one that is of some priority for the international community. One immediate concern about the break-up of the Gaddafi regime surfaced in the press when a number of sophisticated surface-to-air missiles systems supplied to the Libyan authorities appeared to go missing. The fact that the very same missiles had been used in an attempted terrorist attack on an Israeli passenger jet taking off from Moi International Airport in Mombasa, Kenya on 28 November 2002, provides added weight to the concerns. The two Strela 2 (referred to as the SA-7 in a NATO designation) missed, possibly as a result of the deployment of countermeasures against the infra-red seeker employed by the SA-7.

Reporters investigating the loss or removal of these MANPADS found empty crates in a deserted warehouse, some ominously marked with the designation of one of the most modern Russian forms of MANPADS missile, the SA-24 (NATO designation *Grinch*). During the conflict several NATO pilots claimed to have been engaged by the SA-24. The attacks were however defeated by infra-red flares.

General Carter Ham, chief of the United States Africa Command, commented that around 20,000 missiles were believed to have been in Libya at the start of the campaign and that many had 'not been accounted for'. The numbers involved are large. Given NATO knew of these missiles being in Libya it is surprising that many more anecdotal stories have not emerged of their use against NATO aircraft. The reasons why the missiles were not deployed by the Gaddafi regime is a mystery.

Should these missiles fall into the hands of terrorist groups like AQIM, which operate in the area, it would be a grave situation for the international airline industry. AQIM have recently been able to build up their finances through earning ransoms for the release of hostages. For them to procure such advanced MANPADS for Al Qaeda would be a major coup. Given Al Qaeda's widespread use of the United States sourced 'stinger' missile in the campaign in Afghanistan against the Russians, they would relish the chance to be able to use such weapon systems to attack aircraft.

General Ham attended the meeting in Algeria and noted that 'there is a threat of proliferation of weapons from Libya', adding, 'we are greatly concerned about small arms weapons, rifles, and weapons similar to that, but also about explosives and shoulder-fired air defence systems.'

Echoing these concerns, the leaders of four countries whose borders are adjacent to Libya, have spoken of their worries that arms smuggled across their borders may find their way into the hands of terrorist groups. At a meeting in Algeria representatives from the host nation and the countries of Mali, Mauritania and Niger noted real concerns that weapons previously part of the former regime in Tripoli had started to find their way into their countries. Special concerns must exist over the chemical weapon stockpile built by Gaddafi which was estimated to amount to nearly twenty-three tons of mustard gas in 2003 and nine and-a-half tons which were identified in a recent inspection by United Nations teams that visited the facility in the latter part of 2010.

In addition to the obvious concerns over the chemical weapon stocks held by the Gaddafi regime, evidence also started to emerge in reporting from the *Sunday Times* of systemic violations by the regime of its commitment not to further develop its Al-Fatah ballistic missile program. Under the terms of the agreement, by which Libya was brought back into the international community, it was supposed to have restricted the range of its missiles to 186 miles. The discovery of documentary evidence of a program designed to increase this range to 600 miles provides additional proof, if any were needed, of the duplicity of the former regime.

State Building: The New Libya

State building, as the United States and its coalition partners found in Iraq, is not easy. The years of the centralised power of the regime had eroded the kind of governance class in Libya that has held back other countries. The NTC however moved quickly to establish some basic instruments of a functioning society. The announcement of Supreme Court Judges was important. It shows an immediate respect for the rule of law. The NTC had also been active during the military campaign drafting a new constitution for Libya. The timetable for this to be put to the people has also been made clear.

In an opinion piece in the *New York Times* published on 9 September, a similar optimistic note was sounded. Noting the immediate issues of the lack of water and electricity and the shortage of fuel, the editorial went on to highlight the swift release of currency assets, held across the world, after the imposition of the United Nations sanctions once Resolution 1970 had been adopted. The sums of money held in overseas accounts are staggering, totalling many tens of billions of dollars. The speed with which this money can be repatriated to Libya will be crucial.

The *New York Times* editorial did offer two notes of caution. It expressed concern for the safety of many African migrant workers who occupy posts in the Libyan economy. The rumours that emerged during the conflict, of Gaddafi employing African mercenaries, seem to have spilled over into a sense that all those who were not of Libyan descent were directly involved in supporting the regime. Anecdotal stories have emerged in the press of some of these people being badly treated. The editorial called for the NTC to act to 'maintain its international credibility' and ensure those 'those who fought for Colonel Gaddafi are treated fairly'.

The second issue raised by the *New York Times* was the matter of so many armed people currently on the streets of Libya. The potential for some of these to become involved in vigilante groups metering out revenge to those known to have cooperated with the Gaddafi regime, raised a valid point that has a basis in history. It is important for the victors

151

to be magnanimous in their dealings with their former adversaries and ensure they are subjected to proper legal treatment within the boundaries defined by the Libyan constitution.

The NTC also seems rightly bullish that the current situation is not a prescription for an extended civil war. The NTC Chairman, Mustafa Abdul Jalil, offered a positive assessment in a news conference not long after the rebels had seized Tripoli. Speaking on 3 September before himself moving to Tripoli, he thanked NATO for their assistance noting that 'we must not that forget the victories achieved by our revolutionaries would not have happened without the support of the international alliance'. He added that 'the Libyans would not forget the protection provided by the alliance until the aims of the revolutionaries were achieved'.

His assessment of the situation on the ground also sounded a hopeful note as he said, 'we are in a position of strength, and can enter any city and direct our revolutionaries to any area'. The pictures of Libyan policeman returning to their posts, broadcast over the weekend of 10 September, also provided an indication that some aspects of life in Tripoli were returning to normal. Some of the omens look good and contrast directly with the lack of governance and security that led to the insurgency developing in Iraq.

However as the situation in Egypt has shown there can be groups who deliberately decide to manoeuvre to slow up the progress, seeking to obfuscate when it comes to the kind of political reforms based on the principles of democracy that they see as being directly in opposition to their own views of how the country should be operated. Calls for Libya to be run as an Islamist society that is based on Sharia Law appear to conflict with the notion of a modern democratic state in which all of Libya's people have equal rights. The vested self-interests of the major tribal federations also come into play.

Whilst in the short-term the joy in Libya at having been freed from the privations of the Gaddafi regime is untold in some quarters, there are others who lament his death. The final outcome in Libya is not yet assured. Reconciliation and diplomacy will be required in no small measure in the next few months to create the conditions for a stable Libya to play its part in the international community and for it to finally lose that label of being a pariah state. The omens as the NTC embarks upon that mission are mixed.

CHAPTER 8

NATO Post Libya

On Thursday, 27 October the UN Security Council voted unanimously for a resolution 'ending the mandate for foreign military action at 23:59 Libyan time on 31 October'. During the military action the NATO-led coalition had flown 26,000 sorties of which 10,000 were labelled strike missions. Interestingly, the resolution was passed despite an eleventh hour appeal from Libya's NTC to continue the mission, arguing that it needed more time to assess its security needs.

For NATO the Libyan campaign was a success. However, as the leaders of the alliance meet in Chicago in May 2012, there will be some important lessons to be learned. The reliance on the United States for the backbone of the Command and Control system is one that will need to be addressed if other coalitions of the willing are to be deployed at short notice. The combination of low collateral damage, the replacement of the regime and the zero casualty count for their own forces provides an outcome that political leaders entering any kind of war would dream about. The Libyan rebels paid the price in blood whereas the collation paid the price in treasure. The final debate as to the actual cost of the campaign will no doubt be the subject of some discussion as various media sources try and come up with a final and definitive answer. But, by any standard metrics of war, the campaign in Libya was a new form of conflict. One conducted principally from the air and with great precision. But is it one that can be replicated elsewhere?

The answer to that question is a resounding no. Libya had a number of quite specific aspects to it. These need to be appreciated before anyone suggests that suddenly a new form of casualty-free (i.e. painless) warfare can be carried out by NATO at locations across the world where they feel they need to intervene. The horrors of the humanitarian intervention in

Somalia by President Clinton still beckon for anyone rash enough to believe that warfare can be painless.

That air power showed its huge flexibility in OPERATION UNIFIED PROTECTOR is not in doubt. Towards the end of October 2011 the RAF Tornados had flown over 1,400 sorties and amassed over 8,000 hours of flying time. The RAF Typhoons also flew 600 sorties and accumulated over 3,000 flying hours.

New tactics, flying Tornados and Typhoons together as a two-ship configuration, had also been developed. Warfare often sees tactical innovation and OPERATION ELLAMY was no different. The mix of the two aircraft, flown as a two-ship configuration, provided additional versatility in terms of the weapons payloads that were available on a single armed reconnaissance mission. The mix of the 1,000 pounds Enhanced Paveway carried on board the Typhoon and the Brimstone and other Paveway variants on the Tornado provided a huge level of flexibility to address emerging targets. During the campaign the RAF, RN and Army Air Corps (AAC) launched 1,470 guided weapons. The Paveway achieved a hit rate of close to 88 per cent. The bombs that fell outside the immediate designated area missed the target by a matter of a few meters.

Throughout the campaign the French Air Force and the RAF both undertook a large range of missions that showed the inherent versatility and flexibility that now exists in their weapons systems. In the course of the NATO operations over 26,000 missions had been flown. Many of those lasted a number of hours and required a number of visits to tankers to refuel. In the course of OPERATION ELLAMY over 30,000 tonnes of fuel were transferred from VC-10 and Tristar aircraft operating in support of the mission.

When deployed on armed reconnaissance it is hard to forecast the type of targets that might emerge. What appears from an orchard or emerges from the side of a street to threaten civilians, is hard to predict at the point the aircraft is prepared for a mission. Emergent targets were not always single units, such as a MBT, APC, Artillery piece or Pick Up Trucks (PUT). Complex targets also presented themselves in the form of troop concentrations at staging points, ammunition and fuel dumps and mobile command and control centres. Having a range of weapon systems at the disposal of the crews allowed them to be selective in their application of air power.

Being able to select an appropriate weapon system to attack an emergent target, whilst reducing the risk from collateral damage, is a hugely important capability. The Storm Shadows also proved their value working alongside the Tomahawk missiles launched in the course of the campaign by the RN. The RAF and the RN can be very pleased with their current inventory. The future prospects also look good, as the RN adds the Joint Strike Fighter (JSF) into its inventory in the future. Operating from a carrier offshore that ability to project air power will also add an additional level of versatility into the ability to conduct a range of possible intervention missions on a global basis.

That does not mean that lessons cannot emerge from the Libyan campaign that might suggest that Paveway and Brimstone might also have additional versatility built into their warhead designs. The ability to 'dial a yield' before a target is attacked would undoubtedly provide an additional element of versatility when attacking lightly-armed vehicles.

The contribution of naval gunnery, an art that many will think must have gone out many years ago, is still something to be considered. As warships have tended to go for stealthy shapes the guns have always appeared to stand out. In an age of the missile system there may be those tempted to think that removing guns from warships is a good idea. For many the use of naval gunnery in the Falklands conflict is a distant memory. OPERATION ELLAMY was to highlight its enduring contribution to the littoral battle.

Any notion that naval gunnery is a capability that is no longer required should be rejected very quickly. Even though little was made of its use in the media, naval shore bombardment is not a capability that should suddenly be lost. In the course of OPERATION ELLAMY the warships HMS *Liverpool, Iron Duke* and *Sutherland* would fire 240 rounds from their guns. These varied from star shells that illuminated suspicious activity on the coastline to high explosive rounds aimed at destroying coastal artillery installations that had fired upon NATO warships.

On several occasions Libyan Special Forces who had tried to approach NATO warships in inflatable boats were chased away by star shells. Being illuminated at night when you are trying to operate covertly has a huge psychological impact. As the RN develops its thinking for the Type 26

Global Combat Ship, and its export potential, they would be wise to retain that capability.

Their collation colleagues also contributed to the overall effort providing a blend of air power that enabled strike missions to be shared out across many NATO countries. As always in such situations the Danish Armed Forces and the Norwegians made significant contributions, as did the Belgians.

The Libyan Campaign in Perspective

For those in NATO seeking to use the campaign in Libya as a form of new approach to intervention on the international stage, a moment's reflection might be in order. Colonel Gaddafi and his sons were not that difficult a regime to topple.

In order to take an objective view of the outcome it is vital for anyone to analyse the mistakes made by the Gaddafis. Had they played any one of these differently, the campaign may well have gone on long enough to make the international community tire of what would readily be characterised by the media as another failed and flawed attempt to intervene in an overseas country.

Gaddafi made several obvious mistakes. Many of these are reflective of an ego and personality that was deeply flawed. In part these contributed to his downfall. The list of mistakes is long and worth some detailed analysis and discussion. They include:

- The regime appeared to be totally unprepared for war. It was as if Gaddafi had concluded that by making the right noises and gestures to the international community he would be allowed to survive. He dramatically underestimated the will of many of those, including David Cameron and Nickolas Sarkozy, to follow up on their rhetoric. This was a bad misjudgement and typical of a person who is unable to read the international hymn sheet that was being written at the time.
- Gaddafi's rhetoric, labelling of the rebels as members of Al Qaeda, was an attempt to sow confusion into the ranks of the international community. It barely raised an eyebrow in political circles. Certainly many so-called experts in international terrorism

raised themselves from their armchairs to venture into the television and radio studios to echo his narrative. Many opined that the rebels had been infiltrated by Al Qaeda, with the implication that if Gaddafi's regime were to fall woe betide the international community, especially European nations, whose southern flank would be exposed to an Al Qaeda-led government in Libya that their military action had installed.

• Gaddafi should have played for time when the international community was debating establishing a no-fly zone. His offers of a ceasefire appeared opportunistic and insincere. His words and actions appeared out of kilter with each other. Given the degree of ISTAR coverage of Libya he should have known that he needed to visibly show a lessening threat to Benghazi as the second week of March came to a close. Had he done this, and played his long-established ties with Russia carefully, he could have dragged out the debate within the United Nations.

• This mistake was repeated when progress on the campaign slowed to a halt in June. This is a crucial issue for NATO and one that is often overlooked. When conducting military operations of this type it is unlikely that the end game, whatever that means, will suddenly be reached. The 100 hours ground war that brought the Iraqi War in 1991 to an end is not representative. It had taken weeks of bombing to shape the battlefield so that, as the ground forces moved in, the Iraqis surrendered en masse. Gaddafi should have anticipated the stalemate and played for time when some members of the international community started to debate a possible end game where Gaddafi would have stayed in power. He should have seen this as a moment of weakness in the international community's resolve and made gestures that would have seen him remain in some titular position. His intransigence at this point was crucial. It is axiomatic in international politics that delay and obfuscation creates opportunities. This was a lesson and insight that Gaddafi failed to appreciate. Had he played for time, offered a segregation of Libya and then played a longer psychologically-focused campaign, he may still be alive today.

• Gaddafi's employment of mercenaries showed from the outset how unsure he was about the loyalty of some parts of his military establishment. When a leader is so uncertain about such a fundamental point it shows that he is in a very bad situation. As events in Syria and Egypt have shown, when a dictator retains the loyalty of his armed forces it is difficult for a rebellion to gain the kind of traction needed to bring down a government.

• One mistake Gaddafi and his henchmen was to make throughout the campaign was to underestimate NATO's ISTAR capabilities, and the ways in which sensors could rapidly cue aircraft in to destroy emergent targets. All the NATO-wide experiments on sensor cueing that had been undertaken over a number of years suddenly all bore fruit. It was, and remains, an impressive capability and one that NATO should do all it can to maintain for the future. Despite the subordinate role played by the United States in the campaign, its ISTAR assets were essential to the precise nature of the way targets were attacked, helping avoid collateral damage.

• Gaddafi failed to implement the full suite of asymmetric options that he could have done as the campaign unfolded. The efforts of the Libyan military in the maritime sphere were particularly derisory. Despite frequent attempts by Libyan Special Forces to mount operations at sea none were successful. Royal Navy submarines became adept at using their sonar systems to track the Rubber Inflatable Boats as they launched. Each mission was successfully intercepted. The Libyan Navy was almost ineffective and the half-hearted attempts to mine various harbours in Libya using a form of floating IED added little to the military effort. Had the Libyan Navy been able to confront and perhaps sink a NATO warship in Libyan coastal waters, with some loss of life, it may have placed what was an uneasy alliance under some increased pressure. Moreover had he been able to resort to cyberspace or to unleashing acts of terrorism in Europe – as he threatened to do at one point – he would have tested the political cohesion of the NATO alliance and a public wary of being drawn into yet another apparently endless campaign. A suicide bomb attack in London, Paris or any other national capital of a nation involved in the campaign, would have quickly created media comparisons with the backlash from the war in Iraq and its impact of Muslim communities in Europe.

• Gaddafi's harnessing of his terror weapons – the FROG and SCUD missiles – came to epitomise a military campaign that was flawed. The single time a SCUD was launched against the rebel forces it fell short and did not cause any casualties. By owning such weapons Gaddafi could well have terrorised the local people in Tripoli as the campaign moved into its end game. The way the Iraqis camouflaged and continued to fire their SCUD missiles in the 1991 war created huge problems for the coalition – causing the diversion of a great deal of military effort to detect and eliminate the launchers. In Libya on several occasions the launchers were discovered by ISTAR and quickly destroyed by attacks from the air. His failure to adopt the classic tactics of using human shields also missed an opportunity. The exceedingly low levels of civilian casualties during the war are a reflection of a huge effort put into targeting by NATO. But is also reflected the fact that Gaddafi was clearly no student of recent military history.

This catalogue of failures should be remembered and if necessary debated at length as people come to analyse the campaign in greater detail. It was Gaddafi's ineptitude as a leader in a time of war, and the fact that he surrounded himself with family and sycophants, that led to his demise. Had he been more agile and flexible he could well have survived.

The Paradigm of Intervention
For many commentators the outcome of the military campaign in Libya creates an opportunity to redefine the paradigm of intervention that has arisen since the events in America on 11 September 2001. Upstream activities in Iraq and Afghanistan have been hugely expensive, very complicated and difficult for member states with governments created from electoral mosaics across the political spectrum. As military campaigns they have had to learn whilst 'in contact' with our adversaries rather than lay out the doctrine of how to fight a war and then execute that approach.

For David Cameron this was not an approach that was sustainable. It is always difficult during wartime for a political leader to overtly criticize his armed forces. The ongoing military commitment of the United Kingdom provided a huge constraint on the Prime Minister's freedom of manoeuvre. The general public would not wear any challenge to the military in the open. Cameron has insisted on at least one occasion that he has 'robust' discussions with the UK CDS – Sir David Richards.

What the nature of these discussions are one can only speculate, but it is not difficult to imagine that the Prime Minister has a specific set of views on the degree of overlap that exists between some areas of military capability. It is not hard to believe that one of the principles of David Cameron's approach to defence matters is to imagine that the United Kingdom's armed forces did have excess capacity that could be taken out. The question was how to do it?

Any leader who tried to place any blame for failure on the armed forces would pay a heavy political price. Cameron has instead not chosen to provide an audible criticism. He has chosen to be far more subtle. Through the mechanism of the SDSR he chose to take out capability that was felt to be redundant for the kind of balanced forms of warfare that he envisaged, with the ODA, the FCO and the MoD playing specific roles within an overall strategy by which the military instrument of power would be applied in the future.

It the heat of the SDSR, and given the speed with which is was undertaken, it is not difficult to imagine that the implications of the some of the decisions taken around the table were not discussed in any great depth. It was an assumed outcome that the force levels would be cut, the only issue was by how much.

Cameron's doctrine for the United Kingdom's armed forces has therefore been based on a covert recognition by some close members of the Cabinet that there was a little too much overlap built into the United Kingdom's military capability. To state that view would have to receive the opprobrium of the press and the British public at large. To hold it covertly, only for its stealthy hand to be revealed in the wake of the SDSR, is a very different matter.

For David Cameron the outcome of the initial phase of the war in Libya will have reinforced his view that its now time for NATO to take similar 'difficult decisions' and to stop fielding equipment that sustains industries in countries that frankly cannot possibly get value for money out of the investment in equipment. What is needed is bulk buys of equipment from seasoned and expert suppliers. This will be at the heart of the next stage of the reformation on which David Cameron has embarked. It will prove a most difficult challenge. Resolving overlaps in the capabilities of the United Kingdom's armed forces is one thing. Addressing the wider issues at a European and then NATO level is a very different matter.

The Insurgent Backdrop

As the campaigns in Iraq and Afghanistan evolved, new doctrine placed the population at the centre of gravity of the military effort. Gain the trust and support of the population and the insurgency will inevitably wither on the vine. This was the enduring lesson of the British efforts in Malaya between 1948-1960, a campaign that was often quoted in the media as being an example of how to secure the 'hearts and minds' of the population.

What was overlooked was the brutal way in which the ever-pragmatic British also chose to place physical distance between the population and the insurgents by moving large numbers of people into camps; hardly a feasible approach in the kind of media environment in which the military have to operate today. The label ethnic cleansing would be writ large over any effort to relocate people with whom the insurgents might find common ground and support. It was quickly realised in Afghanistan that the so-called panacea of Malaya was anything but a solution. That it worked at the time was down to a wide range of local factors that had little read-across into Afghanistan.

The one enduring lesson to emerge from the campaigns in Iraq and Afghanistan was that in a COIN environment it is difficult to be able to define when the war is over. There is no signing of a peace accord or formal surrender. Those unable to reconcile with any attempt to create bridges across past fault lines will inevitably try to turn to terrorism as a way of coercing local people. The language of the COIN environment is of 'creating the conditions' where the population will seek to reduce their support and succour for the insurgents.

The aim for the military commanders is to capitalise on situations, which are often fleeting in nature, where the insurgents cross red-lines and upset the local people. In Iraq this eventually led to the Tribal Awakening in Al Anbar and the rejection of the insurgents by the local people. What happened saw the increasing marginalisation of the insurgents from the local people to a tipping point at which they were alienated, and physically ejected from the area.

Once that stage had been reached the insurgents support base declined swiftly, creating a situation where they became irrelevant. That Iraq continues to suffer from an on-going level of criminality that sits astride the loose definitions of an insurgency and terrorism, draining political progress and causing disruption across community fault lines, is a testament to the difficulties of bringing a counter-insurgency campaign to something akin to a successful close. What defines the end of an insurgency is a subject that would occupy many academic papers.

One thing is for sure. As long as there is finance available and some people prepared to provide safe houses for those that seek to disrupt an orderly progress towards a new form of government, the potential for trouble exists. In Libya some of the noises emerging from the survivors of the Gaddafi family are less than encouraging.

In Libya there are parallels with the situation in Iraq, although perhaps not quite so dramatic. If a sufficient core of the regime elements is allowed to escape across relatively porous borders into Mali and Niger to the south they may be able, over a period of time, to establish a series of training bases from which they can launch attacks into Libya. The availability of a sanctuary from which to train and mount operations across a border is something that was a feature of the Iraqi insurgency. The channels that brought suicide bombers into Baghdad used the porous border to the north of the country with Syria as its port of entry into Iraq.

In Afghanistan the long and extremely difficult border with Pakistan provides similar challenges. It would be unwise not to imagine a hard core of regime loyalists retreating across the border into Niger, re-grouping, and then sending people back into Libya to target the main assets of the country, its oil reserves and production facilities. Should this occur the likelihood that NATO will have to sustain some form of special forces capability, alongside unmanned aircraft (or drones), to enable the training camps that might appear in Libya's southern neighbours to be targeted.

For NATO it is to be hoped that the lessons emerging from the Libyan campaign are positive and reinforce a new sense of purpose for the organisation. Its reputation has suffered in Afghanistan. Libya offered NATO an opportunity to claw back some much needed credibility, even if the war reserves on bombs and missiles ran seriously low.

A key question for NATO is, does the Libyan campaign create a new basis for liberal interventionism overseas? Given the difficulties that existed in Yemen and Syria at the end of the Libyan campaign, could what has been achieved in Libya be transferred to help topple other regimes?

Syria

For those looking at this question from a truly objective viewpoint, the answer has to be no. Basking in some reflected glory at the success of the campaign in Libya, the United Kingdom's Prime Minister David Cameron did express 'frustrations' with Syria's apparent intransigence and unwillingness to create a more modern society. Was this a prelude to another initiative aimed at maintaining the pace of reforms in the Middle East? Was Cameron starting down the road to another intervention, emboldened perhaps by the success in Libya?

His rhetoric certainly helped stoke the flames in the European Union for placing the Assad regime under greater economic pressure. The speed with which the European Union agreed to increase sanctions on Syria is revealing in itself. Syria does not have a large trading relationship with the European Union. Its largest economic partner is Iraq. So the Europeans hardly had a lot to lose. For Italy, one of Syria's closest trading nations, the restored links with Libya in the wake of the fall of the Gaddafi regime will be seen to more than compensate for the loss of economic ties to Syria.

Watching on from the sidelines is an increasingly nervous Russia. In an interview[1] given by President Medvedev on the 8 September 2011

---

[1] This is based upon reporting from the BBC on the content of an interview given by President Medvedev on 8 September 2011 to the Interfax news agency.

which was broadcast on the Russian news agency Interfax, he said that he had been in discussions with a number of French ministers over the matter of NATO's interpretation of the United Nations Resolution 1973 noting, 'the thing is that we are not quite satisfied with how Resolution 1973 was implemented'. Elaborating on this point he went onto to specifically rule out any similar political accommodation with respect to the crack down that was on-going in Syria. His statement was unequivocal saying 'we definitely would not want the same thing regarding Syria'.

This point was backed up by Mikhail Margelov, the presidential envoy and chairman of the Foreign Affairs Committee of the Federation of Russia, who noted, after talks in Moscow with a delegation from the Syrian opposition, that Russia's stance is 'based on the need to reach a political settlement and not slip into repeating the Libyan scenario'. He went onto state, 'the [Syrian] people have the right to decide what they deem fit. They must reach solutions to the crisis without foreign intervention'.[2]

The Syrian opposition leader at the talks, Ammar al-Quarbi – who also heads the Syrian National Organisation for Human Rights – expressed his satisfaction with the talks, urging the Russians to take on a 'more positive stand' and that, at the talks, the opposition had presented a road map that will 'organise the transitional period in Syria'. All very fine words but they are unlikely to make the Assad regime think a turning point has come in which it has to give up power.

What is more likely is that Damascus will look to develop some concessions on the way Syria is run that will allow an increased level of local democracy, whilst the Assad regime stays on in Damascus. No doubt any such arrangements will be hailed by Russia as a major diplomatic breakthrough. As far as ordinary Syrians are concerned however it will be more of the same, unfulfilled promises. The question is, will they be bought off this time with hollow promises of reform?

Not that President Medvedev was in any way trying to shield the Syrian regime from criticism. His own words, however, seemed ambiguous when he said, 'we see the disproportionate use of force and the large numbers of victims. We are also dissatisfied with this. I have

---

[2] This is based on reporting from the BBC on content published on the website of the London-based newspaper *Al-Hayat* on 10 September.

spoken about this on more than one occasion also in personal communications with President Bashar al-Asad, and only recently sent a deputy foreign minister to him so that he would once again underline our position on the matter.'

This was the Russian President resorting to a soft power approach towards the Syrian regime. It is not in the Russian's interests at all to see President Assad go the way of Gaddafi. They are clearly concerned about some kind of domino effect with first Libya and then Syria moving away from the Russian sphere of influence. Any such outcome would also threaten Russian trade arrangements with Syria, many of which are in the important defence sector.

The President however, also noted the complex societal landscape in Syria, as he observed, 'those that come up with the anti-government slogans are not supporters of a refined European democracy, these are very diversified people'. Offering an olive branch to the international community President Medvedev announced that the Russian side is prepared to support a variety of approaches but, and this is the important part of the language, 'they should not be based on unilateral condemnation of the actions of President Al-Asad's government'. Given the intransigence of the President of Syria this kind of diplomatic language is hardly going to frighten Damascus.

In today's globalised world one of the problems faced by the regime is the ingenuity of the political opposition to use social networking sites to reveal the harsh nature of the actions being taken by the regime to 'restore law and order'. Doing everything they can to prevent material recorded on mobile phones from leaving Syria is therefore hugely important. To that end Syria is not only engaged in a military suppression of its people, it is also pursuing a relentless campaign against those who record and try and post the evidence of the activity of the military to the international community.

In their calculus Russia has simply too much to lose to go beyond some mild diplomatic rebuke of the regime's actions. As far as the Syrian regime is concerned, provided they operate below Russia's threshold of pain, they can count on Moscow to block any attempts by western political leaders to move beyond a few economic sanctions, none of which will have much impact in Syria. The simple fact is that when you have a regime whose behaviour cannot be swayed by nuanced diplomatic language, there are few options that are available other than some form of military intervention. This is where soft power has its limitations.

The other factor that will come into play is the degree of embarrassment experienced in Germany at their lack of involvement in the NATO campaign in Libya. The Germans chose to stay out of the fray, splintering NATO's cohesion over the Libyan campaign. By staying on the sidelines the Germans showed they were in part frightened by the prospect of Libya becoming another Iraq. With elections in the offing the German Chancellor probably thought it wise not to become involved in another military campaign. Besides, economically the Germans have massive issues trying to salvage the project called the single European currency.

That said, the fact that the indications are that another Iraq-style insurgency does not look like gaining traction in Libya, will cause a backlash in Germany. They missed the chance to be involved and to benefit from the contributions made by NATO countries to the displacement of the Gaddafi regime. A swiftness to join in on a bandwagon associated with ratcheting up the pressure on Syria might help restore some of the political clout lost by the Germans because of their attitude towards Libya.

The increased sanctions placed on Damascus might well contribute to what was already an increasingly tricky economic situation in Syria. The economic lever, coupled with the political instrument of power, may well enable the Western powers to avoid any military intervention in Syria.

But can the economic lever of power, even if it is coupled with political opprobrium, actually achieve regime change? Whilst the Syrian regime retains the support of the army it is an unlikely proposition. Superficially therefore it seems that if the regime is to be swept away the only way to do this is to use the military application of power. How feasible might that be? What lessons can we learn from the Libyan campaign?

There are several important differences between Libya and Syria. Some of that is a matter of geography. The NATO intervention to assist the citizens of Benghazi benefited hugely from the east-west divide that existed in Libya. There was a distinct line of separation that helped NATO avoid some of the more worrisome aspects of conducting a bombing campaign.

In Syria the uprisings have tended to focus on a number of quite discrete population centres, several of which have a long history of being rebellious, such as Hama and Homs. The heterogeneous nature of the landscape of the protests in Syria made it almost impossible for NATO to find any point at which it might apply military power. Herein lays a problem.

Across many parts of the Arab world this inability to find a point at which the military instrument of power can be applied is massaged and portrayed as an inconsistency in the policy of the West. The narrative that has developed in some quarters suggests that NATO and the West are selective in their interventions and disregard the plight of the Syrian people. On the surface that might appear to have some legitimacy as an argument, after all if the people of Libya wanted freedom and NATO air power was used to achieve it, why not in Syria?

The answer of course lays in the nuance of how military leverage might be applied. In this day and age where media coverage and associated rumours can take a single event and portray it as a campaign-changing moment, the need to avoid civilian casualties is huge. In Syria the heterogeneous nature of the societal landscape means that with Syrian military forces operating in urban areas the potential for collateral casualties is high, with all its knock-on implications for maintaining the support of the population.

With pressure increasing on the regime, the *Los Angeles Times* reported on 8 September 2011, that twenty-three people died in Homs as a result of the regime seeking out army units that had defected to the protestors. This single event may be the precursor to wider defections that might create a tipping point at which the regime is finally out-manoeuvred. That appears unlikely. Whilst the regime seems able to retain the loyalty of the Syrian Army it is unlikely that the protestors who have largely resorted to peaceful means of demonstrating their discontent, can achieve the kind of advantage that will see Syria go the way of Egypt.

Syria's history also plays a part. President Assad's father had similar problems with that city which resulted in a large military operation and widespread genocide. The uprising was short-lived. A variety of estimates have been published about the overall cost in human lives which ranged from 1,000 – the official figure – to close to 40,000 dead (an estimate by the Syrian Human Right Committee).

Another factor that comes into play in Syria is that during the uprisings linked to the Arab Spring the regime in Damascus did not resort to using its air force to suppress the protestors. The regime relied, as it has done in the past, on the army to put down what it saw as an insurrection that threatened its future. The absence of an air power element to the tactics employed by the regime meant that NATO could not use the stepping stone of a limited no-fly zone as a basis for a wider-ranging mission that might seek regime change.

The one element of the Libyan campaign that is more readily transferable is the naval blockade. In the absence of the ability to apply wider military power, the enforcement of a trade embargo by sea is a useful adjunct to the application of economic sanctions. Whilst the naval blockade cannot prevent Syria using other ways of getting its goods moved overseas, it is a point of leverage.

This approach is also supported by the location of the main port facilities in Syria, which lay along a 100 kilometre piece of the coastline. To the north, the small port of Borj Islam is not capable of moving significant quantities of goods. The single most important oil port on the coast is Banias Oil Terminal, which is slightly to the north of the larger port of Banias. The major commercial ports of Tartus and Lattakia could readily be embargoed by a naval force, providing a limited restriction on the Syrian economy.

The problem for the European Union is that even that military intervention would have a limited impact as Syria exports most of its goods across the land boundary with Iraq (its largest trading partner at just over 30 per cent in value) and to the Lebanon (13 per cent). Germany comes in third at just under 10 per cent with Saudi Arabia and Italy around 5% each. These figures highlight even the difficulty of applying a naval blockade as a way of shaping the situation in Syria.

These factors will be known inside Damascus and will be part of a calculus that is developed by the Assad regime. They will know that it will be hard for NATO to embark upon another military adventure. The aim of the regime must therefore be to use just enough force to suppress the uprisings so as not to bring the kind of international condemnation that will create a political consensus for regime change. That will be the first step along what might become another Iraq. The international community would do well to steer clear at all costs of a military involvement in Syria. NATO's view must be that each situation it faces, where calls are made for intervention, needs to be evaluated on its merits.

In the absence of a military option the simple fact is, that if Syria avoids provoking the international community, it can ride out the immediate aftermath of events in Libya and avoid a situation where the international community decides to act. But that does not mean Syria can act below the international threshold of pain without impunity.

The best chance of any regime change occurring in Syria is to encourage, in any way that is possible, those who have spontaneously taken to the streets in peaceful demonstrations. This is a nuanced application of soft power that lies in the murky world of deniability and underhand dealings involving clandestine operations. The aim of such activities is to encourage a critical mass of people inside Syria so that, despite the imbalance they face with respect to the army, even it cannot resist a national uprising. The key is to create the conditions where Social Movement Theory shows that people will turn on the regime en masse.

This kind of application of soft power, a key element of the Cameron doctrine, would aim to encourage those professional classes inside Syria who have traditionally aligned with the Ba'ath Party, that the time is up and they need to look to themselves to create an effective opposition inside the country. In the immediate aftermath of the campaign in Libya the signs were encouraging. Doctors had started to organise coordinating committees to provide medical assistance to protestors injured in clashes with the security forces. Lawyers and other members of the professional classes were also joining the protestors. Importantly these have the skills and qualifications to run a country should the Assad regime fall.

Syria is not like many countries that suffer from a lack of ability to create governance structures. It has a rich history of professional people that could form part of new democratic institutions. Other members of the professional classes are also deserting the regime including some of those that represent its traditional constituency in the merchant and business classes.

Aleppo traders, who had been widely reported as paying staff to remain away from the protests, have apparently stopped cooperating with the regime. The traders are known to be cautious individuals whose primary motivations are to ensure the long-term health of the business situation. Moving away from the regime, who they may feel now has the stench of failure associated with it, is a classic response.

In September 2011 Syria's future is balanced on a knife edge. If the Assad regime can regain the initiative by reaching out to its main support base in the professional classes it might yet survive. That the main bulk of the army will stay loyal until the last moment is virtually assured, through the kind of patronage networks that bind the senior members of the army into the regime. However, if President Assad does not apply the limited manoeuvre room that he enjoys carefully he may well trip up and create the kind of bow wave that even he cannot resist. Social Movement Theory provides one guiding principle that all political leaders need to be aware of – populations can suddenly turn. When they do, they rarely immediately turn back. Looking at the situation from the viewpoint of the middle of September 2011, the likelihood is that the regime will eventually fall as a tipping point emerges. That NATO may help shape the emergence of that tipping point seems highly unlikely.

However the global political landscape is so difficult to understand. Situations can and do arise unexpectedly. There is one scenario, however unexpected, that NATO needs to bear in mind. Should the uprising in Syria suddenly gain traction it is possible that large parts of the army might defect. The isolated pockets of resistance may suddenly fracture into defined areas of the country that might wish to break away from Damascus.

The regime may try to dig in and barricade itself behind the high stone walls of the capital, even using its own terror weapons against its own people. In Libya there was one report of a SCUD missile being fired by those loyal to Colonel Gaddafi. Syria has significant quantities of SCUD missiles. If the regime was threatened it might well reach to these terror weapons to try and finally turn the tide back in its favour. History provides a number of illustrations of how regimes go through all kinds of contortions when they are under pressure. Saddam Hussein did, after all, use chemical weapons in Halabja on 16 March 1988. There is, therefore, an urgent need at the end of the campaign to ensure the stockpiles of chemical weapons in Libya are secure. If the situation in Libya were not to stabilise they might prove too tempting a target for terrorist groups that operate in the region.

Such actions would go far beyond the kind of events that have been witnessed in Syria until this point. The calls for action on behalf of the international community may grow to a point where NATO felt compelled to act. A limited intervention, aimed at destroying the regime's SCUD missiles could then be justified and might gain sufficient support for a United Nations resolution to be passed. Were a tipping point to be achieved from internal insurrection one thing that cannot be ruled out is NATO throwing its weight into the final stages to help the rebels bring down a faltering regime. The island of Cyprus would provide an excellent launch point for such attacks. Is this a likely scenario? It seems not.

NATO issued a statement on 30 October distancing the organisation from any plans to impose a no-fly zone over Syria. Showing great awareness of the unique circumstances that prevailed in Libya, a NATO spokesman noted that 'the Libyan template in unlikely to work in Syria'. It would appear at the time of writing that there is little appetite to test Syrian President Assad's threat of an earthquake in the region if NATO were to intervene.

The Syrian people have to date been unequivocal about their desire to avoid international intervention. Besides gaining a consensus at the United Nations would almost be impossible with Russia able to veto any proposals for armed intervention. However, there is an adage that seems to apply now more than ever when it comes to international politics, and that is 'never say never' as that other well known statement 'events dear boy, events' has a habit of creating unusual and unforeseen circumstances which can dramatically sway public opinion and necessitate a political and military response.

If there is an enduring lesson to learn from the intervention in Libya it is to be prepared for the unexpected. Whilst it is a cliché, in today's interlinked and complex world it provides at least one guide to those trying to formulate a coherent military doctrine. It also fits well with the kind of agility envisaged by David Cameron and laid out in the United Kingdom SDSR.

If Syria appears difficult the likelihood is that Yemen is impossible. In the book *Yemen: Dancing on the head of snakes* the author Victoria Clark takes the reader on an intensely personal journey into Yemen and its complex societal landscape, providing a detailed historical context of the tribulations of the country. It is a place that is riven with divisions along ethnic and political lines. Any military intervention in the country would be doomed to fail. It would make Iraq look like a walk in the park.

NATO's Future Intervention Strategy

That the NATO countries have grown tired of conflict in the period since the attacks in America in 2001 is a given. Western liberal democracies were supposed to collaborate to prevent war, not to conduct a series of campaigns in a futile pursuit to create the nirvana of a secure homeland.

The situation in which NATO finds itself is also complicated by the economic woes that are besetting the world's economy. NATO's desire to become the world's policeman must be in doubt even though in the wake of the success in Libya it must feel that its purpose has to some extent been renewed. It would be wise for political leaders to pause for breath as Afghanistan winds down and Libya hopefully moves onto a stable footing. More interventions which involve the application of hard power just might prove one step too far. To apply soft power however is potentially cheaper, and it may be that David Cameron's call to other nations to 'step up to the mark' with respect to their international aid budgets, might prove attractive.

Of course military power does not have to be exercised by the full gamut of military forces. What is clear is that specialised forces and unmanned aircraft may well form the backbone of operations that seek to combine the soft power approaches with a laser-like application of precision power using Special Forces and unmanned aircraft. The inherent agility and flexibility of Special Forces mean that they will increasingly become the spearhead of upstream activities. The model of how they assisted the Libyan rebels to become more organised and effective as a fighting entity is one that will be poured over by political and military strategists for some time to come.

That NATO must come to terms with the limitations of how it can apply military force is an obvious outcome from the Libyan campaign. Whilst siren voices will be raised from the right-wing elements in Europe that this is the moment to finally address some of the long-standing issues with countries around its borders, they should not be given a great deal of air time. The campaign in Libya has not provided a brand new paradigm for liberal interventions.

That it should see continued NATO involvement in the development of the Libyan Army is an important step. Creating professional security forces in Libya should be an urgent requirement that is on the action list of NATO leaders. Their continuing engagement with the development of key military leaders in Iraq is an important application of soft power. It needs to be extended into Libya.

Politicians who rather simply declare that there will be 'no more Rwandas' are being far too adventurous. They need to understand and accept the limitations of military power, even when it is jointly exercised with economic and political power. In a world that is a complex mosaic of dynamically evolving relations, set against the rise of some new economic powers like Brazil and India, getting the international community to agree on any form of concerted action at the United Nations is going to be almost impossible.

It is a self-evident truth that whilst dictators are able to use whatever internal levers of power that exist in their countries to assume and then hold power, little amount of demonstrations on the streets of London, Paris or Washington will create situations where they can be deposed. In the short-term the legacy of Iraq and Afghanistan outweighs the relatively short timetable over which progress was made in Libya.

For NATO the Libyan campaign was, and will remain, one that had a number of very specific advantages that enabled contemporary military power to be applied in a successful way. To suggest that this then becomes a new form of confrontation where despots can be removed is to be naive in the extreme. Along that path lies further pain and misery. It is an avenue that the west should at all costs seek to avoid.

Libya and the UK SDSR

So what can the Prime Minister take from the United Kingdom's involvement in Libya? From his own comments he seems to wish to avoid the kind of triumphalism that was associated with the passing of the initial combat operations in Iraq and the start of the insurgency. Whilst Libya faces enormous challenges it would appear that the chances of a full-blown repeat of Iraq can be avoided. That said, when there are lots of armed people with a rich tapestry of alliances on the streets, the outcome is far from certain.

Whilst Gaddafi was in power the rebels had a cause, remove the dictator, and gain the freedom to decide on their own future. Their single mission to rid the country of the man that had led them for over forty years created the bond that gave the rebels their mission focus or a centre of gravity. How they now build a political consensus as to what a post-Gaddafi Libya looks like is a very different challenge. David Cameron was wise to be cautious in his use of language in the immediate aftermath of the seizure of Tripoli.

The RAF can take great heart from its contribution to OPERATION UNIFIED PROTECTOR and to the precursor operations to evacuate entitled persons from the chaos that was enveloping Libya. The RAF was at the spearhead of the international effort targeting regime military assets and, at its best, when shipping money into Benghazi to pay the local public sector workers. If anyone had their doubts about the ability of the RAF to deliver a balance of hard and soft power OPERATION ELLAMY put paid to those concerns once and for all. Its actions were crucial in shaping all aspects of the battlespace. The RAF had lived up to its mantra of being versatile, flexible and agile.

The RN role received less attention in the media. The initial wave of attacks designed to suppress and eviscerate the Libyan air defence systems saw the Royal Navy launch a large number of TLAM from a submarine based offshore. This was part of a concerted initial wave of firepower deployed by NATO against specific military targets. Once that initial phase was over and the Libyan air defences had largely been suppressed, the RN mission settled into a daily routine designed to bring sustained military and economic pressure onto the regime.

As part of an international force of warships deployed off the coast of Libya, the embargo was clearly enforced. Barring an attempt by Gaddafi loyalists to mine the harbour of Misrata, the RN role was defined by a need to ensure that weapons were not smuggled to the regime and to supporting the overall military effort when it was able.

The role played by the Apache helicopters operating from HMS *Ocean* whilst not an overwhelming display of firepower provided an additional level of versatility to the commanders. In the course of the campaign the Apaches were to fire 110 Hellfire missiles and CR-V rockets, and fire more than 4,000 rounds from the 30mm cannon on the aircraft.

Whilst for the British Army, so often the centre of attention in such campaigns, this was a modest return on its investment in the Apache helicopters. But it did provide another example of the flexibility that exists in the equipment program. For UK MoD planners such versatility is priceless but often undefined at the procurement stage. With the modernisation of the MoD high on the political agenda, perhaps a measure of versatility and mission overlap should be introduced when future platforms are being evaluated at the early stages of their procurement.

In its own unassuming way the naval contribution to the campaign, whilst not having the same media profile as the air forces, was nevertheless important. It provided an additional domain in which to manoeuvre. For commanders that is always a nice thing to have at their disposal.

It could have turned out very differently. Had Gaddafi's forces been able to really threaten Benghazi with force, the option to conduct a limited amphibious operation to deploy Royal Marines ashore in support of the rebels may well have had to be launched. Its aim, to provide a short-term piece of assistance to the rebels defending Benghazi, would have been clear. Its legality under United Nations Resolution 1973, which specifically made the point that no ground troops were to be used, might have been hugely contentious. That the British and French may have had to seek another resolution to provide the legal to cover for any amphibious operation is a matter for speculation.

The problem is, in fast moving situations on the ground where non-combatants are suddenly drawn into a terrible situation, that the international community is not known for its political agility. United Kingdom and French forces may well have had to go ashore quickly whilst allowing the international political wrangling to try and find a way of sanctioning the effort. The spectre of Suez would have hung over such an operation. It would have been very tricky territory for President Sarkozy and Prime Minister David Cameron.

Whilst the issues over such an operation remain of interest, the simple fact of the matter, as far as David Cameron is concerned, was that despite all of the criticizm he and his coalition government received for the way the SDSR was conducted, the United Kingdom still retained that capability. He could have authorised the conduct of an amphibious operation to provide humanitarian relief to what would have been the embattled defenders of Benghazi.

David Cameron's assertion that the United Kingdom retains a broad spectrum of military capability has some additional street credibility in the light of the outcome of the Libyan campaign. But, and this is the hugely important point, the conditions on the ground in Libya *favoured* the operations that were conducted. Had that test arisen in Syria or Yemen the outcome is likely to have been so very different.

The other thing the United Kingdom's Prime Minister benefited from was the inherent flexibility and agility that is built into the very psyche of the British military mind set. The professional cadre that is at the heart of the British military gives the Prime Minister an additional element of military power that is very hard to quantify. As Napoleon understood so very clearly, military power is not simply measured by how many combatants and equipment you deploy on the ground.

In time, many anecdotal examples will emerge of the kind of adaptability that goes to the heart of the ways in which the United Kingdom's armed forces use the equipment they have been given to operate outside its intended operational boundaries. The use of Apache helicopters, intended for close air support operations on the German plain against the Soviet Third Shock Army, from maritime platforms against fixed and ad hoc targets of opportunity, provides one example of that operational flexibility.

Another is provided by the use of Sea King ASaC helicopters whose radar systems were originally optimised for over-the-sea detection of threats to a carrier task force in a role to identify and spot those emerging targets and guide in the Apaches, was not in the original specification of the radar. Time and again the armed forces of NATO countries show how equipment brought for a single mission suddenly can be adapted and used in a wider mission set.

Whilst that inherent flexibility certainly worked in Libya a more detailed appreciation of the situation may provide some nuanced understanding. Libya provided the perfect testing ground for Cameron's approach. Had he tried an intervention elsewhere it is likely that the outcome may have been very different. Before drawing too many positive conclusions from the Libyan intervention a cold hard look at the Libyan armed forces capabilities, and the obvious mistakes made by the regime in the way it deployed its forces, is in order.

The Cyber Domain?

Given the degree of media coverage of developments in the cyber world, little has appeared in public about any use of the cyber domain as part of the campaign. Media speculation towards the end of the campaign has suggested that there were voices in Washington urging the President to unleash a cyber attack against the Libyan regime that would have swiftly brought the campaign to a conclusion. In practice this is more likely to be reflective of an opportunistic moment, sensed by those who are arguing for cyber budgets to be increased, to argue for its employment as a way of reducing American military involvement.

Coming against a backdrop where the Obama Administration was clearly seeking a back seat in Libya this is easy to understand. Here was an opportunity to showcase cyber warfare and its ability to bring down a regime. Wiser heads, it would appear, prevailed on this matter and whilst there is little doubt that there is more to emerge on the role played by cyber weapons and capabilities it was not front and centre in the campaign.

Given the way that the Chinese, for example, pour over any United States military venture in detail this was probably a sound approach. If there are advanced capabilities ready to be unleashed should they be required, at best to keep them for the occasions on which they might really provide leverage. To have employed advanced cyber weapons against the Gaddafi regime would simply have given the Chinese and Russians, to name two countries that would be interested, an intelligence field day. Cyber Warfare would have to wait its turn as far as Libya was concerned. Like nuclear weapons, it was sensibly reserved for another day. For Libya the burden would fall on conventional weapons. Using them in ways to achieve military effect, whilst minimising the danger to the civilian population in Libya and the rebels, was the priority. The weapon platforms and systems used were not to disappoint.

Reflections on SDSR from OPERATION ELLAMY

It is possible that at the heart of the Cameron thinking is a basic understanding of this inherent flexibility provided by the equipment program within the MoD. He may have suspected that because of the ways the MoD procure equipment that some inherent degree of overlapping capabilities might have existed in the configuration of the armed forces. The loss of the Harrier element of the Royal Air Force can be seen through this lens. In the Cold War, having aircraft whose missions could be defined in terms of a broad range of categories such as close air support, air defence and ground attack fighters, was a necessary view if you were to retain a national ability to fight.

As the Cold War ended that need to have mission-specific aircraft declined. The adaptation of the Typhoon from a purely air defence fighter to a versatile aircraft with a unique capability to develop on-board situational awareness is a major shift in its capability. Whilst that journey may have been criticized by various groups it is a journey that has produced a highly capable weapon platform.

It might be unwise to suggest that the SDSR was based on a kind of assumption that such operational flexibility would arise should the forces be committed into a combat situation. For many the decision to scrap the Nimrod MRA4 program still rankles and makes little sense. Their use off the coast of Libya would have enabled some of the naval forces to have been scaled back – freeing assets to resume their usual counter-piracy and counter-narcotics activities. This was an area of weakness that many in the press with personal agendas failed to address.

In many ways David Cameron and Nickolas Sarkozy were lucky. The gods seemed to smile on their efforts.

One example illustrates this assertion. David Cameron was very fortunate that the effort in Libya came at a time when the piracy off Somalia was entering a decline as the shipping industry started to deploy armed guards and the success rates of hijackings was reduced. A combination of an increasingly assertive naval presence off the coast of India and the introduction of agreed practises amongst seafarers designed to reduce the levels of hijackings, started to have a real impact in the early part of 2011.

If a surge in hijackings occurred before the onset of the North West monsoon the right-wing media would have been all over the operational stretch being experienced by the RN. When he did go public on his concerns the First Sea Lord was entirely right to highlight to the Prime Minister that the RN would find it hard to maintain its operations off Libya and fulfil its other mandated activities.

The sea blindness that seems to affect political leaders in the United Kingdom is still a vexing question. There remains a complete misunderstanding of the high operational tempo maintained by the RN across the world in the last few years. For the RN, as it quietly and effectively goes about its huge variety of day-to-day tasks, it remains the case that over the horizon is also out of mind as far as political leaders are concerned.

From an SDSR viewpoint OPERATION ELLAMY confirmed that if a British Prime Minister wants to deploy military force against a coastal country, and there are many of them in the world, that he or she will need to be capable of manoeuvring in the littoral. To do that the United Kingdom's government needs a substantive naval presence. This must have the ability to project both hard (kinetic) and soft (influence) power into the littoral and over the horizon into the hinterland of the country involved. The versatile way in which the RN played its role in OPERATION ELLAMY should not be dismissed to quickly. The submarines, minesweepers and warships deployed off the coast alongside their NATO allies provided an important constraint on the manoeuvre room of the Gaddafi regime.

By dominating the maritime domain the naval component ensured the arms embargo was enforced. That had a material impact on the duration of the campaign. Had significant quantities of weapons been able to arrive in Brega, Ras Lanuf or Tripoli from the sea, the pro-regime forces would have been given an extra lease of life in terms of maintaining the campaign. Given that Gaddafi was always convinced that the NATO-led coalition would eventually collapse, it was time that he needed most. By denying him and his forces access to the sea the navies not only compressed the battlespace in a geographic sense, they also compressed it in time.

But the simple fact of the matter is that the operational circumstances allowed the British Prime Minister and the French President to embark upon a short-term military involvement in Libya. They were able to do this as a result of the support from the United States, NATO, allies not directly involved in NATO, such as Sweden, and the contingent of Arab countries who also stepped up to the plate. As a result of this coalition David Cameron was rightly able to claim that they fulfilled the UN mandate provided under UN Resolution 1973 whilst not denuding the focus on Afghanistan.

That is remarkable of itself. It provides some concrete support for David Cameron when he defends the SDSR. But he would be unwise to assume that Libya provides the ultimate vindication of the SDSR. That United Kingdom forces deployed in Libya were able to achieve regime change in the immediate aftermath of the decision making of the SDSR, is not in doubt. That SDSR provides the kind of baseline from which the United Kingdom could then project military power onto the international stage should more complicated situations arise is a very different question. Syria, Iran and Yemen are very different propositions to Libya.

To make the success in Libya the altar on which to shape the United Kingdom's armed forces in the future would be to disavow the one crucial aspect that rarely comes through the kind of numerical analysis that goes to the heart of political decision making. This is the difficult to express and hard to substantiate element that is the inherent flexibility and ingenuity that lies at the heart of the ways that the United Kingdom armed forces go about fighting wars. They are simply very good at it as OPERATION ELLMAY demonstrated. For that there is no magical Treasury formula. Its contribution, however, is beyond measure.

Appendix A: A Summary of the Air Attacks Conducted by the RAF over Libya

The contents of this appendix have been derived from the reporting provided by the MoD through official channels of the nature of the attacks conducted by the RAF through the air campaign in Libya. The start and end dates of the reporting do not align fully with the start and end of the campaign. The data is also based entirely on the 156 press reports released by the United Kingdom Ministry of Defence in the course of OPERATION ELLAMY. It therefore only represents a sub-set of the attacks undertaken by the RAF. An official statement released on 28 October, as the NATO-led campaign came to an end, attributed 640 successful strike missions to the RAF out of a total of 3,000 flown; of which 2,100 were strike missions. This shows that around one in three missions saw weapons released. This appendix therefore covers reporting on one quarter of the strike missions flown by the RAF. It shows the diversity of targets attacked and the tempo of operations that were maintained. A small number of reports of the activities of the Army Air Corps pilots attacking targets in their Apache helicopters are included for completeness. The use of the term 'unknown' in the data suggests that the UK MoD did not report the actual weapon system, target or platform involved.

Date	Platform	Location	Target Type	Weapons Deployed	Comments
5 April	Tornado	Mişrātah	MBT and Armoured Vehicles	Paveway & Brimstone	12 targets were hit in the course of the operation, 6 by Paveway and 6 by Brimstone.
8 April	Tornado	Adjabiya	MBT	Paveway & Brimstone	2 MBT were attacked as they were involved in fighting in the city of Adjabiya.
8 April	Tornado	Mişrātah	MBT	Brimstone	5 MBT were destroyed as they were prepared to be shipped to the front line.
12 April	Typhoon	Mişrātah	MBT	Paveway	2 MBT destroyed.
12 April	Tornado	Mişrātah	MBT	Paveway	1 MBT destroyed.
13 April	Tornado	Unknown	MBT	Brimstone	Footage provided by the RAF of a single MBT being destroyed by Brimstone missiles.
13 April	Tornado & Typhoon	Mişrātah, Brega, Adjabiya	Armoured Vehicles & Air Defence Assets	Unknown	20 targets destroyed by the RAF over a period of several days.
17 April	Typhoon & Tornado	Unknown	Command & Control Facilities	Unknown	Synchronised strike by RAF & RN assets on a range of command and control facilities.
18 April	Typhoon & Tornado	Mişrātah	MLRS & Light Artillery Piece	Unknown	
18 April	Typhoon & Tornado	Mişrātah	Self Propelled Gun & MBT	Unknown	Being brought into the area on a tank transporter.
19 April	Typhoon & Tornado	Unknown	Communications facilities	Unknown	7 attacks were mounted in a 7-minute window to destroy key communications sites.
23 April	Typhoon & Tornado	Mişrātah	APC & Surface to Air Missile Facility	Unknown	3 Armoured Personnel Carriers destroyed.
24 April	Unknown	Mişrātah	MLRS & Support Vehicles, MBT and Rocket Storage Site	Unknown	1 MBT destroyed and 8 MLRS.
25 April	Unknown	Mizdah	MBT	Unknown	1 MBT destroyed
25 April	Unknown	Yafran	Self Propelled Gun (SPG)	Unknown	1 SPG destroyed
25 April	Unknown	Mişrātah	MLRS	Unknown	

April Air Activity Reports: OPERATION ELLAMY

Date	Platform	Location	Target Type	Weapons Deployed	Comments
3 May	Typhoon & Tornado	Brega & Miṣrātah	Various targets	Unknown	Imagery supplied of an attack by a Typhoon on a number of vehicles in what appears to be a synchronised attack that leaves several of the targets burning.
5 May	Unknown	Sirte	FROG & SCUD Canisters	Paveway	20 FROG-7 Rocket Launchers assessed as completely or partially destroyed.
6 May	Tornado	Sirte	MLRS and Missiles	Paveway	Imagery from Litening III targeting pods show secondary explosions in the vicinity.
8 May	Tornado	Miṣrātah	Two floors in a building	2 Paveway	The attack was conducted in a way that destroyed the top two floors of the building only, leaving the rest of the building standing.
12 May	Typhoon	Sirte	Self Propelled Artillery	2 Paveway	2 Self Propelled Palmaria Vehicles destroyed.
13 May	Tornado	Tripoli	Vehicle Storage Facility	Paveway	Imagery supplied by the RAF of the attack.
Unknown	Unknown	Tripoli	Armoured Vehicle Repair Facility	Unknown	
Unknown	Unknown	Miṣrātah	Artillery Piece	Unknown	
18 May	Tornado	Tripoli	Intelligence Agency Buildings and Training Centre for Gaddafi's Executive Protection Force	Paveway	Vehicles at the training base had been associated with the repression of protests on 4 March in Tripoli.
20 May	Tornado & Typhoon	Al Khums	Warships & Dockside Facility constructing Fast Inflatable Boats	Paveway	First time NATO aircraft attacked the Libyan Navy in response to indiscriminate mining to prevent aid flows into Libya.
24 May	Tornado	Brega	Coastal Radar Station	1 Brimstone	Coastal radar station destroyed with a single Dual Mode Seeker Brimstone missile, this destroyed the radar without having a great impact on the rest of the building.
25 May	Typhoon & Tornado	Tiji	Military Complex	9 Paveway	Tornado used five Paveway IV bombs and the Typhoon used four Enhanced Paveway II bombs – the first time the Typhoon had released four bombs against a single target.
27 May	Typhoon	Tripoli	Gaddafi Headquarters	Unknown	Guard towers around a Gaddafi Headquarters were targeted.
29 May	Unknown	Zlitan	MLRS and Support vehicles	Unknown	1 MBT destroyed
29 May	Unknown	Jadu	MBT	Unknown	
30 May	Unknown	Zlitan	Heavy Equipment Transporters (HET) & MBT	Unknown	5 HET carrying MBT destroyed or severely damaged.
31 May	Typhoon & Tornado	Zlitan	Heavy Equipment Transporters & 2S1 Guns	3 Paveway	3 HET carrying 2S1 self-propelled guns were destroyed.
31 May	Typhoon & Tornado	Waddan	Ammunition Storage Bunkers and Military Vehicle	Paveway	Ten ammunition bunkers and a military vehicle destroyed at a depot by Typhoon & Tornado attacks.

May Air Activity Reports: OPERATION ELLAMY

Date	Platform	Location	Target Type	Weapons Deployed	Comments
6 June	Tornado	Tripoli	Intelligence Facility	Unknown	
7 June	Typhoon & Tornado	Various	Various	Unknown	Imagery provide by the RAF to illustrate a wide range of missions being conducted at the time by Typhoon and Tornado aircraft.
7 June	Tornado	Tripoli	Intelligence Facility	Paveway	Detonation of the bomb was set to attack the lower floors in the building.
11 June	Unknown	Al Aziziyah	MBT	Unknown	4 MBT destroyed hidden in an orchard.
11 June	Typhoon & Tornado	Al Mayah	Military base and key installations	9 Paveway	Key military installations around the capital Tripoli
12 June	Typhoon & Tornado	Waddan, Al Qaryat Ash Sharqiyah	Ammunition Bunkers	Unknown	9 underground storage bunkers destroyed.
12 June	Apache	Zlitan	ZSU-23-4 Self Propelled AAA system	Unknown	Coastal strike by Apache Aircraft based aboard HMS *Ocean*
14 June	Typhoon & Tornado	Gariyat	Ammunition Bunkers	Paveway	Images of the ammunition bunkers exploding after being attacked.

June Air Activity Reports: OPERATION ELLAMY

Date	Platform	Location	Target Type	Weapons Deployed	Comments
9 July	Typhoon & Tornado	Mişrātah	MLRS	Unknown	
9 July	Typhoon & Tornado	Mişrātah	Howitzers & APT	Paveway	4 Howitzers destroyed and an Armed Pickup Truck.
9 July	Unknown	Mizdah	Artillery Piece	Unknown	
10 July	Typhoon & Tornado	Tajura	Military Vehicle Depot	Unknown	
11 July	Typhoon & Tornado	Tajura	Military Vehicle Depot	Unknown	
11 July	Unknown	Tripoli	IFF Antenna at Tripoli Airport	Brimstone	Brimstone used to limit the damage to the specific antenna that was targeted.
12 July	Unknown	Zlitan	Mortar Position	Brimstone	
12 July	Apache	Al Khums	Military Checkpoints, Military Vehicles & MLRS	Hellfire & Cannon	Apaches attacked, destroying four military structures and seven vehicles, including on MLRS.
13 July	Unknown	Zlitan	Command & Control Centres, Military Supply and Ammunition and Fuel Storage Facilities	Unknown	29 facilities attacked as a result of detailed intelligence analysis.
13 July	Apache	Al Khums	Large Vehicle Sheds	Hellfire	2 Large Vehicle Sheds destroyed.
14 July	Typhoon	Mişrātah	APC	Paveway	1 APC (BMP) was destroyed.
21 July	Unknown	Zlitan	SPG	Unknown	
21 July	Apache	Al Khums	Military Facilities	Hellfire	2 Buildings destroyed.
22 July	Unknown	Zlitan	Ammunition Sites	Hellfire	6 Ammunition Sites attacked.
22 July	Unknown	Mişrātah	MLRS Base	Unknown	
22 July	Unknown	Zlitan	MBT and APT	Unknown	
23 July	Typhoon & Tornado	Tripoli	Gaddafi Command Complex: Bab al-Aziziya	13 Paveway	Outer walls breached.
23 July	Unknown	Zlitan	Command & Control Centres & Staging Post	Unknown	4 buildings attacked.
23 July	Unknown	Zlitan	Ammunition Stockpile	Unknown	
23 July	Apaches	Al Khums	Military Positions	Hellfire	
24 July	Typhoon & Tornado	Tripoli	Central Organisation for Electronic Research (COER)	Unknown	Major R&D centre operated by the regime for what has been described as 'nefarious activities'.
24 July	Unknown	Zlitan	Staging Posts	Unknown	Area used to muster tanks, artillery and ammunition.
24 July	Unknown	Gharyan	MBT	Unknown	1 MBT destroyed.

July Air Activity Reports: OPERATION ELLAMY

Date	Platform	Location	Target Type	Weapons Deployed	Comments
2 August	Typhoon & Tornado	Zlitan	Command and Control centre	Paveway	
4 August	Typhoon & Tornado	Zlitan	Staging posts and MLRS	Unknown	Two staging posts were destroyed and a Grad MLRS hiding under a tree was also destroyed.
4 August	Typhoon & Tornado	Djebel Nafousa	Buildings hiding artillery firing into Yafran	Unknown	Two buildings attacked and destroyed.
4 August	Typhoon & Tornado	Gharyan	Headquarters and Troop Camp	Unknown	
4 August	Apache	Zlitan	Vehicle Checkpoints	Unknown	Being used to restrict civilian movement in the area. 5 Military Vehicles destroyed in the area.
4 August	Unknown	Tripoli	Bin Ghashir Missile Depot	10 Paveway	
5 August	Unknown	Djebel Nafousa	Building hiding artillery firing into Yafran	Unknown	
5 August	Unknown	Gharyan	Staging Post	Unknown	
6 August	Unknown	Bir al Ghanam	MLRS Base & Ammunition Store & Military Headquarters	Paveway	2 Ammunition Stores destroyed & a HQ.
7 August	Apache	Al Watiyah	Troop Concentration	Hellfire & Cannon Fire	64km inland south of the coast at Zuwarah. One headquarters was destroyed and 12 military vehicles destroyed, including one armed with a SAM. Four other vehicles were seriously damaged.
7 August	Tornado	Tiji	Military Staging Post	Unknown	
8 August	Typhoon & Tornado	Zlitan	Ammunition & Vehicle Store Depot	Unknown	
8 August	Unknown	Brega	APT	Unknown	Two APV destroyed.
8 August	Unknown	Tripoli	Frigate	Unknown	
8 August	Unknown	Bir al-Ghanam	Weapons Depot	Unknown	
8 August	Unknown	Zlitan	Staging Post	Unknown	
8 August	Unknown	Zlitan	Barracks & Staging Post	Unknown	
9 August	Unknown	Al Aziziyah	APT	Unknown	
10 August	Tornado	Sebha	Command & Control Bunkers	Storm Shadow	6 Aircraft attack launched from Marham.
16 August	Unknown	Zlitan	Staging Post	2 Paveway	
16 August	Typhoon & Tornado	Hun	Command Compound	11 Paveway	
17 August	Unknown	Zlitan	Command & Control Post	Unknown	
17 August	Unknown	Sabratah	Commando Base	Unknown	
17 August	Unknown	Al Zawiyah	Armed Vehicles & Tug Boat	Paveway & Brimstone	The tug boat was being used to redeploy troops to attack along the coast.
18 August	Unknown	Zlitan & Al Khums	Staging Areas and Mobile Radar	Unknown	

Date	Aircraft	Location	Target	Weapon	Effect
18 August	Unknown	Al Zawiyah	Unknown Targets	Unknown	3 Precision attacks undertaken.
19 August	Typhoon & Tornado	Tripoli	MoI Operations Room	8 Paveway	Ministry of Interior buildings in Tripoli.
20 August	Tornado	Tripoli	Baroni Intelligence Centre & Communications Facility	5 Paveway	
20 August	Tornado	Tripoli	MBT	Paveway	1 MBT destroyed.
20 August	Unknown	Tripoli	Artillery Piece & Command & Control Centre	Unknown	1 Artillery Piece & 1 Command & Control Centre Destroyed
20 August	Typhoon & Tornado	Tripoli & Sirte	Command and Control Centres	Unknown	3 Command & Control Centres destroyed
21 August	Typhoon & Tornado	Tripoli	COER Facility Command & Control Nodes	Unknown	Return to attack COER after other buildings involved in military activity identified.
21 August	Typhoon & Tornado	Tripoli	Intelligence Centre	9 Paveway	This was close to the Baroni Intelligence Facility
21 August	Unknown	Tripoli	MBT	Unknown	1 MBT destroyed.
24 August	Tornado	Tripoli	Military Facility	Paveway	
24 August	Unknown	Sirte	3 SCUD Missile Support Vehicles	Unknown	SCUD Support Vehicles destroyed.
27 August	Typhoon & Tornado	Bin Ghashir	FROG-7 Ballistic Missile Launch Vehicle	1 Paveway	FROG-7 BM could have been used as a terror weapon.
28 August	Tornado	Ras Lanuf	MLRS, Artillery Piece, APT with heavy weapon	Paveway & Brimstone	1 MLRS (BM-21 Grad).
29 August	Typhoon & Tornado	Waddan	Ammunition Lorry	Brimstone	
29 August	Unknown	Bani Walid	Command & Control & Ammunition Storage Facilities	Paveway	All three targets were destroyed.
30 August	Typhoon & Tornado	Bani Walid	Command & Control Site	Paveway	
30 August	Unknown	Hun	Mobile radar system	Unknown	
30 August	Unknown	Bani Walid	SCUD Missile Launchers	Paveway	
31 August	Tornado & Typhoon	Bani Walid	Barracks	Paveway IV & Enhanced Paveway II	3 SCUD Missile Launchers destroyed.

August Air Activity Reports: OPERATION ELLAMY

Date	Platform	Location	Target Type	Weapons Deployed	Comments
1 September	Tornado	Waddan	Military Command and Control Facilities	Paveway	8 Military Command and Control Facilities.
1 September	Tornado	Sirte	Weapons and Ammunition Facilities	Unknown	9 Weapons and Ammunition Facilities.
2 September	Tornado	Bani Walid	Buildings used as vehicle depots	Paveway	3 Buildings used as vehicle depots.
5 September	Tornado	Sirte	3 Pickup Trucks	1 Paveway	Acting as a command centre for a dug-in artillery piece.
6 September	Tornado	Sebha	Military Communications Facilities & a Surface to Air Missile system facility	Storm Shadows	Long range employment of GR4 aircraft from RAF Marham.
6 September	Tornado	Sirte	Armed Pickup Truck	Brimstone	
6 September	Tornado	Birak	Command & Control Post	Unknown	
7 September	Tornado & Typhoon	Hun	Command & Control Post	Unknown	
8 September	Tornado	Sebha	Military vehicle compound	Storm Shadows	Long range mission from RAF Marham.
8 September	Typhoon	Bani Walid	Main Battle Tank	Paveway	
8 September	Typhoon	Bani Walid	Multi-Rocket Launcher System (MLRS)	Paveway	
13 September	Tornado	Sebha	Armoured Vehicles	Unknown	
13 September	Unknown	Sirte	MLRS	1 Brimstone	
14 September	Tornado	Sebha	Military Vehicle Depot & Military Buildings	Storm Shadows	Long range mission from RAF Marham.
15 September	Tornado	Sebha	Armoured Vehicles	Brimstone	First salvo firing of the Brimstone missile; configuration of 12 fired resulting in destruction of 7-8 military vehicles.
15 September	Tornado & Typhoon	Sirte	MBT, MLRS, Armoured Vehicles	Brimstone & Paveway	1 MBT, 4 MLRS, 4 Armoured Vehicles.
17 September	Tornado	Hun	Military Command Control Centre	7 Paveway	
17 September	Unknown	Sirte	Armoured Personnel Carrier & APUT	Brimstone & Paveway	1 APC, 2 APUT.
17 September	Tornado	Sirte	Ammunition Dump	Paveway	

Date	Tornado & Typhoon	Waddan	MLRS, APUT	Paveway	
18 September					
18 September	Unknown	Bani Walid	MBT	1 Brimstone	
20 September	Tornado	Bani Walid, Hun, Sirte	Command & Control, APC and AAA	Paveway	Tornado formation conducts three separate attacks across Libya against targets.
20 September	Tornado	Hun	Military Vehicle Depot	Paveway	
24 September	Unknown	Sirte	Command & Control Centre, Psychological Warfare Centre, Firing Points and AV	Paveway & Brimstone	In one attack the warhead was replaced with concrete to avoid collateral damage.
25 September	Tornado	Sirte	Staging Post	Unknown	
26 September	Tornado	Sirte	Ammunition Stores	Paveway	
26 September	Tornado	Bani Walid	Psychological Warfare Centre & Firing Position	Unknown	
27 September	Tornado	Sirte	Ammunition and Vehicle Storage Depots	Unknown	
28 September	Tornado	Sirte	Ammunition & Vehicle Storage Depots	Unknown	
28 September	Tornado	Sirte	Headquarters Buildings and Firing Positions	Paveway	
29 September	Tornado	Bani Walid	Ammunition Stores	4 Paveway	
29 September	Tornado	Bani Walid	Ammunition Stores	Unknown	
29 September	Tornado	Sirte	Supply Point for MBT and MLRS	Unknown	

September Air Activity Reports: OPERATION ELLAMY

Date	Platform	Location	Target Type	Weapons Deployed	Comments
7 October	Tornado	Sirte	Firing Position & Supply Trucks	8 Paveway	Two formations of Tornados attacked the targets.
8 October	Tornado	Sirte	Vehicle Supply Point	4 Paveway	
9 October	Tornado	Bani Walid	Armed pickup trucks	2 Brimstone	
10 October	Tornado	Bani Walid	Main Battle Tank	1 Brimstone	
10 October	Tornado	Bani Walid	Armed pick up truck	1 Paveway	
10 October	Tornado	Bani Walid	Missile Depot	7 Paveway	Caused extensive damage to the facility.
12 October	Tornado	Bani Walid	Armed pickup truck	1 Brimstone	
12 October	Tornado	Sirte	Armed pickup Truck	1 Brimstone	
13 October	Tornado	Bani Walid	3 Armed pickup Trucks	Paveway	Hidden beneath trees to the east of Bani Walid.

October Air Activity Reports: OPERATION ELLAMY

Appendix B: Profile of the Attacks on a Number of Key Cities from NATO Reporting

	April	May	June	July	August	September	October	Totals
Tripoli	15, 98	28, 126	30, 171	29, 136	24, 176	0, 0	0, 0	126, 707
Misrata	15, 92	24, 126	17, 86	17, 88	6, 11	0, 0	0, 0	79, 403
Sirte	14, 76	18, 62	4, 6	8, 12	10, 151	30, 288	5, 25	89, 620
Brega	6, 12	15, 49	15, 147	27, 164	15, 95	0, 0	0, 0	78, 467
Zintan	11, 41	15, 59	12, 45	7, 13	3, 7	0, 0	0, 0	48, 165
Misda	5, 28	14, 41	2, 5	0, 0	0, 0	0, 0	0, 0	21, 74
Zlitan	0, 0	0, 0	6, 45	22, 119	18, 57	0, 0	0, 0	46, 221
Waddan	0, 0	0, 0	8, 10	29, 31	11, 15	12, 100	0, 0	60, 156
Hun	0, 0	10, 91	3, 4	0, 0	3, 21	11, 58	0, 0	27, 174
Yafran	0, 0	0, 0	2, 2	4, 10	0, 0	0, 0	0, 0	6, 12
Bani Walid	0, 0	0, 0	0, 0	1, 1	6, 15	11, 32	11, 41	29, 89
Sebha	0, 0	4, 4	1, 1	0, 0	1, 4	9, 32	0, 0	15, 41
Totals	66, 347	128, 558	100, 522	144, 574	97, 552	73, 510	16, 66	624, 3129

Notes:

1. The format of the numbers in the table (n, m) is that the first number (n) is the number of days that attacks reported in the *Guardian* dataset for that specific city or town in Libya for that month. The second number (m) is the total number of targets that were attacked where weapons were released.

2. It is important to remember that the *Guardian* did also report attacks on towns like Ras Lanuf and Ajdabiya. Most of the air attacks in that area of Libya however were over by the time the *Guardian* dataset started on 11 April 2011. By then the first phase of the operations in the east to halt the threat to Benghazi had largely been completed.

3. Please also note that April and October are only partial months.

Glossary

AAC	Army Air Corps
AAG	Air-to-air Gun
APC	Armoured Personnel Carrier
AQIM	Al Qaeda in the Islamic Maghreb
ASaC	Airborne Surveillance and Control
AWACS	Airborne Early Warning and Control System
CIA	Central Intelligence Agency
CJEF	Combined Joint Expeditionary Force
COMUKTG	Commander United Kingdom Task Group
COIN	Counter Insurgency
CSAT	Supreme Council of National Defence
FAC	Fast Attack Craft
FATA	Federally Administered Tribal Area
FEBA	Forward Edge of the Battle Area
GAINS	Global Positioning System Aided International Navigation System
GPS	Global Positioning System
IED	Improvised Explosive Device
ICC	International Criminal Court
IMINT	Image Intelligence
ISAF	International Security Assistance Force
ISTAR	Intelligence, Surveillance, Target Acquisition and Recognition
JFHQ	Joint Force Headquarters
JSF	Joint Strike Fighter
JSTARS	Joint Surveillance and Target Attack Radar System
MBT	Main Battle Tank
MANPAD	Man Portable Air Defence
MRLS	Multi-Rocket Launch System
MoD	Ministry of Defence
NATO	North Atlantic Treaty Organisation
NEOCC	Non-Combatant Evacuation Operation Coordination Cell
NSC	National Security Council

191

NTC	National Transitional Council
OAV	Other Armoured Vehicles
ODA	Overseas Development Aid
OV	Other Vehicles
ORBAT	Order of Battle
PUT	Pick-up Trucks
RAPTOR	Reconnaissance Airborne Pod for Tornado
RFTG	Response Force Task Group
RAF	Royal Air Force
RN	Royal Navy
SAS	Special Air Service
SDSR	Strategic Defence and Security Review
SDR	Strategic Defence Review
SDT	Social Dominance Theory
SIS	Secret Intelligence Service
SPG	Self-Propelled Guns
TARDIS	Tactical Air Reconnaissance Deployable Intelligence System
TIW	Tactical IMINT Wing
TLAM	Tactical Land Attack Missile
TLC	Toyota Land Cruiser
UAE	United Arab Emirates
UN	United Nations
UNITAR	United Nations Institute for Training and Research
UNOSAT	UNITAR's Operational Satellite Applications Programme
UNSCR	United Nations Security Council Resolution

Index

INDEX